SACRED SEXUALITY

OTHER BOOKS BY GEORG FEUERSTEIN

Yoga: The Technology of Ecstasy
Structures of Consciousness: The Genius of Jean Gebser
The Philosophy of Classical Yoga
Encyclopedic Dictionary of Yoga
Enlightened Sexuality (editor)
The Bhagavad Gita: Its Philosophy and Cultural Setting
Sacred Paths
Holy Madness
The Yoga Sutra of Patanjali

SACRED SEXUALITY

Living the Vision of the Erotic Spirit

GEORG FEUERSTEIN

JEREMY P. TARCHER, INC.
Los Angeles

Library of Congress Cataloging-in-Publication Data

Feuerstein, Georg.
   Sacred sexuality : living the vision of the erotic spirit / Georg Feuerstein.
     p.   cm.
   Includes bibliographical references.
   ISBN 0-87477-683-X : $19.95
   1. Sex—Religious aspects.   2. Sex customs.   I. Title.
HQ61.F48   1992   91-37684
306.7—dc20   CIP

Requests for such permissions should be addressed to:

Jeremy P. Tarcher, Inc.
5858 Wilshire Blvd., Suite 200
Los Angeles, CA 90036

Distributed by St. Martin's Press, New York

Manufactured in the United States of America
10 9 8 7 6 5 4 3 2 1

First Edition

Contents

Acknowledgments

The many references in this book bespeak my indebtedness to many professionals in different areas of expertise.

First of all, I am indebted to my publisher Jeremy Tarcher, who saw the potential of this book and allowed me to go well beyond my allotted number of pages. He also helped expand the manuscript's original conception to a point at which it could be more broadly appealing.

Generous financial support came from Laurance S. Rockefeller, for which I am very grateful. Without his kind assistance it would simply not have been possible for me to produce this work in its present form.

As with my other Tarcher publication, *Yoga: The Technology of Ecstasy,* the present volume owes much to the skillful editing of Dan Joy. I have integrated many, if not most, of his editorial suggestions. My profound thanks are due him.

I would also like to thank the respondents to my questionnaire and personal inquiry, as well as the editors of *Common Boundary, Yoga Journal,* and *Magical Blend* for printing announcements about my research. Thanks go also to John White for his moral support and a steady stream of magazine clippings; to Howard S. Levy for his helpful comments about Eastern sexuality and a free supply of his intriguing books on the subject; and finally to my wife, Trisha, for sharing my sexual–spiritual adventure and for her always welcome editorial input.

Preface

Sacred Sexuality is about love—not merely the positive feeling between intimates but an overwhelming reverence for all embodied life on whatever level of existence. Through sacred sexuality, we directly participate in the vastness of being—the mountains, rivers, and animals of the earth, the planets and the stars, and our next-door neighbors.

Sacred sexuality is about recovering our authentic being, which knows bliss beyond mere pleasurable sensations. It is a special form of communication, even communion, that fills us with awe and stillness.

Sacred sexuality is about the reenchantment of our lives. It is about embracing the imponderable mystery of existence, about the curious fact that you and I and five billion others cannot account for our existence and our sexuality.

When we truly understand our sexuality, we come face-to-face with the mystery of the spirit. When we truly understand the spiritual dimension of existence, we come face-to-face with the mystery of sexuality. And when we truly understand anything, we are immediately cast into mystery and wonder.

The average American apparently makes love twice a week. Assuming that the ordinary person commences sexual intercourse at the age of seventeen and can look forward to an active (if perhaps gradually declining) sex life for a period of at least fifty years, this means that he or she will have repeated the sex act some 4,800 times by the age of sixty-seven. For some people the figure will be much higher, perhaps around 8,000 times, while for a small minority it may be as low as a few hundred times.

Why, then, is it that countless people nevertheless feel dis-
satisfied and curiously ill at ease with their sexuality? Why is it
that they feel a sense of shame or guilt about their genitals and
about sex? Why do we generally hide our sexual feelings, sometimes even from our partner?

As Morton and Barbara Kelsey, who have given hundreds
of workshops, noted in their book *Sacrament of Sexuality*, "We
have found very few people who, when they were honest, did
not share real concerns about sexuality." These concerns reveal a
deep confusion about the proper place of sexuality in our lives.
Despite the sexual revolution of the 1960s, and although we
know that "everyone does it," we feel strangely ambivalent
about sex.

This book traces the causes of sexual malaise, showing
how it is rooted in a deeper, spiritual dilemma: the obscuration
of the sacred dimension in modern times. I will argue that there
is another, more rewarding, challenging, and creative option to
contemporary sex as performance. That option is sexuality as a
transformative vehicle of higher human growth: *sacred sexuality*.

The present work has grown out of my own struggle with
sexuality in the larger context of a meaningful life. Like so many
people, I have for many years confused sexual need with the
need to be loved and have passively expected to be loved rather
than taken it on myself to love actively. I have explored many of
the opportunities opened up by the sexual revolution, but these
explorations gave me neither lasting happiness nor inner peace.

My own sexual dilemma did not begin to lessen until I
seriously obliged myself to integrate my sex life with the deeply
felt urge to become a whole person. Ten years ago, I voluntarily
adopted a lifestyle that required me to inspect closely the psychological mechanism that made me a sexual and emotional *con-
sumer* rather than a fully cognizant participant in the play of life.
Luckily I have a partner who was willing to experiment with
different approaches to this problem, which, I believe, lies at the
core of the existential dissatisfaction experienced by numerous
men and women today.

For a period of time we made love daily, working through
our respective problems and learning to be vulnerable with each
other. Then we economized our sexual life and even practiced
celibacy for a stretch. More than anything, that period of voluntary sexual abstinence allowed me to really see my own habit

patterns. Step by step, I succeeded in disentangling the sexual drive from my emotional needs. I became a little freer in myself, a little less guilt-ridden, and more capable of genuine love. In due course, I also found myself more able to invite the sacred into my intimate life.

I looked to such traditional spiritual schools as Hindu Tantrism and Chinese Taoism for practical guidance. My professional training as an indologist specializing in the Sanskrit literature of Hinduism particularly qualified me to investigate the original sources of Tantrism. My research in this area prompted me to contribute a series of articles on Tantrism to the widely read *Yoga Journal*.

The favorable response to these essays subsequently induced me to conceive and edit the book *Enlightened Sexuality,* published in 1989. With that anthology I tried to give voice to a sex-positive spiritual orientation to counterbalance the inherited Christian puritanism from which many of us are still suffering.

Encouraged by the public response to *Enlightened Sexuality* and feeling that there was room for a more systematic treatment of sexuality in the context of a sacred life, I next embarked on the present work.

This book is arranged in three parts. In Part I, I review the stark reality of our contemporary sexual malaise, or what I call the sexual stress syndrome. I also trace the roots of the modern sexual dilemma and unhappiness to what I call *modal guilt* and *shame,* the denial of the body, and the felt sense of being cut off from the ground of existence.

I further show that sex need not be a dull routine or dreaded twice-a-week or once-a-month encounter. It can be a healing event and one that reconnects us to the sacred dimension of existence. I include many first-person accounts of men and women who have experienced the sacred aspect of sexuality, which demonstrate that sex can be a window onto the ultimate reality, whose presence can make us whole.

Traditional cultures, which do not recognize our modern separation between sacred and profane, have always considered sexuality as an aspect of the great mystery of existence. I believe that these cultures contain many important clues for us. Hence the core chapters of this volume, those of II, are dedicated to an overview of the significant ways in which traditional societies—

from the Stone Age to our own era—have integrated sexuality into their religious-spiritual world views.

Men and women once embarked with unshakable faith on the great adventure of the spirit, risking everything for a glimpse of the eternal reality beyond appearances. Today, adventurers of the spirit who boldly scale the mountain of self-discipline and self-transcendence are as good as extinct. We have too limited a view of our humanness; hence we also have too limited a view of our own sexuality.

Yet we cannot live fully as sexual-erotic beings without first recovering our spiritual depth. Our sexuality can help us get in touch again with that depth; it can serve as a gateway to the spiritual dimension. In this book I explain why and also show how this is possible in practice. The extensive historical survey in Part Two shows how other cultures and traditions have dealt with this matter. We can learn many practical lessons from them.

In Part Three I spell out more clearly how we might use the knowledge gained in the preceding chapters. Although it is not intended as a workbook, I believe that this volume contains enough material of practical consequence to inspire you in your personal attempt to reintegrate your sexual life with the sacred.

Within the limited compass of this book, it was possible to present only a selection of materials on sacred sexuality. I have focused on the most salient traditions and, within them, on those features that allowed me to develop a rounded and sufficiently varied treatment of sacred sexuality through the ages. I believe that my discussion is both sufficiently broad and detailed to serve as a reliable introduction to this far-reaching and complex subject.

I am aware that the premise on which this book is based—that sexuality and spirituality are perfectly compatible—might seem revolutionary to some readers. It indeed represents a significant departure from our inherited sex- and body-negative perspective. In pondering with me the age-old alternative approaches presented in this volume, therefore, I invite you to make a courageous leap—the kind of imaginative leap that Democritus made when he insisted that matter was composed of atoms, or Philolaus when he taught that our planet was not flat but spherical, or Copernicus when he boldly announced that the planets were circling the sun, or Darwin when he concluded that Homo sapiens evolved from a more primitive species.

Today the ideas of these ingenious men are commonplace; we also know that they were not the first to hold them. Similarly, the whole notion of an erotic spirituality is not new, but it calls for a quantum leap in those of us who have been exposed to centuries of sex-negativity.

Sacred sex, which is the experience of ecstasy, is the real sexual revolution.

GEORG FEUERSTEIN

I

Contemporary Sexuality: Its Failures and Possibilities

❧

CHAPTER I

Taking Stock:
The Sexual Wasteland

THE AGE OF SEXUAL BEWILDERMENT

Our contemporary society has been called a sexual wilderness. The phrase was coined in 1968 by Vance Packard, an astute observer and tireless critic of modern life. In his book of the same title, he wrote:

> There have been suggestions that we are in the midst of a "sexual revolution." What in fact is occurring seems too chaotic and varied to describe yet as a revolution. A revolution implies a clear movement in an understood and generally supported direction. As I have examined my evidence the phrase that kept springing to mind as more appropriately descriptive of the state of male-female relationships in the late 1960s is "sexual wilderness."[1]

In the nineties, we find that the promised sexual revolution is in actuality still little more than a matter of widespread perplexity about sex and the moral issues connected with it. Perhaps a more apt image than wilderness today would be that of a wasteland, for so many of us are not merely sexually bewildered but also curiously lost in a cultural landscape that does not seem to be able to sustain us morally and spiritually.

Twenty-five years ago, when I was in my early twenties, a woman telephoned me. She had read one of my books on Hindu philosophy and wanted to talk to me about it. Still inexperienced at this sort of request, I rashly invited her to my home. I soon discovered that she was a desperately unhappy woman in her forties who had been married for many years. Going through her midlife crisis, she had recently embarked on a quest for self-understanding and had turned to diverse Western and Eastern spiritual traditions for illumination and help. Her husband, who was much older than she, did not share her newfound interest at all; in fact, he tried to undermine it in various ways.

It turned out that the greatest conflict between this woman and her husband revolved around sex. He insisted on his twice-weekly lovemaking, whereas she, an ex-Catholic, had always found sex unappealing and now was worrying whether it could impede her inner progress. I felt awkward about being cornered into advising a woman twice my age about her intimate life, particularly since as a newlywed I had my own share of sexual and emotional issues to deal with. I don't recall what wisdom I managed to dredge from my own limited experience of life to ease the woman's pain, but I am certain I reassured her that sexuality and spirituality were not necessarily incompatible. Later on I often pondered the curious fact that a woman her age should be at such a loss about her sexual life; it struck me as rather tragic and symptomatic of the moral disorientation of our culture.

Since that incident I have had numerous other opportunities over the years to get glimpses of a similar confusion and desperation among my friends and business contacts. And, of course, I myself was not spared this experience either. I had to work through my own problems, which, I found, were not all that different from those of other people. Whether we are sexually inactive, active, or overactive, we cannot deny the fact that sex plays a dominant role in contemporary life. Our era has correctly been characterized as being one of sexual overkill. I call this emphasis on sex, which puts varying amounts of pressure on different people, sexual stress.

In his book *The American Sexual Tragedy*, psychologist Albert Ellis summarized his findings by saying that "Americans have many sexual conflicts and are thoroughly confused and confounded about their sex, love, and marriage views and behavior."[2] Sexual and moral conflict does not stop at the borders of the United States, of course. The nations of Europe share the same syndrome, as do other so-called modern or modernizing countries around the world. Ellis's statement encapsulates the frustrations, anxieties, doubts, and hopes of countless people. What precisely is it that we feel so bewildered about?

THE SEXUAL STRESS SYNDROME

In the mid-1970s, as part of my graduate work in anthropology, I spent a prolonged period in the Middle East. After only a few weeks I found myself experiencing what anthropologists call culture shock. I was jarred by the onslaught of the Arabs' alien ways of doing things and the unfamiliar thought patterns that informed their behavior. Although I tried very hard to adjust to my new situation, I don't think I ever overcame that sense of shock.

I believe our Western civilization as a whole is in a comparable state of psychological upheaval. The twentieth century has witnessed social change on an unprecedented scale. Alvin Toffler has even spoken of future shock to describe the intensity of this experience of acute cultural transmutation, in which people are overwhelmed by change.[3] We have become alienated by the rapidly shifting ground of our culture. To borrow science-fiction writer Robert A. Heinlein's well-known phrase, we have become strangers in a strange land, even though that land is of our own collective making.

In his book *Doesn't Anyone Blush Anymore*, Manis Friedman argues that we are morally and sexually adrift because we have lost our familiar boundaries.[4] In the past, tradition told us how to behave and what to think. Today we are instead bombarded with options and are freer than ever before in the choices we can make, yet by and large we seem to lack the wisdom to make good use of that freedom. Some of us are beginning to appreciate that freedom brings with it a tremendous demand for personal responsibility. However, this lesson is not easily learned, and many people are therefore still enmeshed in confusion and suffering.

The sexual malaise experienced in the so-called civilized world is evident in many ways. Perhaps the most widespread problem is that of the routinization of sex. This is the engagement of sex as an unfeeling, mechanical performance with the goal of achieving orgasmic release, often only by the man.

Routine sex is a brief encounter between the sheets at the end of a long, tiring day. According to one source, three-fourths of men ejaculate less than two minutes after inserting the penis into the vagina.[5] To add insult to injury, many men then roll over and fall asleep, which proves a terrible disillusionment for millions of women. Generally speaking, American women participate, often as reluctant victims, twice a week in this anticlimax. Understandably, women often feel raped but may find it hard to admit this. The situation is duplicated in Europe and other parts of the world.

The sex act is seen as a biological necessity (usually by the man) or a necessary evil (usually by the woman). Routine sex can be both a sign and a cause of emotional dissociation and boredom in one's relationship. It leaves both partners unfulfilled, frustrated, and unloved. Instead of being relaxing and vivifying, as hoped, the orgasmic release is experienced as a letdown. It may even lead to depression, or it may deepen the depression that prompted coitus in the first place.

What is so unfortunate about routine sex is that it involves a depersonalization of oneself and one's partner. In routine sex, people treat each other as puppets, with the sex drive as the puppet master. They preempt the possibility of deepening their relationship and growing as persons.

Sexual frustration is especially true of women whose lovers do not appreciate their different biological makeup and emotional needs. While men can reach ejaculation in a minute or two, most women take considerably longer to reach orgasm through penile penetration, even though many can come to climax also within minutes by masturbating. A large number of women—according to some statistics, as many as 50 percent—are unable to attain orgasm through vaginal intercourse alone.

Then there are men who go to the other extreme by insisting that their partner reach orgasm as well—ideally in a couple of minutes—and so some women have become expert at "faking it." Some men are even obsessed with having their partner climax in perfect synchrony with their own orgasm. On the other side, there are women who have become firm believers in multiple orgasms and demand that their partner gratify this desire by turning into a thrusting machine.

Such attitudes have caused performance anxiety in both men and women, leading to impotence or orgasmic dysfunction—emotional gridlock. In some instances, this dissatisfaction leads to actual *sexual burnout*. This includes the feeling that sex is a frustrating experience, a source of conflict and emotional pain, to be avoided at all cost. People experiencing sexual burnout tend to shut down not only their genitals but also their emotions. They may become frigid and rigid, repressing their sexual drive rather than mastering it. They become their own victims. Only a few people who go through the crisis of sexual overload find a creative solution, such as voluntary celibacy for a period of time until the fog has cleared. Of course, they may find to their own surprise that they are far happier people without sex.

To break out of the pattern of routine sex, some men and women seek sexual and emotional fulfillment with another partner outside their established relationship. More often than not their quest merely leads to further disappointment, because they failed to realize that sex cannot be isolated from the rest of their lives. Sex outside one's established relationship is seldom fulfilling and may in fact add to one's overall stress. A sexual relationship must involve the total person to be satisfying and regenerative.

This insight also eludes those thrill seekers who, in an attempt to overcome their basic boredom, explore the farther reaches of sex—from bondage to sadomasochism, to sex with minors, to group orgies, and so on. Their search is always for *the* ultimately satisfying experience, which, wisdom tells us, does not exist. Such people allow sex to dominate their lives more and more, until they are so deep in the quagmire of their pleasure hunt that they feel trapped. Theirs is a special brand of sexual addiction.

Another route explored by a growing number of people seeking to escape sexual conflict is same-sex relationships. In some cases, these men and women become extremist advocates of the separation between the male and female genders. The anger harbored by some lesbians against men is certainly understandable. However, their emotional wounds hardly justify a social philosophy that radically dismisses the male gender. They confuse the right of sexual self-expression with their own peculiar brand of sexist ideology. Obviously our society has much to learn about homosexuality and also about practicing tolerance, but militant homosexuality is no answer to the age-old conflict between men and women. Here the social ideal of partnership, as ably proposed by Riane Eisler in her popular book *The Chalice and the Blade,* can serve as a valuable guidepost.[6]

I have mentioned sexual addiction, which is almost the obverse of sexual burnout. *Addiction* has become a popular label in recent years. The spate of books and articles on addiction that has been unleashed on the public is part of the bandwagon effect that seems to be a staple feature of the popular marketplace. Nevertheless, as there is a certain usefulness to the notion of addiction in the context of sexuality, I will avail myself of this concept in subsequent sections of this book.

Our consumeristic culture uses sex to merchandise anything from cars to beer to such seemingly innocuous products as toothpaste. Ads on television and billboards as well as in newspapers and magazines constantly seek to stimulate our sex drive. Our garments and women's makeup also frequently convey a sexual message.

In contrast to this public preoccupation with sex, our laws and official mores—as upheld by State and Church—still largely reflect the buttoned-down morality of our Victorian ancestors. This discrepancy was first pointed out by the American sexologist Alfred C. Kinsey. Writing in 1948, Kinsey and his team observed that "at least 85 percent of the younger male population could be convicted as sex offenders if law enforcement officials were as efficient as most people expect them to be."[7]

In their subsequent report on female sexuality, Kinsey and his collaborators reiterated that if our outmoded laws were consistently applied, many women would find themselves prosecuted as well. Indeed, they incurred much displeasure among state and ecclesiastical authorities for maintaining that "our culture considers that social interests are involved when an individual departs from Judeo-Christian sex codes by engaging in such sexual activities as masturbation, mouth-genital contacts, homosexual contacts, animal contacts, and other types of behavior which do not satisfy the procreative function of sex."[8]

For instance, while few cases of fornication or adultery are prosecuted nowadays, in many states they are still on the books as crimes. Considering that numerous divorces are granted on the basis that adultery was committed, these laws are evidently antiquated. While most states do not regard homosexuality itself as illegal, Lady Justice is by no means blind when it comes to homosexuals. They are more frequently charged with so-called crimes against nature than heterosexuals who break the law by performing oral or anal sex with their partner. The gap between law and social practice is considerable. Law is notoriously slow in adjusting to new social realities.

While the existing archaic laws oblige most Americans to be sex offenders in the strict legal sense, more and more people are discovering that sex is not all that it is pumped up to be. Fulfillment cannot be found in the sex act alone, however frequent, varied, or momentarily relieving it may be. Therefore, people—especially women—are beginning to express more their desire for greater intimacy and communication in their sexual relationships. In her widely read 1976 report on female sexuality, Shere Hite concluded that women overwhelmingly want sex with feeling. She observed that in the early sexual revolution, "tender feelings were often considered to be something only 'neurotic' women wanted."[9] In the meantime, the ideology of the sexual revolution has progressed beyond the philosophy of sex as an end in itself or sex for the moment and without commitment—at least in some quarters.

The women's call for intimacy did not fail to elicit a strong echo from sensitive men. Books such as Rollo May's *Love and Will,* Harold Lyon's *Tenderness Is Strength,* Herb Goldberg's *The New Male,* Sam Keen's *The Passionate Life,* and George Leonard's *The End of Sex* (now reissued as *Adventures in Monogamy*) all articulate very well the male contribution to the discussion.[10]

Inevitably, there has been a counterswing to this movement away from male machoism. Thus, poet Robert Bly has recently expressed his fears about what he terms a feminization of the male gender. He used the old German fairy tale of Iron John to register his concern about what he calls the soft male, who is sensitive and sympathetic but enervated and unhappy. "What I'm proposing," says Bly, "is that every modern male has, lying at the bottom of his psyche, a large, primitive man covered with hair down to his feet. Making contact with this Wild Man is the step the '70's male or '80's male has not yet taken: this is the process that still hasn't taken place in contemporary culture."[11] The Wild Man is not merely a savage but a resource of creative energy, which men must encounter and integrate to go beyond both machoism and sissyism.

A central part of the struggle for self-definition witnessed among American and European men and women, and increasingly also in other parts of the world, concerns the question *Who am I as a sexual being?* People consult sex therapists, counselors, Eastern gurus, and newsstand magazines, as well as joining encounter groups and sex-positive religions, in search of an answer. The question is motivated by a sense of dissatisfaction and unhappiness but also by the hope that there is indeed a solution to the problem.

As theologian-sociologist-novelist Andrew M. Greeley rightly affirmed:

> Most men and women know that they are capable of much more in their sexual lives than they permit themselves to experience and that there is immense room for growth and development in sexual pleasure and playfulness if they can find the time, the energy, and the courage and honesty to seek such development.[12]

The sexual revolution of the 1960s has made us aware of our widespread sexual misery, but it has failed to provide us with a convincing remedy for it. If anything, it has aggravated our situation by encouraging us to look in the wrong directions for personal fulfillment.

Now, twenty-odd years later, we know that open marriages, multiple orgasms, and vibrators do not add up to happiness. We can recognize more clearly the so-called sexploitation by the mass media. We can also better appreciate the wide gap between the sexual free-for-all promised by the sexual revolution and the lackluster reality of our own bedrooms. In other words, we are at last able to gaze deeper and see farther.

Among the first things our dispassionate glance encounters are the curious psychological mechanisms called guilt and shame. They are formidable and pervasive obstacles that block our path to sexual and emotional wholeness. We will examine these two stumbling blocks next.

◈

CHAPTER 2

Tracing the Roots of the Modern Sexual Dilemma

GUILT: THE FEELING OF BEING FOUND OUT

Everyone has experienced guilt at one time or another. In fact, millions of people are burdened by feelings of guilt of all sorts, especially sexual guilt. But what is guilt? What, in particular, is sexual guilt? Where does it come from? How does it differ from shame? What is the effect of guilt on us? Can we ever completely rid ourselves of guilt? Should we even attempt to do so?

The word *guilt* stems from the Old English term *gylt*, which refers to a fine for an offense. Today, guilt signifies the *objective* state of having done wrong, of being in breach of a law, and hence of being liable for a penalty. In the *subjective* sense, guilt stands for the nagging feeling of having done wrong, of being culpable. It is the concern over the rightness or wrongness of one's action. This concern implies a worry that one might be found out, or caught, and as a consequence be suitably chastised. This worry can manifest even without a person having committed a wrongful act; the mere intention to do so is sometimes enough to provoke feelings of guilt.

Not infrequently our guilt feelings are quite disproportionate to their causes and any consequences arising from them. It is as if we had an inborn guilt trigger that goes off at the slightest provocation.

Not all guilt is inappropriate and unhealthy, however. Guilt, like anger or jealousy, is a normal emotion. Only exaggerated and persistent feelings of guilt are a sign of neurosis. We must distinguish between *situational* guilt and *modal* guilt. The former is the result of actually having committed a wrong; the latter is the pervasive but nebulous sense of having violated a law, or of having sinned, which adheres to one's person like an unpleasant odor. Situational guilt is healthy, but modal guilt is neurotic.

Modal guilt is the feeling of having done wrong frozen into a habitual pattern, which is dysfunctional because it tends to arrest the free flow of our actions and thoughts. Wayne W. Dyer, in his popular book *Your Erroneous Zones,* therefore called guilt "the most useless of all erroneous zone behaviors" and "by far the greatest waste of emotional energy."[1]

Psychotherapists know that even those clients who are not aware of any guilt feelings or who deny having them soon discover, if confronted with their unconscious, that they are in fact sitting on a Pandora's box of guilt. Guilt is apparently a universal phenomenon in the human family. Whatever race or culture we belong to, we are all apt to make mistakes and errors of judgment that bring us in conflict with existing laws, mores, or etiquette and that can cause us to feel temporary regret or remorse, perhaps mixed with fear of discovery and punishment.

As you will shortly see, guilt has even deeper roots, which reach down into the human condition itself. First, however, it is necessary to look at the feeling of shame, the second stumbling block to sexual and emotional wholeness.

SHAME: THE FEELING OF BEING UNWORTHY

Guilt is closely connected with shame but must be distinguished from it. Guilt is the painful feeling resulting from our awareness that we have *done* something bad or unworthy. Shame, on the other hand, is the painful feeling that we *are* bad or unworthy. The expression "I could die from shame" describes this sense of self-abnegation well. The distinction between *doing* something unworthy and *being* unworthy has come to play an important role in the recent literature on addiction and recovery. In their valuable book *Letting Go of Shame,* Ronald and Patricia Potter-Efron offer these clarifying observations:

> There are important differences between shame and guilt. First, shame concerns a person's failure of *being,* while guilt points to a failure of *doing.* Shamed people believe something is basically

wrong with them as human beings, while the guilty people believe they have done something wrong that must be cor-
rected. . . .

A second major difference is that the shamed people usually are bothered by their *shortcomings,* while guilty people notice
their *transgressions.* . . .

The third difference between shame and guilt is that the
shamed person fears *abandonment,* while the guilty person fears
punishment. The reason the shamed person fears abandonment is
that he believes he is too flawed to be wanted or valued by
others. . . .

Shame can be more difficult to heal than guilt, because it is
about the person rather than specific actions. The shamed person
heals by changing her self-concept so that she gains new self-
respect and pride.[2]

It is easy to see how shame may follow upon feelings of
guilt or how it can feed guilt. The two emotions can be like a
revolving door that keeps the person trapped in a perpetual spin.
Hence we must deal squarely with guilt and shame if we want to
grow and overcome our sexual malaise.

Our Heritage of Sexual Guilt and Shame

The experience of guilt and shame is especially pronounced, if
not omnipresent, in the area of sexuality. Not a few men and
women feel guilty about sex itself; they think sex is dirty or in-
human. They avoid making love, or if they do have sex, it is in
the form of a hasty encounter in the dark while wearing pajamas
and nightgown. Such people never talk about sex or their suffering. Their sexual paranoia and frustration spills over into their
marital and family life as well as into all their other relationships
and activities. This sex-negative disposition is especially prominent in religious fundamentalist circles.

Generally speaking, women feel guilty when they aren't in
the mood to make love but don't know how to say no. Men, statistics tells us, desire sexual contact more frequently than
women. How many men feel vaguely or openly guilty when
they insist on their conjugal right even though their partner
shows no interest? Women often experience guilt and shame
when they feel aroused but do not dare to communicate this to
their husbands. Married men feel guilty when they resort to

masturbation because their wife claims to have another head-
ache, and they feel ashamed when they are caught in the act. Or
perhaps they feel guilty because they want to see their partner in
the nude.

Women may suffer from guilt because they allowed their
husband to try out different sexual positions and practices, or
because they derived pleasure from these variations in their
otherwise so-called straight sex life. Conversely, men may feel
guilty for asking their partner to commit such supposedly ab-
normal acts. Women frequently experience tremors of guilt
about their premarital sexual relationships. They may also feel
guilty about using contraception, because the Church de-
nounces this as a sinful practice. Men feel ashamed when their
wife discovers the pornographic magazine hidden in the bedside
table.

Many men suffer from what is called a Madonna complex,
finding it difficult to see in their wife a sexual partner after she
has given birth to a child. They confuse their wife with their
own mother, conveniently forgetting how they themselves
were conceived. Such men tend to shun marital sexual intercourse after their wives have borne children.

Mothers feel ashamed when their young child fondles its
genitals in public, and shame is a more intense feeling than mere
embarrassment. Parents tend to feel too ashamed about sex to
educate their children about sexual matters, leaving it to teachers who are similarly ashamed and guilt-ridden and to their
children's ignorant and misinformed peers. Children feel too
ashamed to talk to their parents and too guilty to confess they
are experimenting sexually. And so on.

As psychotherapists and marriage counselors can vouchsafe, the forms of sexual guilt and shame and their permutations
are nearly infinite. It appears that sexual guilt is particularly
troubling to those who know the least about sex,[3] and sexual ignorance often bedevils the lives of religious puritans; to coin a
phrase, those who are religiously rigid also tend to be sexually
frigid.

The sexual revolution notwithstanding, we, as Westerners, are still suffering the backwash of centuries of sexual repression under the Christian Church. Alex Comfort, a physician who was one of the movers of the sexual revolution, commented:

Whatever Christianity may have contributed to the growth of our culture in other fields, it seems undeniable that in sexual morals and practice its influence has been less healthy than that of other world religions.[4]

Comfort also observed that the "fact of having made sex into a 'problem' is the major negative achievement of Christendom."[5] We do not have to be anti-Christian to concur with this statement. Some of the finest advocates for Christianity have rebuked the overly sex-negative attitudes of the Christian heritage.

THE DENIAL OF THE BODY

When we inspect the Christian view of sex more closely, we find at its bottom a stubborn denial or denigration of bodily existence. The body—or the flesh—is regarded as the enemy of the spirit. Kenneth Leech, an Anglican priest, has this passionate criticism:

> It is through the flesh that salvation comes. And yet so much in Christian spirituality and Christian life is flesh-denying, flesh-despising, flesh-devaluing. It is head-centred, ponderous, life-extinguishing, devoid of passion. . . . It is disturbing to see how Christian history and Christian spirituality has been so marred by a highly ambivalent tradition which, while officially rejecting gnostic denials of the goodness of the flesh, has nevertheless been affected to a great extent by those gnostic tendencies within orthodoxy itself.[6]

According to the classic Christian model, the body is innately impure and thus is inimical to religious or spiritual life. This view of embodiment has caused immense trauma among Christians, and it continues to do so. We are supposed to feel guilty and ashamed about our body. We are meant to feel especially guilty and ashamed about our sexual organs and their functions. And a good many people, though they may consciously reject puritanism, have unconsciously accepted this negative message, which comes to us across the centuries from Platonism, Gnosticism, Christianity, and finally from the dualistic philosophy of Descartes on which our whole scientific edifice is built.

As historian and social critic Morris Berman has argued in his breathtaking study *Coming to Our Senses,* we in the West have lost our bodies. We are largely out of touch with genuine somatic reality. There is a frightening conspiracy of silence about bodily processes, including death. Because we are "out of the body," we seek to ground ourselves by resorting to substitutes—secondary satisfactions—such as success, reputation, career, self-image, and money, as well as spectator sports, nationalism, and war.

But these substitutes offer no ultimate fulfillment, and consequently, as Berman notes, "our defeat shows in our bodies: we either 'prop ourselves up,' so to speak, or slump in a posture of collapse."[7] Although we disregard our own somatic reality, we are paradoxically preoccupied with the body and how it looks. We seek to improve it through makeup, fine clothes, hairdos, plastic surgery, deodorants, health foods, vitamins, and jogging.

Yet this improvement is often a means of concealing the *lived body,* that is, the body as we *feel* it when we do not abstract ourselves from it and treat it as an object. To what degree we hide our somatic reality is especially demonstrated in our sanitized approach to death.

Philosopher Drew Leder explained this apparent contradiction between simultaneous denial and preoccupation with the body as follows: When our body functions normally, it tends to disappear from our awareness.[8] However, when it ceases to work smoothly we quickly become aware of it. Our present-day consciousness is ill at ease with bodily reality, and hence we are constantly paying attention to the body as object. In the process, what phenomenologists call the lived body continues to be obscured. In other words, we tend to withdraw into our heads and assume a more abstract relationship to life. Men are not alone in this conspiracy. The female gender, though subject to the bodily dramas of menstruation and birth, also succumbs to denial of the body.

Our obsession with sex can similarly be understood as arising from the absence of true sexuality: the authentic rhythm of sexual desire and its spontaneous expression as part of a full embrace of our embodied condition. We distrust the body, and so we constantly watch it as if it were something separate from us. Hence we can perform sexually without being truly present in the act.

If we are religious, we identify with what we call the spirit because we distrust the body. If our orientation to life is a secular one, we identify with mind or consciousness because we feel threatened by the body. In either case, we suffer a diminution of our being.

Finally, our fear of the body is expressed in our irreverence for nature at large, which we tend to exploit and use as a dumping ground for the discards of our consumerist civilization. As the feminist movement has made clear, the same alienation from the body is also evident in our disregard for the female gender, which symbolizes nature and embodiment. The correlation body:nature:woman:sexuality is a very important contemporary insight. Unless we become fully cognizant of it and its many implications, we cannot understand our postmodern world and the challenge before us, both on the personal and the societal level.

GUILT, SHAME, AND ECSTASY

In a previous section I distinguished between situational and modal guilt and shame. A further distinction must now be introduced, namely that of existential guilt and shame. The former two can be explained as deriving from personal experiences of transgression or inadequacy or a combination thereof. Existential guilt and shame, however, are dispositions that are an integral aspect of the human constitution itself. They spring from our universal experience of alienation and finitude or imperfection: we, as individuals or ego–identities, experience ourselves as separate from everything else.

When we consider this situation profoundly enough, we find that this mood of separateness is equivalent to unhappiness. Existentialism speaks of this mood as anxiety. At a certain level of human maturity, this sense of separation is even felt to be wrong and reprehensible, because we intuit that it does not express the wholeness of our being. That is to say, we feel guilty about living below our capacities. In fact, neurosis has been defined as the inability to heroically transcend oneself, to go beyond one's present appearance. Psychological health, as psychologist Abraham Maslow has persuasively argued, implies the impulse toward wholeness and self-transcendence.[9]

Similarly, we are filled with existential shame at denying

our own potential, our innermost impulse toward self-transcendence. In his well-known book *The Art of Loving,* psychoanalyst Erich Fromm commented:

> The awareness of human separation—without reunion by love—is the source of shame. It is at the same time the source of guilt and anxiety.[10]

Fromm further noted that our deepest need is the need to overcome our separateness, the prison of our aloneness. In a similar vein, Andrew M. Greeley observed:

> Some feeling of personal and physical inadequacy is probably part of the human condition. Man becomes conscious of himself by individuating himself over against others, and in that act of "alienation," he acquires fears that in his attempts to accomplish union now as an individuated person, he may not have all that it takes.[11]

Greeley contrasted this innate existential shame with what he called psychic shame:

> Some cultures and societies greatly reinforce the existential shame by placing strong emphasis on the evil of the human body and the risks of human sexuality. Within these societies certain kinds of early childhood experience produce intense feelings of guilt and inadequacy. Thus, in contemporary America, despite our happy talk of "permissiveness," many (indeed, most) people approach the physical and psychological stripping that marital intimacy demands with a combination of fear and disgust.[12]

This emotional overlay on our existential disposition of guilt and shame is essentially neurotic. Both neurotic guilt and shame are states of mind that, given a chance, depress our life energy. "Shame eats the soul," writes social theorist Victor J. Seidler.[13] Guilt likewise grinds away at our being. Both guilt and shame countermand our native creativity and exuberance of life.

People who are chronically guilty tend to be walking "black holes." Their outlook on life is bleak. They are complainers, blamers, and failures. They absorb the energies of others but fail to project and share their own. They are ill-equipped for the rigors of a life dedicated to personal growth, which demands a great deal of self-confidence, willpower, courage, and, above all, the intent to change and grow.

Psychoanalysis has given us a rather somber but essentially correct vision of our Western civilization as a giant template producing millions of guilty and ashamed consciousnesses. As Sigmund Freud proposed in his classic work *Civilization and Its Discontents,* civilization conspires to make us inauthentic and anti-ecstatic.[14] According to Freud, we are individually motivated by the need for happiness, the pleasure principle, while civilization perpetually seeks to direct that need along acceptable channels. Thus we end up choosing security over self-expression and freedom. Freud speculated that perhaps all of humanity is neurotic on this score.

Because of our ambivalent attitude toward embodiment, we are prone to converting our innate drive for happiness into what we might style the fun principle. To be sure, fun is as far removed from happiness as voyeurism is from actual sexual intimacy. As psychoanalyst Alexander Lowen noted:

> To the casual observer, it would seem that America is a land of pleasure. Its people seem intent upon having a good time. They spend much of their leisure time and money in the pursuit of pleasure. . . .
>
> The question naturally arises: Do Americans really enjoy their lives? Most serious observers of the current scene believe that the answer is no. They feel that the obsession with fun betrays an absence of pleasure [or happiness].[15]

In his "passionate ethnography" entitled *Culture Against Man,* anthropologist Jules Henry made the point that fun is a way of staying alive in a culture that is riddled with boredom. Commenting on his fellow Americans, Henry remarked:

> Fun, in its rather unique American form, is grim resolve. When the foreigner observes how grimly we seem to go about our fun, he is right; we are as determined about the pursuit of fun as a desert-wandering traveler is about the search for water, and for the same reasons.[16]

Henry was wrong in assuming that this grim pursuit of fun is uniquely American—pleasure-seekers are an integral part of other postindustrial societies as well. He was also wrong in suggesting that fun is "a clowning saboteur undermining the very system fun was meant to sustain."[17] On the contrary, fun supports the status quo. It is merely a safety valve for the pent-up frustrations of those living in a competitive society such as ours.

Fun is based on make-believe: we experience pleasurable sensations, but we do not really experience deep pleasure and joy, not to mention happiness or bliss. In fact, many of us fear the kind of pleasure that seizes the whole body. As Lowen remarked:

> How can anyone be afraid of that which is beneficial and desirable? Yet many people avoid pleasure; some develop acute anxiety in pleasurable situations, and others actually experience pain when the pleasurable excitation becomes too intense.[18]

Lowen explained this fear of pleasure in bodily terms: when pleasurable sensations spread through the body, they may encounter blockages in the average individual who suffers from chronic tension and tightness. These blockages then convert the pleasurable sensations into pain. Unless a bodyworker or therapist stands by to help a person to stay with the pain and go beyond it, achieving release, that person may never experience the other side of pleasure. The typical reaction is to recoil from the pain and thus to contract more. Of course, the bodily blockages have their emotional equivalents.

When pleasure sprawls through our body, it threatens to overwhelm us emotionally; and if we are emotionally constipated, this prospect can cause us a good deal of anxiety. It is not easy to let go and to trust the pleasurable sensations in our being. We may, as Lowen points out, first have to "fall apart" before we can arrive at bodily and emotional wholeness. On the other side of pain or resistance is happiness, ecstasy, or bliss.

In its normal state, as dictated by society and imbibed habit, our body is relatively shut down. Wilhelm Reich spoke of the body being armored—from hunched shoulders to furrowed foreheads to tight abdomens.[19] We are barely capable of feeling pleasure and when we do, we tend to feel it only in localized areas, notably our genitals. But it is well established that when we are open bodily, pleasure is experienced throughout the body. The big toe is capable of tingling with delight as much as our genitals, as paraplegics have testified.

Whole-body pleasure coincides with the relaxation of emotional stress. As the body's rigidity is broken down through

deep-tissue massage, for instance, flexibility returns to our emotions. We feel open-hearted and open-minded. Psychologist
Ken Dychtwald, who has studied extensively the remedial effect
of bodywork, writes:

> I know that the existential conflicts I have felt regarding my own
> sexuality are reflected throughout my bodymind. Sometimes, I
> find myself wanting to open up and embrace the world; at other
> times I am closed, afraid of being hurt and rejected. . . .
>
> In terms of my own sexual experience and expression,
> however, I have discovered that the more conscious I become and
> the more healthy my bodymind is, the more dynamic and beau-
> tiful are the sexual feelings I experience. *I have especially found that
> when my body is well tuned, and unblocked, it is capable of heightened
> sensitivity and expanded emotional experience.* And when I am hon-
> est and aware, I find that my interactions with my lover are more
> direct, more nourishing, and more loving. [20]

We can consider ordinary life as the habit of living below
our human potential, below our capacity for experiencing genuine happiness, even ecstasy. Psychologist Robert A. Johnson
made these pertinent comments in his best-selling work *Ecstasy:*

> It is a great tragedy of contemporary Western society that we
> have virtually lost the ability to experience the transformative
> power of ecstasy and joy. This loss affects every aspect of our
> lives. We seek ecstasy everywhere, and for a moment we may
> think we have found it. But, on a very deep level, we remain un-
> fulfilled. [21]

We remain unfulfilled because, on the whole, we no longer
intuit the nature of happiness. We confuse it with spurts of pleasure or, more exactly, with fun arrived at mechanically, whether
it be through genital friction, and ingestion of alcohol, or TV
voyeurism.

SEXUAL ADDICTION AS AVOIDANCE OF BLISS

One form in which we express and perpetuate our personal and
societal "dis-ease" is by our cleaving to genital sensations, especially orgasm. Through orgasm we seek to punctuate the

monotony of our life while at the same time reducing nervous tension.

Actual sexual addiction, like nicotine, alcohol, or drug addiction, is simply a more exaggerated and therefore more conspicuous version of that same basic disposition to settle for short-lived thrills of the nervous system rather than a penetrating transmutation of ourselves that attunes us to the larger reality and fills our body-minds with the bliss "that passeth all understanding." The addict, observed the cultural philosopher Jean Gebser, "tries to belie his own nature with elements foreign to it."[22]

Sexual addiction comes in many forms and guises, which have been presented by psychotherapist Anne Wilson-Schaef in her book *Escape From Intimacy*.[23] At one end of the spectrum of addictive behavior described by Wilson-Schaef is "Molly," who is described as a sexual anorexic. She was the typical "prudish tease," who liked to come across as sexy and thought incessantly about sex but was afraid of sex and men. She first had to accept her co-dependency before she could recognize her own sexual addiction.

Next, Wilson-Schaef presented the case of "Julian," whose addiction to sexual fantasies threatened to destroy his marriage and family. Then there is "Leslie," an inveterate masturbator who took greater and greater risks with her secret habit until she started to live for the next orgasm in a socially or physically risky situation. At the other end of the behavioral spectrum is sexual violence—from rape to incest to child molesting to sadomasochism.

Sexual addiction is a special way of avoiding happiness, or ecstasy. It substitutes local pleasure or instant thrill for abiding happiness.

The Quest for Transcendence

Civilization has always sought to inhibit and regulate our instinctual life, and it has surrounded sex and aggression with a great variety of restrictions and severe prohibitions, called taboos. Consequently, civilization has been a breeding ground for pervasive feelings of guilt. Freud deserves credit for making us aware of our pervasive guilt feelings and for exposing some of the mechanics behind them.

However, with the hindsight of the past five or more decades, we must now acknowledge that Freud's model of the human being was sadly deficient. It still owed too much to the materialist ideology of the nineteenth century, which interpreted the body-mind as a machine. A more penetrating view is today espoused by transpersonal psychology. This young discipline maintains that beneath our hunt for fun or fleeting pleasure there lies buried a deep desire to realize our ecstatic potential. But to realize ecstasy means to transcend ordinariness. In fact, it means to transcend all experiences conditioned by space-time—hence *transpersonal,* which means "beyond the personal," or beyond the ordinary limited sense of identity.

This brings us to a consideration of the profound theme of what the religious traditions call the spirit or the spiritual dimension of existence. The spirit refers to that aspect of human life which participates in the larger reality that is named God, Goddess, the Divine, Absolute, Tao, Shunya, Brahman, or Atman.

The Chinese word *tao* means "way" and stands for the ultimate thing, or process, which includes all visible and invisible processes or realities but is not confined to them. The Buddhist Sanskrit term *shunya* means "void" and refers to the ultimate reality insofar as it is devoid of all characteristics and hence is finally incomprehensible to the finite human mind. The Sanskrit word *brahman* comes from the root *brih,* meaning "to grow, expand." It is that which is infinitely large and all-comprising—the transcendental ground of the universe. The Sanskrit term *atman* means "self" and designates the ultimate subject, or transcendental self, concealed deep within the human personality, which is infinite and timeless.

The Divine, or ultimate reality, is inherently sacred. That is to say, it is set apart from conventional human life and our ordinary presumptions about existence, and it fills us with awe. The Divine has variously been envisioned as the Creator of the world (as in Judaism, Christianity, and Islam) or as the very foundation or essence of the universe (as in Taoism, Hinduism, and some schools of Buddhism). Belief in a great being was virtually universal before modern times. Today, as we witness the godlike accomplishments of technology, some of us have grown doubtful of the existence of the Divine.

The widespread attitude of skepticism notwithstanding, however, talk about God is rather tenacious, and it has even reentered the scientific world view. This brings us closer again to the age-old spiritual traditions of the world.

Thus, borrowing from Hindu philosophy, transpersonal psychologist Ken Wilber speaks of the Atman project, which he explains as follows:

> We have seen that psychological development in humans has the same goal as natural evolution: the production of ever-higher unities. And since the ultimate Unity is Buddha, God, or Atman (to use those terms in their broadest sense as "ultimate reality"), it follows that psychological growth aims at Atman. . . . From the outset, the soul [psyche] intuits this Atman-nature, and seeks, from the start, to *actualize* it as a reality and not just an enfolded potential. That drive to actualize Atman is part of the Atman-project.[24]

In other words, at the bottom of all our individual and civilizational enterprises lies a spiritual impulse, the will to go beyond appearances, beyond the conventional human personality and its motivations, beyond even the Freudian unconscious and its resident passions.

In keeping with Wilber's concept of the Atman project, we can understand existential guilt and shame as the products of a diminished response toward, and responsibility for, our potential as human beings. Contrary to much of modern philosophy and scientific ideology, the spiritual traditions tell us that we are capable of realizing the ultimate reality. We can do so by means of the process of self-transcendence, of stepping beyond the boundaries of the ego-personality.

As Wilber affirms, we are not only capable of realizing the ultimate reality, but are secretly propelled to do so. However, this subconscious push generally takes a somewhat circuitous route, because we seldom consciously collaborate with it. In other words, the primary spiritual impulse is subverted and contorted. Each person, according to Wilber, "wants only Atman, but wants it under conditions which prevent it."[25] We subvert that impulse by finding substitutes for it, such as our hunt after fun or temporary experiences of pleasure, including sexual diversion, or our quest for security in finite things.

We are afraid of the sacred just as we are afraid of deep pleasure or bliss, because they all threaten to undermine our familiar identity, which is the ego-personality, our sense of being a particular, limited body-mind.

The ego, one might say, is the primary Atman substitute. It is responsible for all subsequent substitutes, which are then experienced in relationship to this artificial center of subjectivity. The ego is responsible, in other words, for our peculiar experience of reality: we experience reality as external to ourselves; we objectify life as a separate event. We objectify our own body and thus separate it from the person we deem ourselves to be.

As we grow, our urges become more refined and we wean ourselves away from our pursuit of this or that Atman substitute, until the spiritual impulse presents itself in its purity and the Atman project comes fully into its own. It is only then that we begin to value ecstatic self-transcendence, or spiritual enlightenment, above all momentary satisfactions. It is only then that we fully realize that we *are* the body and that the body is not external to ourselves or separate from the rest of the world. Ecstasy is the realization of the essential interconnectedness of all existence.

FROM SEXUAL MALAISE TO THE LOSS OF THE SACRED

Through a long chain of arguments, we have traced the roots of our present-day sexual malaise to a fundamental rift in the modern psyche. This self-dividedness is evident in the way we objectify the body as if it were a thing that we, as ghostly entities, inhabit. That "thingified" body then becomes an object of ambiguity for us. Just as we split the body from the mind, we exclude it from the rest of the world. In that process, we also come to feel ambiguous about many aspects of life. In particular, we cannot fully enjoy our sexuality because we are out of tune with our body, which is the vehicle of sexual experience, and also because we are out of touch with the body of the world, which is the medium in which all our social and intimate relationships occur.

In the final analysis, our sexual malaise turns out to be a spiritual problem. We experience ourselves at odds with the universe at large, alienated from what theologians have called the ground of being. In many ways, we have lost sight of the sacred. Our lives are marked by an unhappy rift between the sacred and the profane.

There is, however, a growing awareness in our Western civilization that in order to heal our psyche and our ailing society, we must repair this multiple breach. In particular, we must reconnect with the sacred.

Luckily, the sacred proves to be a pervasive power in the universe that cannot be easily ignored. The Atman project exercises its potent influence within us. Hence we find that even rather secular individuals are surprised by experiences of the sacred. Suddenly—sometimes at the oddest times—there is a momentary breakthrough when the spiritual or sacred dimension of existence makes itself known to us. We may be listening to a Beethoven sonata, tending our garden, hiking in the wilderness, or passionately making love. In that instant, we are healed at the core of our being. There is joy, happiness, bliss, ecstasy.

CHAPTER 3

The Hidden Window:
Spiritual Breakthroughs in Sex

SEX, LOVE, AND TRANSCENDENCE

According to a national survey conducted in 1973, four out of ten Americans have experienced what they described as a powerful spiritual force that seemed to lift them out of themselves.[1] One in five of these people claimed that he or she had this experience more than once. Fifty-five percent said they partook of "a feeling of profound peace" and 43 percent spoke of "a sense of joy." It is clear from their descriptions that not a few of them had been the beneficiaries of a full-blown mystical experience, in which the sense of body-encapsulated identity is lost.

The high incidence of such religious or mystical experiences in our secular, materialistic civilization has come as a great surprise to some people. However, another survey finding is at least equally amazing: most of the respondents never talked about their extraordinary experiences until the time of the survey. This self-imposed silence on the part of closet mystics may well be one of the principal reasons why our unspoken cultural taboo against ecstasy continues to be so strong and influential. How our society would change if we were to tell one another freely about our most sacred moments and our happiest and most remarkable experiences!

I believe we all have the potential for such uplifting experiences of total happiness, when all self-centeredness is suspended. Abraham Maslow, the great pioneer of humanistic psychology, has shown that such moments of self-transcendence occur frequently in mature, well-integrated persons.[2] He called them peak experiences.

In the mystical state (*unio mystica*) there is no sense of being divorced from anything, and all opposites are transcended. Self and other are merged into a single whole, and there is no within and without, no space and time. No words can adequately portray the content of the mystical experience, and it harbors depth upon depth of revelation that the intellect cannot fathom. But, above all, it is a state that is felt to be vastly superior to, and more desirable than, the ordinary state of being and consciousness.

The unitive condition comes always as a surprise. As popular writer Joseph Chilton Pearce would say, the unitive experience affords us a glimpse through the crack in our cosmic egg, our particular mind-set or interpretation of reality.[3] It opens up a new view of reality—a view that is qualitatively so different from our ordinary perspective that it cannot but surprise us and put us in wonderment.

Sometimes this kind of breakthrough happens when we are in love and during or as a result of sexual intimacy. Indeed, sexual love is the most intense and tangible way in which ordinary men and women strive for a union that transcends the boundaries of their everyday experience. In the sexual act, we seek to forget ourselves, if only for a brief spell. We seek to make a deeper contact with our lover. We want to escape the sense of being imprisoned by skin and separated from the rest of the universe.

Often, however, this desire remains quite unconscious, and then sex is engaged in as a mere diversion from the concerns and stresses of daily life. Our contact is only skin-deep, and we fail to give that primal impulse toward union full expression. Consequently we continue to feel alone, abandoned, betrayed, and unloved. Yet we are again and again pushed to repeat sexual contact. Since we are not, like animals, blindly subject to the reproductive cycle, this urge can be understood only as having deep psychological as well as physiological roots.

Sex is the ordinary person's substitute for a spiritual or sacred way of life, with orgasm being a surrogate for the utterly blissful unitive state. In that state, extolled by mystics of all ages and cultures as the pinnacle of human experience, reality is encountered in its nakedness, without conceptual blinders. As Greeley noted:

> Intercourse does deautomatize somewhat our ordinary reality
> orientation. It does take us out of ourselves; it is an experience of
> passionate unity; it is an attempt at sharing, a temporary immer-
> sion in fundamental life forces.[4]

My investigations—conducted by questionnaire, interview, and a careful study of various cultures—have convinced
me that sex can be an important gateway to mystical experiences
or encounters with the sacred. Sex has long been considered in
this positive way by many religious traditions, even those, like
Christianity, that are known for their puritanism. My conclu-
sions are confirmed not only by Greeley and McCready but also
by Marghanita Laski, a British writer. In her classic book *Ecstasy
in Secular and Religious Experiences,* she made these comments:

> Among contemporary secular people of the kind that composed
> my questionnaire group sexual love appears to be a common
> trigger. In this group sexual love was named as a trigger by 33
> percent of people (18 women and 8 men). Eleven of these people
> (6 men and 5 women) made unmistakable references to sexual
> intercourse, and of other references to 'love,' 'being in love,' etc.,
> sexual intercourse was probably implied in several cases.[5]

Surprisingly enough, Laski's finding that sexual love appears to be a common trigger does not seem to be confirmed by
the research of that other intrepid collector of mystical self-
reports in Britain, Sir Alister Hardy. Hardy, an emeritus professor of zoology at Oxford who is well known for his contribu-
tions to marine biology, has been pioneering the rapprochement
between spirituality and biology since the 1920s. In 1969, at the
age of seventy-three, he established the Religious Experience
Research Unit at Manchester College in Oxford. Ten years later,
he and his collaborators had collected over 4,000 first-hand accounts of mystical and psychic experiences. The team's provi-
sional analysis of a large bulk of these materials is contained in
The Spiritual Nature of Man.[6]

Of the 3,000 cases so far analyzed by Hardy, only 12 are
stated to have had sexual love for their trigger. If correct, we
must wonder whether the British have no love lives, which is
clearly absurd, or whether they do not mix sex with love or passion. The most likely solution to the problem posed by the low

figure in Hardy's survey is that his fellow British were simply reluctant to write about their sexual lives.

In the following, I will present a number of first-person accounts by people who have courageously broken the existing taboo and divulged their extraordinary experiences during sex, including mystical union. Since most of them still preferred to remain anonymous, I have, with the exception of my wife's case, preserved the anonymity of all respondents to my questionnaire and personal inquiries.

THE POWER OF LOVE:
EROTIC AND SPIRITUAL BREAKTHROUGHS

The following self-report shows that the feeling of love, as it thrives between young lovers, is a powerful means of slipping through the eye of the needle into the bright world of joyous communion with, and attunement to, another person. Monica is a pretty, petite woman in her late thirties. She is divorced and works as a secretary. She has lived an active spiritual life for many years and has experienced a variety of meditation states.

> I was sitting at the edge of my bed waiting for my lover. He had just called, and I was looking forward to his visit. As I was thinking about him and how much I loved him and valued his love, I grew determined to just love him that night, to be concentrated in loving rather than allowing myself to be distracted about worries about our future. In that moment I simply accepted that he was not yet ready to make a long-term commitment to me.
>
> My lover arrived shortly after I had made my resolution, and for some reason it was not difficult at all to focus on that feeling of love. As we were making love, I remember looking into his eyes and being "undone" by the love and naked vulnerability I saw in them.
>
> All of a sudden I felt no separation between us. I was startled by that and wanted to draw back. But realizing that I was cutting myself off from him and the love that we were feeling for each other, I continued to look into his eyes and to simply be present with him.
>
> I "fell" into the fullness that had arisen in and between us. It was so uncomplicated and natural, and my mind was amazingly calm and quiet. A simple joy! And our love-making wasn't passive either. In fact, it got rather boisterous and passionate.

I have had the experience of losing myself a few times in meditation, but this was the only time it happened during lovemaking. That day I was undoubtedly emotionally more open than usual, but also his depth of feeling seemed to draw me into a deeper feeling. Afterward he asked me whether I had noticed anything different and nodded in agreement when I told him what I had felt. He said that for him it was as if we had been encased in a large bubble of energy.

The bubble of energy experienced by Monica's lover probably represents a far more common experience than is assumed. While it cannot be called a mystical experience in the strict sense, because there is still a sense of duality, it does signal an important spiritual opening.

A thirty-four-year-old divorced man was converted from agnosticism to a metaphysical perspective on life by just such an energy experience during sex. As he described:

I have known this particular woman for almost three years. I always felt a special type of connection with her since the time we met, and she claims the same feeling. Our friendship grew deeper as time went on, and we became lovers. We both felt a profound deepening of our love for each other.

I had not had many sexual relationships with women before meeting her, and it was with her that I first experienced what it was to make love. This I feel deeply. I know what it is to make love, because it was her, because of her. My relationship with her has caused a change in me that I am very thankful for.

For personal reasons I had to move across the nation, while her life was in California. We had to separate. The weekend prior to my departure, we took a beautiful room at an inn. We dined, walked, and made love that evening. With her I had experienced what lovemaking could be. However, it was during this particular evening that I experienced what I feel was the beginning of a joining of our spirits.

We were making love, and while I was kissing her, I felt a strong desire to be a part of her, and for her to be a part of me. Our kissing intensified, and I began to experience the sensation that my physical senses were falling away. My body was disappearing, as was the sensation of her body against mine. I began sensing energy swelling and flowing toward her, and in my mind's eye I saw a white shapeless form, moving and growing. As the form grew, the energy grew and intensified.

This lasted just a few seconds, before I pulled away from

her lips. I was as startled by this as she was. We both gasped in surprise and looked at each other for a few seconds, not knowing what had happened and not knowing what to say. She then told me that she had never been kissed like that before, and I confessed the same to her. She had experienced the same physical sensations, though she did not visualize the white shape. Then, after collecting ourselves for a few moments, we resumed our lovemaking.

In his book *Tenderness Is Strength,* Harold C. Lyon, Jr., related an incident that involved a parapsychological phenomenon of mutual visualization during a moment of self-surrendered sex. Early one morning, he went fishing. For three hours he trolled for lake trout, using all his skills to perfection, and was about to head back home when he had a strike. He had caught a twenty-six-inch trout. Excitedly he shared his adventure and joy with his wife, who was still in bed. He recollects:

> We had not been comfortable in our relationship for the past few months, struggling to resolve our differences and blaming each other for them. How silly. How useless. Our lovemaking had become mechanical, lacking the flow and fulfillment we both sought. An hour after I had climbed back into bed, we found ourselves making love with incredible passion, spontaneity, and tender joy, flowing from orgasm to orgasm. There was a letting go, a total surrendering to our own inner rhythms, which had eluded us for months. In the midst of my orgasm I had a vision of the big lake trout, organic and beautiful in the depths of the lake, and I realized that I could not *make* her take my lure even when it was presented with perfect technique. *She* had to be ready to strike the lure, with no holding back. This was a natural flowing instinct, not something I could force or manipulate.
>
> Incredibly, in the afterglow of our loving, Eta shared with me that she too had seen a vision of the organic lake trout in the throes of *her* orgasms! We both realized in a flash that with all the technique in the world, we couldn't make our love flow until it was ready to flow, any more than I could make the lake trout take the lure.[7]

Of course, the shared visionary experience is not the point. The crux is the mutual lowering of the couple's ego defenses, which allowed love to flood their hearts and transform their lovemaking into an ecstatic affair.

This happened in a very dramatic way to another respondent to my questionnaire whom I will call Mary. Her breakthrough, which involved a more advanced stage of unitive consciousness, happened just a few months prior to my completing this book. Mary, who is in her mid-thirties, was brought up as a Catholic and predictably felt, as she put it, "rather divided about sex and spirituality." She had tried several times to break away from her tradition but was always drawn back to it, although she married a non-Catholic during one of her phases of involvement with Catholicism.

In 1989, her husband, Carl, went to an office Christmas party on his own, met a woman to whom he felt deeply attracted, and exchanged a long, passionate kiss with her. When he asked her to go to bed with him, she refused because he was married. Carl confessed the brief encounter a couple of days later. Mary was understandably shocked. In her own words:

I was devastated. Carl had never done anything like it, though he had not promised anything either, merely said it was unlikely that he would have an affair. I had been afflicted with jealousy before, unreasonably so. Even though Carl assured me that his love for me was deep and lasting, I was disillusioned and depressed, and lost interest in anything but our relationship. I had no appetite and no orgasms.

But then I started to see this incident as an answer to my prayers. I had asked God to show me how to love. A short time before I had read Meister Eckhart. He wrote that love is its own reward: when you love other people, then you really do share their joy, and so it multiplies your own joy. I wanted this very much, but was too self-involved to really feel it.

Carl told me that something happened to him that day. He felt a weight had been lifted from him, and he started to feel stronger in other areas of his life—like his job. He wasn't going to be hung up about money and security anymore.

I flitted between being loving and understanding and being full of worries and what-ifs. I loved him a lot but tortured myself wondering where I would draw the line. I was afraid of being a martyr. Nevertheless, a few days later I decided not to leave him. Not only did I love him, but I trusted the depth of his love for me.

That night after our daughter was asleep, we continued our dialogue. He told me many things, including the ways he loved me. He also told me that he worried if I were unable to have orgasms anymore, blaming himself.

Until that evening, I was never able to have orgasms without using my fingers on myself. Our usual way of getting me to come was with him lying on top of my back. But the dam broke that night. I had powerful, easy, beautiful orgasms in all sorts of positions.

The pleasure I felt was throughout my body. I had no conscious control over it, and I didn't feel limited by my body. It was like I was overflowing—swimming through Carl, swimming through God. I felt totally ecstatic. Carl was telling me he worshipped me—that I was a goddess. We were praising God together. I felt finally at one with my sexuality. And I felt the closeness of God as never before. I felt completely accepting of Carl and of myself. Pure love. It went on and on.

We both felt the momentousness of that night. We stayed up till 5 A.M. talking and making love. It was incredible to me that I could now look him in the eyes and have glorious orgasms without even trying.

I was in a bit of a daze in the weeks that followed. There were some downs, but the feeling of being transformed has stayed with me. We both feel that we have fallen in love again, but in a deeper, even more exciting way. Before I had tried to link up my spirituality and my relationship with Carl, but it never really worked. He didn't share my Catholicism, and it was hard to talk to him about spiritual things. But now I feel like we have come from different directions and met on new ground.

Soon after that evening I realized that I was wasting my time with Catholicism. As liberally as I was interpreting it, it was still holding me back, giving me an excuse (when I wanted it) not to think for myself, not to listen to God-in-me.

I feel clearer, freer, less conflicted, and happier this year than ever before. I am rid of most of the self-hatred and guilt that I had carried for so long. I have practically given up the word "should." It is clearer to me what I should do with my time and what is dispensable clutter. Closeness to God has been important to me most of my life, but this year, God is in reach, daily, more than ever before. I am more open to finding God everywhere.

My interest in sex has skyrocketed. I now understand sex as a God-given ecstasy as much as any mystic's. I have given up much of my shyness, as I feel so much better about myself. I also have more interest in other people. I find God deep within myself and by encountering Carl, I find a new dimension of God.

Mary obviously succeeded in pulling down a number of walls in that single spiritual experience. It was Mary's deep love of her husband that opened for her the gate to the realm of delight, which then healed her psychic wounds.

Love was also the trigger for a spectacular experience that my wife, Trisha, had several years before we met. She was twenty-five years old when it struck her like a lightning bolt and for three weeks obliterated her ordinary sense of self:

My mystical experience was initiated by falling in love with a man I had known, deeply respected, and more or less placed on a pedestal for almost two years prior to dating him. He was one of the most mentally and emotionally uninhibited individuals I had ever met, and this resonated with my own desire at the time to move beyond all my own conditioning. I had had no prior spiritual experiences, nor did I know or even suspect that such a thing existed. Up until this time, I had experienced only life's ordinary highs and lows.

I have no specific memories of our lovemaking, only that it was, from the beginning, totally uninhibited, frequent, and never enough! My body-mind was completely trusting, open, and receptive.

My first memory of that incident is of awakening one morning after a night of lovemaking and feeling as if I had not been asleep. I felt as though I was conscious or constantly awake on some higher plane. That entire day I remember feeling *totally* and *perfectly* relaxed.

In this perfect relaxation I stood outside of time. It was as if time normally flowed in a horizontal plane, and I had somehow stepped out of this horizontal flow into a timeless state. There was absolutely no sense of the passage of time. To say there was no beginning or ending of time would seem irrelevant. There was simply *no* time.

I remember coming home from work a few days later, standing in the living room of my little studio apartment, and suddenly realizing that I had no edges. There was no me. The thought arose, and these are the exact words, "This is what I AM in truth." I remember looking over at the door to my apartment and thinking, "There is no difference between door jambs and smog." There is no difference between anything whatsoever. Everything is the same. There is only apparent difference. I remember that the thoughts also arose, "The body is a joke. You could shoot me in this moment and I would laugh."

Everything material seemed superfluous. It was all spontaneously and playfully arising from one great source, and it could just as well cease to arise in any moment.

Somehow I had become infinity with eyes. I felt as if I had just been born in that moment, or that I had been asleep all my life and had just awakened. I also remember thinking that this was the true condition of everyone and that everyone could know this. Arms or legs were not necessary—all that was required was conscious existence.

This particular moment remains, seventeen years later, the single most significant moment of my life. It was also the most ordinary, simple, happy, normal, neurosis-free moment of my life. I was simply being what I AM, and what everyone else IS, in truth. I also recall having a vision at the time of five young men and women standing side by side, joining hands, and then leaping off a cliff into infinity—that is what it seemed like I had done.

I remained in this state of edgelessness for about three weeks, and life was intensely magnified. When I walked, I felt so light it was as if my feet did not touch the ground. I had no appetite for food—in fact, most of what I tried to eat left a strange metallic taste in my mouth. And although I ate almost nothing during this period, I lost no weight. I remember telling my lover that it felt as if my spine were plugged into the "universal socket" and that it was a source of infinite energy.

During this time I was more creative than I had ever been (or have been since) both at work and outside of work. All the limits on my thinking were no longer in place. I also became prescient—seeing into the future and then later experiencing the scenes I had foreseen down to the last detail. This astonished me.

I also remember sitting at my desk at work one day and turning to look at one of my officemates. In an instant I was drowning in bliss, overwhelmed with love and compassion for my fellow worker, and for every being and thing I looked at. I loved everyone, including my lover, the same, infinitely. There was really no one separate to love. Tears silently rolled down my cheeks. I felt infinite love and infinite pain at the same time, the pain arising from realizing the power and primacy of love, yet how little we love.

I remember thinking that this universal love is what the Madonna symbolizes. Then suddenly I felt as if I were the source of all creation, that the universe was arising from me, or through me—from whatever this infinite thing was I had become.

Then, at one point I felt as though I were moving into, or becoming blinded by, brilliant white light. It literally felt like the molecules of my body were flying apart and that if I allowed the process to continue I would simply fly apart and disappear. There would be no trace left of me. I knew in this moment that some kind of atomic release of energy would occur, that it would have no gross physically destructive effect, but that inconceivable energy would be released. I also knew that it meant I would leave this realm for good and that I was not ready to do this.

In that instant, I felt fear, and whatever is "me," that isolating, binding force, grabbed hold mightily, and suddenly I had edges again. I felt separate, complicated, neurotic, and unhappy again—all in an instant. It felt as if infinity had been stuffed into a 5'7" container, as if my connection to the universal source of life had been torn asunder. It was so devastating that I even contemplated suicide in the days that followed.

My relationship with my lover slowly deteriorated after this. I wanted desperately to understand what had happened to me, and most of all to regain that brilliant state of edgelessness. For years, my entire life was spent urgently searching for understanding of this event. I have gained a great deal of knowledge and some wisdom about what happened, and have even lost my edges again for moments at a time, but that perfect and continuous state of self-transcendence remains elusive.

A respondent to my questionnaire, whom I will call Deborah, offered the following remarkably similar account of her extraordinary experience of what is often referred to as cosmic consciousness.[8] The experience happened when Deborah was thirty-two years old. Again, the trigger was love. Deborah had been unhappily married for several years when she fell head over heels in love with Bob. She was unable to sleep, eat, or function at work; all she could do was think of Bob. Here is Deborah's vivid description of the events that followed, which not only shows an incredibly complex and rich mystical experience but also her retrospective sense of humor, perhaps a sign that she is beginning to integrate the experience:

My heart chakra [psychic center in the middle of the chest] was like a giant flower, opening and closing and loving Bob. I felt an invisible cord stretch out and something opened very softly, yet there seemed to be joyous music—sounds, happiness, and love. It was shaped like a morning glory flower that would open and close. All I knew was that I had to be with Bob, and after a week of talking together on the phone it happened.

Sex with him only enhanced the love I felt for him. It is quite embarrassing for me to admit that I was transformed into a nymphomaniac. I couldn't get enough sex with Bob, and my genital "chakra" was like a malfunctioning buzz-saw! It wouldn't turn off! I lost thirty pounds in eight weeks! We made love three times a day, and poor Bob didn't know what had hit him. I always wanted more, which after a while left him tired and frustrated. This went on for several months. In the end Bob threatened to break up with me. He bought me a vibrator to play with so that I would leave him alone. I ran the batteries out the first night! Yet, I never had a conventional orgasm until three months later. It was always a matter of cosmic fireworks.

Our love-making was incredible. Every time we made love, I had an out-of-body trip. It was like moving through a tunnel at warp speed, moving through space, passing stars and planets until I seemed to be at the center of the cosmos. The universe opened up to me. I saw the Earth being created, saw the early volcanic eruptions and the most angry storms and explosions. It was almost like watching a Nova program, except I was *there*!

All the beautiful colors of the rainbow would pulse through me at times. Also, while I was watching great swirling stars, there was an accompanying sound, which rang like a deep grinding engine in space, or perhaps it was a giant vibration I felt.

I experienced such love the whole time and was awestruck and in loving tears during our love-making. My love enveloped everything from the microscopic to the most gigantic galaxies. My love seemed to be mirrored: Whatever love I felt for the All came back to me in great multitudes.

At times my entire body shook and vibrated like a rocket during take-off. All kinds of knowledge and mathematical equations were passing through me. I understood them all in a split second and forgot them just as quickly. I even saw myself in a giant pyramid working with those equations.

After three months of this, I had to shut down . . . or die. I couldn't possibly handle the knowledge and information that was passing through me. The experience slowly declined over a period of six months. I stopped meditating, reading and study-

ing. I focused completely on mundane things. It was like holding
back a great flood.

Although Deborah had studied metaphysical subjects all
her life and was a frequent meditator, she was nonetheless quite
unprepared for the powers unleashed in her by that experience.
Her fear of death was very real. It is experienced at the threshold
between the kind of spectacular cosmic consciousness that she
enjoyed and the full-fledged unitive experience of mystics. The
latter experience is possible only when the ego-personality (the
entity who we think, feel, and sense we are) is dissolved to make
room for the realization of perfect oneness. Deborah was unable
to cross that threshold, stopped by her fear.

Yet, Deborah's story has a happy ending in ordinary terms:
Three years after this experience, she and Bob got married.
Prior to her mystical awakening, Deborah's sex drive was not
very strong. Since then, however, her sex life has accelerated,
though her orgasms are more conventional than cosmic now.
She is relieved that the frenzy has ebbed, adding "for now any-
way." Most important, Deborah is feeling grateful for the experience, since it made her grow in ways that she would have
thought impossible. She admits that she is not ready for a repeti-
tion of the experience just now but hopes that one day she can,
as she put it, open herself again to the universe.

SEX: THE HIDDEN WINDOW

Sex—or, to be more precise, sexual love—*can* be a hidden window onto the spiritual reality. That window or opening can
manifest all of a sudden in the solid walls of our conventional
existence. At the height of passion or in the fullness of love, we
might suddenly feel transported to a different plane of existence
where all our sensations, experiences, and thoughts occur
against the peaceful backdrop of an overriding sense of at-
oneness. In the case of the well-known writer George Leonard,
the opening happened spontaneously *after* lovemaking, when all
the built-up tensions of the day were eased and his awareness
stood at the threshold of sleep. In his own words:

There was once a moment in the deepest hours before dawn, after a night of love, when consciousness itself began to change.
Awareness of the different parts of our bodies which earlier in
the evening had brought such delight had faded away, leaving
only a generalized awareness of luminescent smoothness and
sinuosity. Separate acts had blended into a prolonged single
movement. Even the divisions between waking and sleeping had
become unclear. Please do not misunderstand me. I offer no expertise in these matters; such nights may be rarer for me than for
you. But I must tell you that the moment did come when our
own once separate and private emotions began to appear on each
other's faces. Just that. Every flicker of feeling I might expect to
originate inside me appeared instead on her face. I was left no
sensation, no emotion, no existence apart from her. There was
nothing metaphorical about this merging. In the faint light from
another room, each of us could see our actual selves embodied in
another—and we were terrified.[9]

Leonard's experience captures for us the very essence of love,
which is experiential participation in the other person. In this
case, there was a wonderful mutuality of experience that blurred
the customary egoic boundaries. This unexpected loss—or expansion—of identity filled Leonard and his wife with terror.
This moment of fear was undoubtedly the point at which they
slipped back into their respective skins to reoccupy their own
familiar inner landscape.

We simply cannot know when such openings will occur,
or whether they will ever occur in our life. But we can certainly
prepare ourselves for them. More than that, we can actively *invite* them by adopting an orientation to life that is sensitive to the
presence of the sacred in the world.

Sexual love, to use Aldous Huxley's phrase, can indeed be a
"Door in the Wall."[10] The wall consists of preconceptions about
and predispositions toward reality, which we must penetrate in
order to see what is on the other side. Of course, when we succeed in this, we realize that the other side is on this side as well.
Reality is a continuity, and that continuity is broken up only by
the mind that perceives and cognizes in piecemeal fashion.

This truth has been obscured by our inherited dualistic
philosophies, but it is a truth that is fundamental to the sacred
traditions inspired by mystics and sages before they were re-
worked by theologians and other intellectuals. Prior to the rise

of dualism, the sacred and the profane were not experienced as radical opposites, nor was sexuality excluded from spiritual life. On the contrary, the further back we go in human history, the more we encounter a life philosophy that was distinctly affirmative of both sex and God or Goddess. And so we will next turn to those erotic-spiritual traditions for illuminating our own modern quest.

II

Sacred Sex
Through
the Ages

CHAPTER 4

❧

Sacred Sex and the Goddess: Ancestral Wisdom

THE EROTIC CULT OF THE GREAT MOTHER

At the dawn of history, God was a she—or so it appears. Our paleolithic forebears, thirty or more millennia ago, conceived of Nature or the Divine as a cosmic female. They delighted in immortalizing her image on cave walls and in the form of statuettes carved out of stone, bone, ivory, or coal. Undoubtedly, they also used more perishable materials to depict the Great Mother, though these did not survive the ravages of time.

Archaeologists have found nearly two hundred statuettes from that period, the most famous being the so-called *Venus of Willendorf,* which dates back to 25,000 to 30,000 B.C. This figurine, standing under five inches tall, shows a female with gargantuan breasts, broad hips, ample buttocks, and a clearly visible vaginal cleft. Head, legs, and arms are highly stylized, suggesting an advanced level of artistic skill. The same message of sheer competence can be surmised from the other statuettes and not least from the cave paintings of that period. Who was this Venus, and what role did these figurines and images play? Above all, what, if any, was her connection to sexuality?

There is no dearth of interpretations of the paleolithic Goddess images. The British historian J. G. H. Clark, for instance, saw in them "characteristic products of unregenerated male imagination," dolls to be ogled and fingered by sexually aroused men.[1] A similar opinion was entertained by Richard Lewinsohn, another European scholar. He remarked:

One reason for the pleasure which men obviously found in these
sexual pictures may have been a lack of opportunity to see the
organs in real life. . . . The inclement climate allowed them to
leave their twilit caves only during a few months in the year,
when they were hunting; the women most likely showed themselves abroad more rarely still. The sight of a woman naked was
therefore an unusual experience for a man.[2]

Lewinsohn seems to project modern male attitudes into the remote past. It seems far more likely that our Stone Age ancestors
had their sexual curiosity satisfied as children, when they were
presumably running around naked.

In her book *When God Was a Woman,* art historian and
sculptor Merlin Stone proffered a far more plausible explanation. She suggested that the Venus figures are representations of
the Divine Ancestress:

In these Upper Paleolithic societies—in which the mother may
have been regarded as the sole parent of the family, ancestor worship was apparently the basis of sacred ritual, and accounts of
ancestry were probably reckoned only through the matriline—
the concept of the creator of all human life may have been formulated by the clan's image of the woman who had been their
most ancient, their primal ancestor and that image thereby deified and revered as Divine Ancestress.[3]

It was women who witnessed the miracle of birthing. It was
they who understood the connection between their monthly cycle and the phases of the moon. And it was probably the women
who, in the neolithic age and maybe earlier, discovered the connection between impregnation and pregnancy. (The anthropo-
logical literature contains descriptions of tribes in modern times
who are still ignorant of the reproductive function of semen.)

Although male scholars have always assumed that men
were the great cultural innovators of the past, there is growing
evidence that women were just as instrumental in the ascent of
human civilization. In particular, they may have greatly advanced early humanity's knowledge of plants and the healing
arts. This idea is supported by what we know about many so-
called primitive societies. It is also not hard to image that wom-
en's sensitivity and intuition were behind the evolving symbolism of the Great Mother and its attendant ritual expression.

Some scholars have seen in the Venus figures representations of a female deity or a fetish associated with a primitive fertility cult. But why can we not assume that in the religious imagination of our Stone Age ancestors the Great Mother played all these roles, rather than attribute to her any exclusive function? The Great Mother was venerated as the origin of life—not only of the clan but of the earth as a whole. Hence art historian Elinor W. Gadon has also called her the Earth Mother.[4]

Informed opinion views the Venus figures not as sex objects but as artifacts that once had a sacred function, and they were an important aspect of a fairly complex metaphysical understanding of the world. This point of view has been argued with particular cogency by the French prehistorian André Leroi-Gourhan.[5] After painstaking analysis of the art found in sixty-six out of one hundred known paleolithic caves, Leroi-Gourhan concluded that male and female symbols were commonly juxtaposed, with the female symbols tending to be central and the male symbols tending to be at the periphery. All this suggests an elaborate sexual metaphysics, which unquestionably had its ritual manifestations.

Here we have, then, the earliest beginnings of an erotic spirituality in which ideas of earth fecundity and human fertility, cosmic creativity and human procreation, as well as the biological cycles of the female body and seasonal change were woven into a practical way of life.

Contrary to popular opinion, the paleolithic clans do not seem to have been dominated by the male gender. From the extant artistic images, we know that women not only went to hunt with the men but even acted as shamans. Nor was cave art necessarily a male prerogative.

However, if the available evidence does not suggest the presence of a patriarchal social arrangement, do we need to assume for that early period a kind of matriarchy? The nineteenth-century Swiss historian Johann Bachofen proposed that in the Stone Age, women were in charge. Most contemporary scholars disagree, though some feminist historians have sought to vindicate Bachofen. From what we know about hunting-and-gathering societies, it is very likely that in the Stone Age, men and women were more or less social equals, with the balance dipping toward the male gender.

The reason for this is that hunting-and-gathering economies depend on a high measure of economic cooperation between the sexes. This has led Riane Eisler to develop what she calls a partnership model. Although she primarily addresses the early neolithic society in her popular book *The Chalice and the Blade,* she appears to imply that her arguments are also valid for paleolithic social organization. She observed:

> The fact that women played a central and vigorous role in pre-historic religion and life does not have to mean that men were perceived and treated as subservient. For here both men and women were the children of the Goddess, as they were the children of the women who headed the families and clans. And while this certainly gave women a great deal of power, analogizing from our present-day mother–child relationship, it seems to have been a power that was more equated with responsibility and love than with oppression, privilege, and fear.[6]

Eisler characterized prehistoric societies as being based on the ideal of partnership rather than domination. Even if one were to confine Eisler's remarks to the neolithic age, her interpretation is open to questioning, for she appears to read prehistory in terms of contemporary sentiments, ideas, and aspirations tied to our notion of individualism and personhood.

It might be more appropriate to employ terms such as social equality or complementarity rather than partnership when speaking of prehistoric societies, including the neolithic cultures of Eisler's focus. Partnership implies a fully intentional collaboration between individuals with clearly articulated personal rights. We cannot assume such a highly differentiated and conscious mode of social functioning for that early period. Nonetheless, Eisler's partnership model, which has a pronounced political thrust, is eminently valid and valuable as a program for our own contemporary situation.

How was this fundamental social equality reflected in the intimate sexual life of our paleolithic forebears? We can only guess. As an illustration, I proffer the following hypothetical scene set in a small European cave twenty thousand years ago. It shows a young couple furtively making love while the clan is asleep. Their lovemaking involves no acrobatic frills, no striving for mutual orgasm, no whispering of endearments into each other's ears. Nor is it a sacred ritual in which they raise each other's inner force to untold ecstatic heights. It is much simpler, less self-conscious, and more instinctive. Yet the sense of the mystery of life, embodied in the potent image of the Great

Mother, is never far from the couple's awareness. Certainly she is uppermost on the woman's mind, for her man turns out to be an innovator, secretly breaking a tribal custom in his approach to her.

AN EROTIC FLASHBACK TO 20,000 B.C.

The clan had settled down for the night. The fire near the cave's entrance cast a reddish glow over the sleepers. He could barely make out their shapes. A child was coughing. Several of the adults were snoring. He lay wide awake with excitement about tomorrow's big-game hunt. The elders had decided to track down the mammoths that had strayed into their vicinity. The excitement had traveled down into his genitals, and his penis was stiff with life.

He reached across, tugging at his young mate's fur covering. She made a sleepy sound. He tugged at the covering more insistently and moved closer to her. The young woman rolled over, giving him her back. He ignored her signal. He wanted her. He lifted the bear cover and pulled her to him. Her naked skin felt warm against his, as he knew it would. Brushing aside her long tangled hair, he sniffed at the nape of her neck. Ripples of urgency ran through his whole body. Then he wetted his hard penis with saliva and penetrated her swiftly in her drowsiness. His clan usually made love with the man lying on top, since only animals mate facing away from each other. He felt vaguely uneasy about breaking this rule.

She yielded after a few moments of reluctance.

His father had found him a good wife. He pulled the cover tighter over them. He didn't want to wake the others. The clan elders would be surly tomorrow if he were to bring them back from their dream world before the sun was up. Besides, they thought it was not very auspicious to copulate the night before the hunt. He didn't know why he was defying them.

She reached beside her bearskin and clutched the Great Mother's bone-carved image to her breasts. The smooth carving had been given to her during her initiation into womanhood. She whispered a short prayer to the Great Mother, the source of all life and the protectress of couples. Too many children had died recently. Not even the old medicine crone had been able to save them.

She prayed silently to the Great Mother to render her womb
fertile and to let her child grow into a strong adult. She was
secretly hoping for a girl, because there were too few women in
the clans. The women had initiated her into the mystery of conception, and she knew that she was in the right cycle for receiv-
ing life into her. Perhaps her grandmother would be reborn in
her womb. She knew that her mate was ignorant of how life entered her womb, and she could never tell him. It was the
women's great secret.

He kept on thrusting rhythmically but quietly. He could
think of no other sensation that gave him as much pleasure. He
felt manly and safe entering her womb like that. He gently
stroked her long, tousled hair as if to placate her. He sensed she
was displeased with him, and he did not want her displeasure to
grow into a magical spell woven against him. Women were
powerful, he knew. They were favored by the Great Mother.

Momentarily, he poured his life force into her. He heard
himself groan. The glow of satedness inside him didn't last
long. It never did. Then a familiar feeling of pleasant lethargy
came over him. He lay still, his arms around her body.

She pressed her back into his stomach, faintly moving her
hips. She quietly enjoyed his embrace and being penetrated by
his horn. It made her belly tingle with power. She knew the
Great Mother was alive in her just as she was alive in his throb-
bing member deep inside her. The Great Mother was everywhere, filling all space with her power.

His erection subsided quickly, but he didn't want to leave
the warmth of her womb yet. Then he fell asleep, dreaming of
tomorrow's hunt. She was unable to go back to sleep. She was
still vaguely aroused, and her thoughts churned.

What kind of mate had been selected for her? He always
flouted tribal customs. He had broken a taboo tonight, and she
had let him. He had not even waited for her to paint a red tri-
angle on her organ or invoke the Mother. The young woman
felt a shiver of excitement at his boldness, and at her lack of pro-
test. She was proud of her new mate, but he also scared her
sometimes. Some of the crones were saying he might be chief
one day. Still, she decided to tell the other women tomorrow
and prepare a special sacrificial offering to the Great Mother to
ensure her continued blessings for the clan.

SEX, MAGIC, AND THE LIFE-FORCE

To properly understand the paleolithic and early neolithic beliefs about fertility and sacramental sexuality, we must first
grasp their underlying magical philosophy. We need not be surprised that our Stone Age ancestors sensed a deep mystery
about sex just as they felt a deep mystery about fertility. The discovery that sexual intercourse and human fertility are causally
connected gave rise to a plethora of beliefs and rituals in which
the connection between sex and fertility was affirmed and
dramatized.

The common link, as our ancestors saw it, was the magical
notion—or intuition—of sacred power, or what in the Melana-
sian tribal culture is known as *mana*. This is how Ninian Smart, a
professor of religious studies, characterized *mana*:

> *Mana* is a hidden or secret force which operates silently and invis-
> ibly in things and persons that are in some way especially power-
> ful, impressive, or socially important. *Mana* is somewhat analo-
> gous to the idea an ignorant person has of electricity—powerful
> and unseen, capable of doing much for his benefit, yet capable
> too of destroying him. As a person, or speech, can be said to be
> "electrifying" in impact, so *mana* is ascribed to people and events
> of a striking nature. It resides in the tribal chieftain, in animals,
> plants, and rocks of a significant kind.[7]

Special beings, objects, or events are thus endowed with
great *mana*. It was a comparatively small step to arrive from this
archaic notion to the related idea that *everything* is charged and
maintained by a universal life-force. This cosmic power is what
the ancient Germans called *Od*, or what the Hindus have for millennia named *prana*. It corresponds to the *orenda* of the Iroquois,
the *oki* of the Hurons, the *ton* of the Dakotas, the *wakonda* of the
Sioux, and the *megbe* of the Pygmies. According to this view,
the cosmos itself is a manifestation of the sacred—a hier-
ophany—and hence is a manifestation of power, or kratophany.

Our early ancestors thought of sexuality and fertility as
expressions of sacred power, as focal points of the universal life-
force. They experienced sexual intercourse as a sharing of the
multifarious life-force, and they looked upon human fertility

and the fertility of the planted fields as conduits of that same pervasive power. Moreover, by way of analogical thinking, ritual sexual intercourse was felt to be directly linked to the natural cycle of the seasons and the growth of crops.

The world view of early humanity was thus thoroughly magical. Our ancestors experienced the world around them as being replete with profound powers and deep connections, which filled them with a sense of mystery but also with fear. Although we have largely lost that sense of mystery and wonder, despite our technological control of the environment we are still subject to much fear. However, even though we have reduced mystery to little more than a puzzle or a conundrum of detective novels, our existence and the world we live in are still as mysterious as ever. Mystery has not diminished, only our sensitivity to it. And one of the manifestations of this all-embracing mystery is our sexual life.

THE SEXUAL TRAGEDY OF AGRICULTURE

The symbol of the Great Mother, it appears, was the pivot around which paleolithic culture revolved endlessly. We must assume that it dominated the waking life and the dreams of our early ancestors, inexorably moving them toward a more lucid self-awareness. This more focused consciousness was the humus in which grew the ideas and practices that led to the neolithic revolution.

About 11,000 B.C., the ice cap that had covered much of the Eurasian continent began to retreat to the north, exposing precious land yielding edible grains. Our forebears learned to cultivate the soil. Women appear to have been crucial in this development. What they could not have known was that their innovative genius would, in a comparatively short span of time, lead to their tragic subjugation by the male gender for millennia to come.

The invention of agriculture and domestication of animals, accompanied by the sedentary life, dramatically redefined the relations between men and women. The hunting-and-gathering groups of the paleolithic era had been relatively egalitarian. Now, however, the larger agricultural settlements depended for their survival on a steady population that could be put to work in the fields. In the period from around 11,000 B.C. to 3000 B.C., the world population is estimated to have grown from three to 100 million.

As Gerda Lerner has convincingly argued, women gradually came to be regarded as a precious tribal commodity, since they alone could guarantee future laborers.[8] Once this idea had taken root, it proved ineradicable. Thus objectified, women were henceforth almost universally treated as property that could be exchanged between tribes or, where an exchange was impossible, simply stolen. This presumably was also the beginning of the tacit condoning of rape, an act that is possible only so long as the woman is looked upon as a thing: the ultimate brutality within the patriarchal mind-set.

With such a general disempowerment of the female gender, individual relations between men and women could not have but suffered. This shift in balance caused a profound distrust between the sexes, leading to the male control over, and regulation of, women's sexual life and, at times, to a complete suppression of women's sexual needs.

However, the neolithic revolution and its accompanying process of female degradation did not occur simultaneously or evenly. There is mounting evidence that there were early neolithic societies in which women were accorded a status similar to men, if not higher in individual cases. It is here that we may hope for signs of a sound erotic spirituality.

THE GODDESS AND HER LOVER

The subordination and denigration of women did not immediately lead to the dethronement of the Great Mother venerated since time immemorial. The belief in the universal Female was deeply ingrained and vital. However, it underwent a significant transformation during the neolithic age. For, as human experience and conceptual capacities leaped forward, the Great Mother became increasingly personified. She was endowed with special characteristics, a personal if legendary history, and a name.

The Great Mother, or *magna mater,* appeared under different names in the villages of the Near East and Europe. We do not know her earliest names, but later, after writing had been invented, she was celebrated as Inanna in Sumer, Ishtar in

Babylon, Anath in Canaan, Astarte in Phoenicia, Isis in Egypt, Nu Kua in China, Freya in Scandinavia, and Kunapipi in aboriginal Australia.

Thus, the Goddess became multiple, while retaining the universality that had been associated with her for countless generations. Each Goddess, while having her own name and distinct attributes, was hailed as the source of life, the life-granting power behind vegetation and fertility. Her splendor was celebrated in many myths, and her favor was sought and her wrath appeased through numerous rituals.

The Goddess was still supreme but no longer alone, for people's imagination and religious feeling had made room for other personifications of the sacred reality. These included a virile male God, who was, however, at least temporarily still subordinate to the Goddess. Further anthropomorphic thought yielded the notion of the male deity as a lover of the great Goddess.

At Çatal Hüyük in Anatolia, one of the earliest known neolithic settlements, numerous shrines were found containing sacred relief sculptures and wall paintings. Most of these artistic creations represent the female principle, or Mother Goddess, and the male principle (often depicted in the shape of a bull's head or horns). The shrines—of which no two were alike—served four or five surrounding buildings, indicating the kind of deep and pervasive religiosity encountered throughout the ancient world. There is not the least sign of the modern split between the sacred and the profane; ritual practice was closely interwoven with daily life.

The pervasive presence of both male and female symbols in the shrines of Çatal Hüyük suggests a complementary ritual widely practiced in antiquity: the annual celebration of fertility at the beginning of the year. A specially chosen man and woman—originally perhaps the chief priestess and the chief priest and later queen and her consort—enacted the divine intercourse of the Goddess and God, which was thought to ensure the fertility of the soil and of the village women. This curious institution will be examined in more detail in the next chapter.

This ritual of sacred marriage (*hieros gamos*) and the myths connected with it were imprinted on the minds of the neolithic agriculturalists, and they must have had a certain influence on their sex lives. Perhaps not every occasion of sexual congress in the privacy of their homes was felt to be a sacred event in the moment, but it may have been so ideally.

For our neolithic forebears, religion was not a matter of a Sunday morning service with the rest of the week spent in godlessness. Their whole life was pervaded by religious notions and sentiments, and worship of the deities, especially the great Goddess, was a daily event of lasting significance. It is likely that in this almost contemplative atmosphere, people's sex lives entailed a certain ritualistic element.

When they came from their sacred shrines touched by the Goddess's grace, our ancestors did not rush to their beds to lose themselves in brutish, mechanical copulation. This does not mean, of course, that they did not know passion, merely that the great God and Goddess were not expelled from their hearts when they made love. It may never have occurred to them to consciously identify with the divine couple during their lovemaking, yet how can we doubt that they enjoyed a sense of participating in the divine marriage act through their embrace? After all, the myths they heard and told each other were, for them, not just entertaining stories; rather, they were accounts of the universe, which gave meaning to all aspects of their lives.

Anthropologist Walter A. Fairservis has taken a different point of view. He conjectured about the culture of Çatal Hüyük as follows:

> Sexual love and its relationship to birth were apparently not nearly as important as the birth itself. There seems to have been little or no ritualism as regards sexual relationship.
>
> In societies where there is a relatively clear separation between men's and women's work, the degree of common relationship between the sexes is greatly reduced. Sex for purposes other than reproduction is therefore far less common than in societies where the separation is less sharp.[9]

Fairservis's argument seems to limp. In a culture such as Çatal Hüyük, which is thought to have had a marked separation between the genders, we would rather expect that its omnipresent ritualism also left its mark in the sphere of intimate relations. Thus a measure of stylized sex seems far more likely than a casual romp in the hay.

CHAPTER 5

❧

Sacred Marriage
and Sacred Prostitution

HIEROS GAMOS: THE SACRED MARRIAGE

Religious life in the early agricultural societies, as has been seen, had at its center the potent image of the Goddess and her divine lover. Their celestial congress, which was believed to guarantee fertility on earth, was celebrated annually in many different cultures of the ancient world. In most countries, it was the core of the harvest festival, but some cultures celebrated it to usher in the new year. The holy intercourse between God and Goddess was reenacted on the human level by the temple priestess and the divinely appointed king or the high priest. This ritual, as stated previously, is known as *hieros gamos* in the Greek language, here rendered as "sacred marriage."

To appreciate this practice, one must understand that the ancients thought of their deities as actually dwelling in the temple. Since human welfare was considered to be dependent on the goodwill of the divine powers, our ancestors felt obligated to provide their gods and goddesses with ample food and drink, as well as to entertain them with music and dance and, not least, to cater to their sexual needs, which were crucial to the fertility of the earth. The touching poetry of the Sumerian priestess Enheduanna (2300 B.C.) records how her life lost its meaning and beauty when she was forced to leave the Goddess upon whom she had waited for many years and how strength and joy returned to her body and soul when she was permitted to serve the celestial Lady again.

We do not know exactly how the earliest neolithic peoples

celebrated the annual fertility rite in honor of the Great Goddess
and her divine paramour. The first written documents that talk
about this popular event appeared around the third millennium
B.C. By then the sacred marriage rite was well established.

From Sumeria have survived some valuable texts that give
us a glimpse of the sensuous nature of the *hieros gamos* ritual. In
one hymn the Sumerian Goddess Inanna (the later Babylonian
Ishtar) candidly expresses her sexual longing for her brother and
lover, the divine Dumuzi (the later Babylonian Tammuz):

> My vulva, the horn,
> The Boat of Heaven,
> Is full of eagerness like the young moon.
> My untilled land lies fallow.
>
> As for me Inanna,
> Who will plow my vulva?
> Who will plow my high field?
> Who will plow my wet ground?
>
> As for me, the young woman
> Who will plow my vulva?
> Who will station the ox there?
> Who will plow my vulva?

Dumuzi answered her:

> Great Lady, the king will plow your vulva.
> I, Dumuzi the King, will plow your vulva.

Then Inanna, Queen of Heaven, responded impatiently:

> Then plow my vulva, man of my heart!
> Plow my vulva![1]

And Dumuzi-Amaushumgalanna, the Great God, fulfilled her
heart's desire, leading the ox to the field, and ensured the fertility of the land and all its creatures.

In another Sumerian hymn, which probably was also re-
cited during the sacred marriage ceremony, Inanna describes
how she bathed and perfumed herself for her lover, how she
applied kohl to her eyes and cleansed her mouth with sweet-

smelling amber. Then she describes their love play in vivid imagery as follows:

> He shaped my loins with his fair hands,
> The shepherd Dumuzi filled my lap with cream and milk,
> He stroked my pubic hair,
> He watered my womb.
> He laid his hands on my holy vulva,
> He smoothed my black boat with cream,
> He quickened my narrow boat with milk,
> He caressed me on the bed.[2]

There is an appealing earthiness and directness about these Sumerian hymns. However, they are apt to be found distasteful by those who confuse eroticism with pornography.

The great Goddess of life was also the harbinger of death. Life is movement, change, and for change to be possible there must be loss and gain. This motif is beautifully captured in the myth of God Shiva's cosmic dance. However, long before this male deity reached supremacy in the Hindu pantheon, the life-and-death cycle was intimately associated with female deities.

Thus, we have the fascinating Babylonian myth of Goddess Ishtar's descent into the underworld, where she recovered her son and lover Tammuz. While Ishtar was held captive in the underworld, animals did not mate and men and women did not make love. Nature's procreative energy had come to a standstill.

A similar idea runs through the myths woven around other divine couples, such as Isis and Osiris, Aphrodite and Adonis, and Persephone and Demeter. Their association with fertility rites suggests that the neolithic cultures had become aware of the role of the male gender in procreation. The myths of the divine couple celebrate the mystery of sex and fertility in Nature.

The Egyptian Goddess Isis was heartbroken over the death of her divine spouse Osiris, who had been killed and dismembered by his brother Set. Isis cut off her hair, tore her robes, and went in search of her husband's body. She found all the limbs except for his penis, which had been eaten by a crab. She carefully crafted an artificial phallus and then resurrected Osiris. No sooner had Osiris returned to life, God and Goddess embraced in love. The new penis was found to work very well, because

from this union the falcon-headed God Horus was born. The
Queen of Heaven's virginity, however, remained intact—a mir-
acle that was later attributed to Mary, the mother of Jesus of
Nazareth.

Osiris was associated not only with vegetation but also
with death. Isis was particularly the patron deity of the fertile
Nile delta, but she was also the first to practice embalming.
Again we have the clear association of life with death.

For the rational mind, this conjunction of life and death is
a paradox, as is the ancient notion that the Goddess, in all her
overwhelming sexuality, was a virgin. Because her sexual intercourse with the male deity was a sacred event, she was believed
not to have forfeited her chastity, or virginity. It was, in fact, her
virginity that ensured perpetual fertility, for virginity meant
the preservation of creative power, which was celebrated in the
hieros gamos ritual enacted by priest and priestess. Jungian analyst M. Esther Harding has spelled out what this means in terms
of female psychology:

> The meaning of this sacrifice in the temple, of this *hieros gamos,*
> thus begins to emerge. Through it the woman who has been ini-
> tiated is released from the domination of her own unconscious
> instinct with its desirousness and craving for power. Through
> submitting to her instinct instead of demanding that the man
> submit to it, she becomes virgin. In this ritual the woman recog-
> nizes and asserts, in the most emphatic and incontrovertible
> manner possible, that her sexuality and the emoluments it can
> bring are not her own, her possession, but represent the de-
> mands of life itself, which flows in her, and whose servant she is;
> her body, her psyche, is but the vehicle for life's manifestations.
> This is her submission to instinct. Until she has submitted in this
> way she is no virgin in the religious meaning of that term and
> cannot be united to the Eros, the feminine principle, the Magna
> Dea, which should rule her from within.[3]

We might add that a similar attitude of self-transcendence
was incumbent on the male participant in the hierogamic rite.
He too had to submit to instinct, or the force of life, without
expecting to "possess" the woman who was not merely acting
out a role but who *was* the Goddess. In his submission, the man,
who *was* God, was animating the feminine, or receptive, side of
his psyche. It is, therefore, not entirely surprising that in some

cultures, the male partner in the rite was dressed up like a woman or was a eunuch.

Originally, the sexual union between God and Goddess was conceived as a temporary, if cosmic, event celebrated annually. Only later were these deities thought to be married in perpetuity. What is more, in the beginning it was the Goddess who was hailed as the more important of the two. However, gradually the rise of the patriarchy in all spheres announced itself in the area of religion and theology. After millennia of unswerving veneration, the great Goddess, the Mother, was at last dethroned by the male deities embodying the phallic principle.

THE PHALLIC PRINCIPLE

In the paleolithic age, the figure and symbol of the Great Mother was predominant throughout the Old World. However, often the artistic renderings of the Great Mother were—as in the astonishing cave art of southern Europe—associated with symbolic representations of the male creative principle: phallus, bull, bison, buffalo, and horns. This custom continued into the neolithic era.

The neolithic Goddess, as a symbol of fertility, was associated with all kinds of animals—especially wild beasts, birds, and snakes, but also butterflies and bees. Her pregnant belly symbolized the fertile fields. Remarkably, the Goddess was felt to embody both the male and the female principle, and her androgynous or bisexual nature was frequently expressed in art. Thus, some representations show her with an elongated phallus-like neck and head; in other images, she is shown holding an upright phallic snake, which, like the butterfly, is a symbol of regeneration and metamorphosis.

For reasons that are still not completely understood, male and female principles became severed from one another after the flowering of the great civilizations of the East—not only in art but in life. Many historians connect this disjunction with the elevated social status of the male in nomadic communities. It was these aggressive pastoralists who, about the middle of the second millennium B.C., began to invade the territories of, and triumph over, the sedentary peoples of India, the Middle East, and the Mediterranean who worshipped the Great Goddess and her lesser male counterpart. As historian Reay Tannahill noted:

> In the pastoral society, man was dominant, and woman as much his chattel as the beasts he herded. It is no coincidence that the male-oriented society of the West today should be in a direct line of moral and philosophical descent from a few tribes of Hebrew nomads, or that of modern India from the Indo-European pastoralists of the *Rig-Veda*.[4]

The pastoralist invaders brought their own mythologies and religious beliefs with them, and in their view it was not the Goddess but the male God who reigned supreme. Their warlike attitudes and ideas proved incredibly resilient, surviving the changes brought about by their adoption of a sedentary lifestyle. In fact, war became a formidable force in history. Until the pastoral era, the neolithic societies had apparently enjoyed millennia of peace. The phallic principle—the ideology of male supremacy—became fairly installed as a modus operandi for urbanized humanity. We are only now beginning to comprehend the tragedy of this development, as we are reaping the consequences of a ravaged earth and millennia-long conflict everywhere on our planet.

PHALLIC WORSHIP

For a long time, it appears, our earliest ancestors—like some modern tribal peoples—believed that women alone were responsible for the creation of new human life. This belief undoubtedly secured for women a privileged position in the social game. All this changed dramatically when men discovered their own function in the reproductive process. They quickly claimed that it was their semen that planted life in the female womb, and that the womb was little more than a protective cave wherein that nascent life could germinate and grow until it was ready to emerge to claim its place in the world. Of course, given this chauvinistic view of male superiority in the creation of offspring, boy children soon became a social preference while girl children were often put to death lest they prove burdensome for the tribe or clan.

This social change also manifested in the area of religion

and metaphysics, as the male generative organ came to be viewed as a particularly potent locus of the numinous reality. The penis—in its nature as *phallos*—was regarded with as much reverence as had been the female organ for thousands of years. This attitude is commonly referred to as phallic worship or phallicism, which, in some cultures and eras, led to the development of fairly complex ritual practices. Animal symbols of the male organ—the bull, goat, snake, and cock—started to populate people's imagination, and in some cases, distinct rituals evolved around them. But pillars, mountains, and trees served the same symbolic purpose. Physician C. G. Berger noted in *Our Phallic Heritage:*

> In his [man's] own body, the object of his adoration was the penis. He knew that all other organs could be controlled at will, but not the penis. Its erections were dependent on stimuli and physical vigor; ejaculations and subsequent relaxations were involuntary. Try as he might, erections could not be repeated after one or several completions of the sex act, although any purely voluntary act could be repeated as many times as desired. This difference, then, in the sexual part of his body caused him to feel that some powerful outside force operated within it and that it was a god. Even in later times, after he had conceived the idea of sky deities or other kinds of gods, the sex organs were held sacred to these deities, were looked upon with wonder and veneration, as creators of life. Since the sexual part of the body was the only part that could create, just as we now say that only God can create, the worship of sex seemed logical and right.[5]

In its creative potential the male organ was deemed an aspect of the male God, or divine creator. Thus, not surprisingly, the mythopoeic ingenuity of our ancestors before long invented myths and images of Gods with oversized phalli and insatiable sexual appetites. There were Osiris, Pan, Hermes, and not least Priapus, Aphrodite's deformed son. Priapus's deformity—consisting in a huge ever-erect penis—proved magnetically attractive to women, who became swiftly enamored of him.

According to one myth, the men of the Lampsacenians were jealous of the God's enormous success with their women. They succeeded in getting the priapic deity expelled from the island of Lampsacus in Greece. However, they did not reckon with the women's passion for Priapus. In one voice, they prayed to the gods, with the result that all the men were afflicted with a genital disease. When the men consulted the oracle of Dodona, they were told that the only way they could restore their health and marital or extramarital bliss was to invite Priapus back into their midst. Realizing that this was an unwinnable situation, the men gave in. In memory of the disease and to honor Priapus they fashioned phallic images for themselves. Of course, Priapus returned to the island to resume his divine play. A similar story is told of Dionysos, who cursed the Athenians with a genital disease when they failed to pay him homage.

It should be noted here that, generally speaking, in premodern times nudity—the exposure of male and female organs— was not surrounded by the feelings of shyness and guilt that characterize much of our own era. Our paleolithic and neolithic ancestors had a far more down-to-earth attitude about nudity and sex than we do. Likewise, images of the genitals, however grossly exaggerated or distorted, were by no means deemed obscene. This explains why representations of the vulva and phallus can be found in countless ancient temples and holy sites throughout the world. Obscenity is a modern notion. As George Ryley Scott observed about archaic phallicism:

> It is important to realize that in these phallic symbols there was, to the people of those races and in those days, nothing in the slightest degree obscene. The obscenity motif was supplied and read into phallic worship by observers and critics a thousand years later. It is purely a question of the individual viewpoint brought about through current usage, morals, philosophy and fashion.[6]

The same moral code that not very long ago misunderstood and condemned phallicism is today responsible for dismissing the emergent sacred eroticism with its body- and life-positive philosophy. That code is a survival of the Victorian morality, which was itself informed by earlier Christian puritanism.

THE RULE OF THE PHALLUS IN GREECE

Nowhere can the reign of the phallic principle be seen more vividly than in classical Greece. As classicist Eva C. Keuls has shown in her path-breaking work, the Athenian society of the fifth century B.C. was haunted by what she called phallocracy, the rule of the phallus. She wrote:

> In the case of a society dominated by men who sequester their wives and daughters, denigrate the female role in reproduction, erect monuments to the male genitalia, have sex with the sons of their peers, sponsor public whorehouses, create a mythology of rape, and engage in rampant saber-rattling, it is not inappropriate to refer to a reign of the phallus. Classical Athens was such a society.[7]

The phallus—the erect penis—is here not so much a symbol of fertility or creativity as of sheer aggression and violence: It is a weapon. This can be fully appreciated only when we observe the Athenians' fear of women, as it is evident in the numerous artistic depictions of battle scenes in which the Amazons are slain. The war between the Greeks and the Amazons was possibly the charter myth of Athenian society, which can be taken as signifying the violent displacement of the old agrarian cultures with their worship of the Great Goddess and their love for peace. Their fear of women is also apparent from the surviving dramas, notably Aristophanes's *Parliament of Women*.

In a society in which women were treated on a par with slaves and constantly subject to rape, we should not expect happy sex lives. Men turned to other men for self-affirmation as well as for romantic and sensual gratification. Women, consequently, turned to other women for intimacy.

As is shown in many paintings, male fantasy suspected that women gratified their reputedly insatiable sex drive with dildos (called *olisboi* in Greek). Women, if they ventured out into the public, were required to veil themselves; they were not supposed to be seen or heard. Men, on the other hand, were expected to be outdoors most of the time and were free to strut about with their genitals on display. It appears that the Greek women did not even disrobe during sexual intercourse. We can guess that such occasions were seldom a matter of pleasure, never mind uplifting delight. It would not have occurred to a Greek man to gratify his wife; in his eyes, she was simply a bearer of *his* children and a domestic servant. He sought his pleasure among the slaves and prostitutes and, not least, among young boys. Homosexuality was widely accepted.

The Greek phallocracy could not last in its extremeness.

However, it set the tone for much of our patriarchal and andro-centric Western civilization. It is telling that it took a female scholar, Eva Keuls, to uncover the historical roots of this cultural bias and rewrite a significant part of Greek history—and thus of the past that made us into what we are today.

SACRED PROSTITUTION IN ANCIENT GREECE

Prostitution was a thriving business in classical Greece and most of the other city-states of the ancient world. It was made possible through the invention of slavery, which was itself a horrible consequence of the ascent of militaristic phallocracy: The perpetual strife between states often led to war, and war meant for the victor not only new land but also goods, livestock, and not least slave labor, including prostitutes.

In the Greece glorified by modern historians, a surplus of prostitutes redefined social life. The wife was locked up at home and forced to be eternally industrious and virtuous, while the courtesan (*hetaera*) was romanticized into a woman of great refinement; she was viewed as a happy hooker who could titillate the educated man. Undoubtedly there were highly talented and educated women among the courtesans, and some of them would, under a different social system, undoubtedly have made great philosophers, scientists, or politicians. Some had prospered sufficiently from their trade to be able to buy their freedom. They were wooed and fawned upon by their male suitors and would pick and choose freely from among them. Often long-term relationships developed that led to marriage. These courtesans must be held apart from the prostitutes in the marketplace.

Courtesans and young boys were desired objects at the Greek love feasts (*symposia*), where the participants would openly copulate. These feasts generally were a scene of music and dance as well as gluttony and drunkenness. Vase paintings show crude orgies, with men taking unfair advantage of slaves and prostitutes—scarcely a setting for sacred sentiments.

The ancient Greeks' penchant for homosexuality, notably pederasty, is well known. Plato, who was himself a homosexual, all but eulogized this practice in his dialogues. In the *Symposium,* he has Pausanias make a distinction between sacred and profane love, of which the former is achievable among men alone. This Platonic bias notwithstanding, bisexuality rather than homosexuality was the rule in classical Greece. Indeed, bisexuality may have been widely practiced in pre-Christian times. And prostitution was by no means confined to the female gender. Enslaved men, too, were forced into prostitution, if only to eke out a living for themselves.

Prostitution and religion were close allies in ancient Greece. For instance, the harlots of Corinth, who numbered over one thousand, were owned by the sanctuary of Aphrodite, the radiant Goddess of Love and sexual passion. They were re-garded as sacred slaves, or *hieroduli*. However, their services were probably rather prosaic, without any ritualistic component. Their status was low, and their choice of trade was prompted more by economic necessity than by religious vocation. Their clients paid the temple officials, who thus effectively functioned as pimps.

But the ancient Greeks regarded temple prostitution proper as a special form of sacred sexuality. Here, the motive was sacred and moral rather than economic. The woman offered her body in service to the Goddess of the temple. Nancy Qualls-Corbett's imaginative re-creation of an encounter between a priestess of Venus (the Roman name for Aphrodite) and a stranger visiting her temple offers a glimpse of this profession:

> Behold the priestess of the temple of Venus, the goddess of love. She is the sacred prostitute.
>
> She is a mystery, concealed by veils. We see her only dimly. Yet in the flickering light we discern her shapely feminine out-line. A breeze lifts her veils to reveal her long black tresses. Silver bracelets adorn her arms and ankles; miniature crescents hang from her ear lobes and lapis lazuli beads encircle her neck. Her perfume with its musklike aroma creates an aura which stimu-lates and enriches physical desire.
>
> As the sacred prostitute moves through the open temple doors she begins to dance to the music of the flute, tambourine and cymbals. Her gestures, her facial expressions and the move-ments of her supple body all speak of the welcoming of pas-sion. . . . She is full of love, and as she dances her passion grows. In her ecstasy she forgets all restraint and gives herself to the deity and to the stranger. . . .
>
> The sacred prostitute leads the stranger to the couch pre-pared with white linens and aromatic myrtle leaves. . . . The gentle touch of her embrace sparks a fiery response—he feels the

quickening of his body. He is keenly aware of the passion within this votary to the goddess of love and fertility, and is fulfilled.[8]

Whenever sacred intercourse lived up to this great ideal, it was inevitably a transformative ritual that profoundly affected both the priestess, acting on the Goddess's behalf, and her visitor. Perhaps he left her couch feeling something of the sacredness of his own embodiment. The priestess, or *hierodule,* will have welcomed the stranger as an ambassador or incarnation of the male deity, the Goddess's heavenly spouse. If he left as a mere fornicator, she would have failed in her calling.

Naturally, the priestesses of love did not always act selflessly and with the Goddess at heart. They are known to have turned away poor men but, in the words of Aristophanes, to have "turned their buttocks toward" those with a full purse.[9] Aristophanes's curious phrase may refer to a preferred sexual practice among the sacred prostitutes of Corinth. It implies that they practiced either anal intercourse (perhaps a method of birth control) or dorsal intercourse.

We must carefully distinguish between sacred and profane prostitution, regardless of whether the prostitutes were associated with a sanctuary. Sacred prostitution was probably the invention of the matriarchal cultures of the neolithic. By contrast, profane prostitution has its social roots in the phallocratic desire to overpower and demean women—a desire that is typical of patriarchal societies. As Qualls-Corbett observed:

> Prostitution outside the precincts of the temple was thus apparently a cruel and brutalizing sport. The degradation of the profane prostitute—who represents the dark side of feminine sexuality—was profound; she was the very antithesis of the sacred prostitute, whose sexuality revered the goddess; yet they existed in juxtaposition.[10]

"One wonders," Qualls-Corbett asked next, "what led some women and men to the temple of love and others to the brothel." The answer seems self-evident. Those who intuited and longed to experience the great mystery and sacred power behind sexuality went to the temple. Those who settled for less, who lived to satisfy a momentary itch of the flesh, went to the brothel to claim their substitute nirvana from a hapless woman, often a mere girl.

The Sexual Servants of Mesopotamia and Egypt

Already in ancient Sumer and Babylon, long before the Greeks visited their *hieroduli,* the temple staff included prostitutes who acted as intermediaries between the Goddess and her votaries. According to the Greek historian Herodotus, the reputed father of history who lived in the fifth century B.C., the Babylonians had a "most shameful custom": Every woman born in the country had once in her life to offer herself at the temple of Mylitta [Aphrodite] to any man who would ask her. Herodotus did not mention whether these women all had to be virgins or whether a woman could postpone this sacred duty until after marriage.

Among the Phoenicians, as among so many other ancient peoples, women had to succumb to ritual defloration by a stranger—often a high priest, king, or other notable—before she could get married. It is not unlikely that the Babylonians expected women to sacrifice their virginity at the temple as well. There was obviously no shame attached to this custom; on the contrary, it was a matter of honor and religious necessity to do the Goddess's bidding.

In the remarkable Sumerian *Epic of Gilgamesh,* a temple harlot is sent to seduce the brutish Enkidu. For six days and seven nights, the epic reports, she made love to Enkidu and drained his strength. Then, when he was sated and sufficiently tamed, she like a mother started to indoctrinate him into more civilized ways and prepare him for the encounter with the hero Gilgamesh. This part of the story is a symbol of the transformative power of sexuality and can be regarded as a mythological key to our understanding of the phenomenon of sacred sexuality, which is to ennoble and liberate men and women, but especially men, from unbridled lust.

In Babylon, sacred prostitutes were classified into three types. The *ishtaritu* was a temple prostitute who exclusively served the Goddess Ishtar and was a virgin, having intercourse only with the Divine. The *qadishtu* was a sacred prostitute who pursued her calling at a temple, serving countless men in her lifetime. The name *prostitute* ill fits her religious status and profession. Merlin Stone remarked about the *qadishtu:*

> Sumerian and Babylonian documents reveal that these women, through their affiliations with the temple complex, owned land

and other properties and engaged in extensive business activities. Various accounts report that they were often of wealthy families, well accepted in the society. . . . One inscription from Tralles in western Anatolia, carved there as late as AD 200 by a woman named Aurelia Aemilias, proudly announced that she had served in the temple by taking part in the sexual customs, as had her mother and all their female ancestors before them.[11]

The *harimtu,* the third type of prostitute known in Sumeria, was probably a hybrid between the sacred and the profane harlots who frequented the taverns. Her piety was shallow, and she pursued her trade with profit in mind. As Reay Tannahill put it:

> The sacredness of the tavern courtesan, in effect, appears to have been strictly nominal, her dedication to Ishtar neither more nor less meaningful than that of the modern motorist to the St. Christopher whose medal gleams from his dashboard.[12]

The *harimtu* was as widely frequented by men as she was despised by society at large. Popular maxims advised against marrying such a woman, such as "He who marries her will find neither happiness nor prosperity." By contrast, young priestesses who desired to marry were considered a good match. They often came from noble families, were of good character, and were well schooled in the amatory arts.

In pharaonic Egypt, both sacred and profane prostitution were as prevalent as elsewhere. Prostitutes were mainly recruited from among the slaves. However, although free women enjoyed a somewhat greater status than in other cultures of the ancient world, they were not always exempted from service at the temple.

Temple prostitution was especially associated with the worship of the God Amon and the Goddess Bast (the Egyptian equivalent of Aphrodite). Queen Hatshepsut, who lived circa 1500 B.C., claimed to have been the offspring of the sacred union of her mother with the God Amon. As Fernando Henriques remarked:

> Few queens, whether of Egypt or elsewhere, could claim so divinely august an origin. Something of this divine afflatus must have invested even the most humble of the temple harlots as they submitted their bodies to the priests and worshippers.[13]

The Egyptians were not alone among the Semitic peoples to know the institution of sacred prostitution. The custom was recorded even for the Hebrews, though if we can trust Ezekiel (23:27), they adopted it from the Egyptians. Jerusalem was notorious for its whores, and Ezekiel made prostitution the symbol of what was wrong with the holy city. In the Old Testament, the prophet Hosea's wife is reported to have dressed up in all her finery for her regular visits to the temple, where she made love to men other than her husband.

Such practices were a thorn in the flesh of those who sought to uphold the Hebrew patriarchy. But old habits die hard, and temple prostitution had been a part of female experience for millennia. Nor was it necessarily always a bad or demeaning experience. Perhaps Hosea's wife chose to continue in the old ways because it afforded her a modest measure of freedom in an otherwise oppressive patriarchal environment. Of course, not all harlots were of the sacred variety. Most of them simply tried to stay alive by selling their bodies to those men who could not afford expensive concubines or spoiled courtesans.

The official religion of the ancient pastoralist Hebrews centered on the worship of the male God Yahweh. However, certainly prior to the Babylonian exile, folk practice—probably largely sustained by the female gender—knew much else besides burning incense, sacrificing lambs, and offering prayers at the altar of Yahweh. This great Father-Deity was so remote as to be nearly abstract and unapproachable, quite unlike the Goddess whose warm breath enlivened the hearts of her worshippers. There were above all the cults of Astarte, Goddess of Fertility and Sexuality, and Baal ("Lord"), with whom Astarte (as Baalat, or "Lady") was associated. These two cults were native to Canaan before the arrival of the Israelites who conquered the indigenous population.

THE TEMPLE PROSTITUTES OF INDIA

It appears that wherever there were temples and a priesthood, prostitution was also to be found. We need not adduce cynical motives for this association, for, as we have seen, sexuality and religion have been in close kinship since time immemorial, long before temples were erected and priests were appointed (or appointed themselves) as messengers of the Divine. In India, too, we find temples harboring sacred prostitutes. They bear the colorful Sanskrit designation *deva-dasi,* which means "slave of God," a *deva* being a shining superhuman entity.[14]

Prostitution in India dates back to the time of the Indus civilization. A well-known bronze statuette known as the Dancing Girl seems to represent a prostitute. She is naked, with her vagina clearly visible, and stands provocatively with one hand resting on her hip. It is almost certain that prostitutes were associated with the great temples in the cities of Mohenjo Daro and Harappa, where the Goddess was worshipped.

The collapse of the Indus civilization, probably by earthquakes, flooding, and climatic changes, signaled the end of the great temples in the north of India. However, the destruction of buildings and monuments does not necessarily obliterate the religious tradition that was responsible for their creation. There is a remarkable continuity between the ancient Indus civilization and modern Hindu symbolism, beliefs, and customs. The native Indian cultures proved incredibly resilient and, in the course of centuries, considerably reshaped the religion of the Aryan (Vedic) peoples who are thought to have invaded the peninsula in the second millennium B.C. Thus we find that by the middle of the first millennium B.C., the brahmins were constructing temples and, presumably, thereby contributed to the revival of the archaic custom of temple prostitution.

The tradition of *deva-dasis* thrived until the twentieth century. In 1950, the Indian legislators abolished this time-honored custom. The government assumed responsibility for the perpetuation of the classical heritage of music and dance in South India, which hitherto had been the prerogative of the temple prostitutes. However, while the institution of temple prostitution was thus demolished, the *deva-dasis* sought refuge in common brothels. Prostitution was never made illegal in India.

The following is a fictional account of the sacramental service of a *deva-dasi,* set in the sixth century A.D. in South India, the heyday of Hindu culture.

THE STORY OF SUNITA

Sunita, born into a merchant family, had been orphaned early in life. Until her twelfth year, a benevolent uncle took care of her. But, like so many of his peers, he had one great vice: the playing of dice. At one point he gambled away his entire fortune. Destitute and shunned by everyone, he was unable to look after his immediate family, never mind his young niece Sunita.

He felt he owed it to his late brother not to abandon Sunita to a life on the streets, and so he took her to the local temple priest. Sunita's life was to be dedicated to the Goddess Uma, the heavenly spouse of Shiva. The head priest was a kindly man, and, seeing Sunita's spiritual potential, he took her in and continued her education. She was an intelligent child with a capacity for great faith and quickly adjusted to her new situation. Thus, she spent three years learning the temple arts and all the while blossomed into a beautiful maiden. She became a devout worshipper of the Goddess, and the head priest was well pleased with her.

Then the old priest died, and his successor quickly recognized not only Sunita's natural beauty and charm but also her economic potential. He took the girl to the matron of the *devadasis,* and forthwith Sunita was groomed to be a temple prostitute. She came to believe that to serve the Goddess and her temple in this way was the most noble thing any girl could do. And no time was wasted in teaching her the amatory arts thoroughly. She knew every line from Master Vatsyayana's *Kama-Sutra* by heart and was well studied in his various forms of kissing and positions of lovemaking. She had learned to dance, sing, and play a variety of musical instruments, as well as to read omens and cast spells. Age sixteen and still a virgin, Sunita was already more knowledgeable in the art of lovemaking than most mature women.

Then arrived the day when Sunita was to serve her first Uma worshipper. Because of her exceptional beauty and fine bearing, she had been chosen to bless the local ruler with the favor of the Goddess. Although she had never seen the man, she felt no fear of him nor any shyness about what was to occur. The Goddess was with her. In fact, she felt certain that when the time came the Goddess herself would move her body elegantly, put the right words into her mouth, and be able to delight her visitor in all the countless ways she had learned. Her only desire was to please the Goddess by pleasing her visitor—who was, after all, Uma's spouse in human form.

At nightfall, the rajah was ushered into her little room in the temple precincts. He was a tall, handsome man in his mid-thirties and was decked in finery. He uncannily matched Sunita's mental image of God Shiva come to earth. The only disturbing thing about him were his eyes, which were cold like the eyes of a reptile. Sunita invoked the Goddess inwardly, and then began her charming dance of gestures and words, weaving a sensuous magical spell over the rajah.

Her royal visitor made himself comfortable on a big cushion but kept staring at her silently. Sunita waited on him as if he were Shiva incarnate, serving him sweets and tea. She danced and played the sitar for him, while singing a traditional song of praise to the Goddess. She could not tell whether he was pleased with her service, and a slight shadow of anxiety fell over her heart, but she was careful to hide her feelings from him. Again, she silently called on the Goddess for help.

The room was heavy with incense. A row of candles in front of a small altar cast a golden light over everything. The sounds of Sunita's sitar were still lingering in the air. Then the moment for the sacred union arrived. Sunita gently took the rajah's hand and conducted him to the couch. He followed her willingly, inhaling her aromatic perfume. He had still not uttered a single word. Artfully divesting her garments save a gossamer vestment that revealed more than concealed her youthful, lissome figure, Sunita gingerly started to disrobe him, and he nodded his assent. There was now a strange fire in his eyes. She knew she had lit the flame of passion in him. Kama, the God of Desire, had entered him. Now she could proceed with the love-play of the Goddess she felt so strongly in all her limbs. She felt her own readiness, and cooing sounds escaped her lips.

No sooner had she joined him on the couch, the rajah suddenly grasped her shoulders and roughly pressed her down. Holding her in place with his massive weight, he mounted her with the least ceremony. She felt a piercing pain as he thrust his member deep into her. She shrieked. Through a veil of tears, she could see him smile. It was a cruel, triumphant smile. She had been warned of men who confuse pleasure and pain and whose sexual passion left no room for the Divine, who were deluded enough to think that they could conquer or possess the Goddess. Surely the Great Mother was testing her by sending such a one to take her virginity.

The rajah, who paraded his refined manners only outside the bedroom, had been eager to meet this girl. He was hungry for true innocence, and he was not disappointed. His own wives and courtesans could not give him what this maiden was able to deliver. He ruthlessly brutalized her.

Sunita endured the onslaught stoically but in her mind cursed the rajah for his unforgivable transgression. Then she swooned. Her consciousness welcomed the nurturing void, which she knew to be the Great Mother's bosom. When she awoke, a concerned matron was bending over her. The rajah had left. Sunita's body bore many bruises, and there was a trickle of caked blood on her thighs. Yet her eyes shone brightly. The Goddess had blessed her with a glorious vision. All would be well, and her assailant would be punished by Mother Uma in due course.

Sunita did not know who her first visitor would be. He was a perfect stranger, and so were all the men she would meet in her life as an honorable temple harlot. This anonymity was essential to sacred prostitution. In this regard, sacred prostitution mirrored the archaic practice of sacred marriage between God and Goddess at the annual celebration of fertility.

THE CONTEMPORARY REAPPRAISAL OF SACRED PROSTITUTION

After centuries of phallocracy, our present age is undergoing a sweeping reappraisal of the feminine. The revival of Goddess worship, often referred to as neopaganism, is one of the aspects of this reevaluation. So are the feminist and lesbian movements, the advocacy of creativity and intuition, as well as the occasional plea for a sensuous or erotic way of life.

Thus, in 1983, Deena Metzger wrote an article that was widely disseminated in New Age circles. Two years later it was picked up by the editors of the nationally read magazine *Utne Reader,* and since then the article has been reprinted many times in various publications.[15] Metzger's essay is a concentrated statement of the idea of sacred prostitution developed in her 1978 novel *The Woman Who Slept With Men to Take the War Out of Them.*

Metzger observed that sacred prostitution was integral to the Goddess religions of antiquity and that this custom came under attack by the priests who spoke for the new God-centered religions. She argued as follows:

If the priests wished to insert themselves between the people and the divine, they had to remove women from that role. So it was not that sexuality was originally considered sinful per se, or that women's sexuality threatened property and progeny, it was also that in order for the priests to have power, woman had to be replaced as a road to the divine; this gate had to be closed. And it was, we can speculate, to this end that the terrible misogyny that we all suffer was instituted.[16]

Thus, Metzger rightly associated the suppression of sacred prostitution and the attendant Goddess worship with the arrival and subsequent victory of what I have earlier called the phallocratic mentality. For that mentality, the Great Goddess was at best the spouse of the Great God-Father; women were inferior creatures; sex was problematic and at least potentially detrimental and sinful; the human body was undesirable and pitted against the mind and the spirit; and nature was separated from the otherworldly Divine. "In a sacred universe," observed Metzger, "the prostitute is a holy woman, a priestess. In a secular universe, the prostitute is a whore. In this distinction is the agony of our lives. . . ."[17]

Metzger then argued passionately for the need to resacralize our lives. As she put it:

And so women must all become Holy Prostitutes again.

When contemporary Feminism was established sufficiently to offer real hope and possibility, women who had formerly considered themselves atheists turned to spiritual matters. . . .

As part of this new spiritual order, we must engage in two heresies. The second is to re-sanctify the body; the first even more difficult task is to return to the very early, neolithic, pagan, matriarchal perception of the sacred universe itself. But to overthrow secular thought may be the heretical act of the century. That is why we are in so much psychic pain. . . .

The task is to accept the body as spiritual, and sexuality and erotic love as spiritual disciplines, to believe that eros is pragmatic, to honor the feminine even where it is dishonored or disadvantaged. . . . We must allow whatever time it takes to reestablish the consciousness of the Sacred Prostitute. We must allow ourselves whatever time it takes to restore eros.[18]

CHAPTER 6

꧁꧂

Erotic Spirituality in the Mystery Traditions

THE MYSTERY CULTS OF THE ANCIENT WORLD

The rise of the phallocratic mentality and the almost complete victory of the stern male God over the embracing Goddess had far-reaching social, political, and religious consequences for the Old World. As male dominance was established in the public domain, there was a growing distrust between the sexes, which made itself felt also in private life. The war between the sexes had seriously begun. Many a bedroom became the scene either of male desertion, as we have seen in the case of classical Greece, or of marital rape. Under these new cultural standards, women were rarely allowed to express their sexuality. A noteworthy exception was the Roman elite, which was utterly self-indulgent, as has been recorded for posterity in the murals of Pompeii and Herculaneum.

The progressive victory of the phallocratic mentality by and large destroyed the age-old link between sexuality and the sacred. It left the female gender sexually repressed, while it gave men abundant opportunity to pursue their sexual needs with concubines, slaves, and prostitutes. At the same time, it at least potentially deprived women of their characteristic religious self-expression, which had for millennia revolved around the worship of the Mother Goddess and which involved visceral rituals celebrating the fecundity of Earth and womb.

The annual sacred marriage rite, or *hieros gamos*, had for generations provided a guiding ideal that was also kept alive by the widespread practice of sacred prostitution. There had been a

77

deep acknowledgment of the life-giving and healing role of the female gender in society but especially also in spiritual matters. Now, with the ascendancy of the ideological *phallos,* the once-honorable institution of sacred prostitution was increasingly desecrated. A prostitute was no longer a mediator between man and the Divine but simply a whore who could be exploited for personal gratification. War and slavery ensured a steady supply of these unfortunate women.

Of course, the psychic forces that had created Goddess worship in the first place could not totally be repressed. Therefore we find that the venerable tradition of ecstatic worship and celebration of fertility did not become completely extinct but continued in the shadow of the official religion devoted to the Male God, although in some cultures or periods it had to go underground. This secondary current of spiritual activity, which preserved something of the ancient fertility and erotic religions, is known as the mystery cults.

These cults, which had their adherents throughout the Mediterranean culture area, were based on voluntary and secret initiation rituals and vows. Their principal purpose was to allow their members to personally experience the sacred at the climax of the ceremonies, to encounter the Divine and be blessed and transformed by that event.

The mystery religions attracted primarily women and other underprivileged members of society—male and female laborers and, not least, slaves. The only important exception to this rule was Mithraism, which admitted only men—and preeminently misogynist soldiers—into its mysteries. This syncretistic religion devoted to the worship of Mithra, which was Christianity's most formidable rival, emerged around 100 A.D. in the Roman empire, though its precise origins are still obscure.

In the ecstasies of the mystery cult, women and other oppressed members of society found sanctuary from the pressures and hostilities of the world. In the company of the erotic Divine and their enthusiastic fellow initiates, all distinctions of social or economic status were wiped clear. Particularly women could be fully expressive and demonstrative and temporarily forget that in their everyday lives they were obliged to be invisible, living in the shadow of their husbands or owners. The mystery traditions served as a much-needed outlet for the pent-up emotions of women, slaves, and the destitute.

Not infrequently their celebrations assumed orgiastic proportions in which all the ordinary conventions were suspended and all the common rules broken. In his classic work on the subject, the Australian professor of historical theology S. Angus remarked:

> Men [and women] entered the Mystery-cults for different purposes: there were all degrees of belief and unbelief, morality and laxity, mysticism and realism. The carnal could find in orgiastic processions and midnight revels opportunities for self-indulgence; the superstitious would approach because of the magical value attributed to the formulae and sacraments; the educated could, in the material and physical, perceive symbols of the truth dear to his [or her] heart; the ascetic would look upon initiation as a means of buffeting his [or her] body and giving freedom to the spirit; the mystic would in enthusiasm or ecstasy enjoy the beatific vision by entering into communion with God or by undergoing deification. Then, as always, "many are the wandbearers, but few are the mystae."[1]

The most notable of mystery cults were those dedicated to the worship of Demeter and Persephone, Aphrodite and Adonis, Cybele and Attis, Isis and Osiris, and Eurydice and Orpheus, as well as the androgynous God Dionysos. Some of these cults will be examined more closely.

THE CORN MOTHER DEMETER AND HER VOTARIES

In Greece, the official religion and the most genuine manifestation of the Greek spirit was the religion of a pantheon of Gods as so imaginatively portrayed by Homer. However, many people were drawn to the religious cult of Demeter at Eleusis near Athens in Attica. The mystery cult of Demeter, which means the "Corn Mother" or "Grain Mother," has very ancient roots. This is borne out by Demeter's association with serpents, which links her to the neolithic Snake Goddess of Europe. Demeter's cult flourished in Greece until the Christian emperor Theodosius I suppressed it in 389 A.D.

Demeter is a form of the Earth Mother (Gaia) worshipped since the Stone Age. The principal myth about her is simple: One day Demeter's daughter Persephone was abducted by

Hades, the Lord of the Underworld. Demeter went in search of her and meantime neglected her divine duty of blessing the Earth to be fertile. Finally Zeus, afraid that the Earth might perish, intervened. Hades released Persephone, but because she had taken food in his house she was obliged to return to the Underworld during the four winter months.

Demeter's long association with fecundity and the cycle of seasons acquired a new dimension in the mystery cult dedicated to her: Now she was made the pivot of personal renewal—symbolic death and rebirth.

In the classical period under the phallocracy of the Athenians, Demeter was given a male counterpart: the youthful God Iakchos (or Triptolemos). However, this theological upstart never quite managed to dethrone the Goddess in the respect and veneration she commanded from the pious.

Demeter was especially honored and worshipped in the fertility ritual exclusive to women—the *thesmophoria*. This three-day ritual, which was celebrated in October and November, lifted many of the rules that normally kept Greek women under male control. The ritual involved a symbolic copulation between snakes, pine cones, and other facsimiles of male genitalia and decaying piglets (representing the female reproductive organs). The high point of the ritual occurred when women who had especially purified themselves descended into the pit to salvage the remains of the piglets and offered them on the altar of Demeter, mixed with the seeds to be sown in the new year. Behind this fertility ritual, one can sense both the dark, death-dealing aspect of the Great Goddess and the women's deep and probably concealed pain. Yet the ritual also preserved a vital link to the archaic tradition of erotic spirituality.

At the high point of the esoteric ritual in the temple of Eleusis, the initiates were blessed with an experience that lifted them out of ordinary experience and above ordinary mortals. The ancient writers tell us that the participants experienced vertigo, cold sweat, and tremor of the limbs followed by the hoped-for glorious revelation that made ordinary vision seem dull and dark. As the Greek bard Sophocles is reported to have said:

> Thrice happy are those mortals who, having seen those rites, depart for the hereafter; for they alone are granted to have a true life there. All others merely experience evil.[2]

Every initiate was under oath to preserve the secret of the vision granted at the peak of the ceremony, and, remarkably, we have no written account of the ultimate mystery at Eleusis. "Silence was maintained with such admirable strictness in antiquity," observed Joscelyn Godwin, "that the inquisitive researcher can discover very little of what went on in the rituals of these religions."[3] However, although their work is quite controversial, thanks to the painstaking researches of R. Gordon Wasson and his collaborators, we now have an idea how the worshippers of Demeter may have come by their revelation. As Carl Ruck explained:

> Clearly an hallucinatory reality was induced within the initiation hall and since at times as many as three thousand initiates, a number greater than the population of an ordinary ancient town, were afforded such a vision annually on schedule, it would seem obvious that some psychotropic drug was involved. . . . And indeed, we do know that the drinking of a special potion, the *kykeon,* was an essential part of the Mystery.[4]

Wasson's investigations have made it very likely that the mysterious potion was derived from a fungus (ergot) growing on barley, which is known to have psychotropic properties. This makes sense when we recall the essential connection between Demeter and grain, and when we consider that barley was thought to be especially susceptible to ergot. There are obvious parallels to the Mexican shamanic mushroom rites, which also seek to achieve a visionary state with the aid of plant chemistry.

Here we may also note that the Greek word for mushroom is *mykes* and that the mushroom was used to symbolize the *phallos.* According to some old traditions, the Mycenean culture of Crete was founded when the native priestess–goddess was conquered by the supreme male of the new, conquering dynasty who had picked and brought with him a mushroom. The word *Mycenea* is traditionally derived from *mykene,* the bride of *mykes,* the mushroom. It is suggestive of the sacred marriage between the resident priestess and the invading mushroom-eating ruler. Neolithic Crete was probably the historical birthplace of Demeter worship.

Participation in the Eleusinian mysteries gave Demeter's votaries a powerful spiritual vision that must have influenced the rest of their lives. The climactic rite was known as beholding (*epopteia*). In cases of married worshippers, their ingestion of the reddish, consciousness-altering ergot of barley could well have proven beneficial to their marriage and sexual relationship, because it revealed to them the sacred reality serving as a unifying and harmonizing common ground between the genders. Although outsiders have periodically accused adherents of the Demeter cult of indulging in orgies, this was more true of the cult of Dionysos, which will be reviewed next.

DIONYSOS: GOD OF WINE AND ECSTASY

The Greek women's psychic wounds and rebellion against the severe repression in their lives as well as their passion for transcendence are very evident in the ritualized madness of maenadism associated with the cultic worship of Dionysos (or, Latinized: Dionysus).

The androgynous figure of Dionysos reaches back into the hoary past of Greece and the splendid Minoan culture of Crete. The Dionysian cult was the second-most-popular mystery tradition in Greece. The name of this deity is a composite of the Greek word *dios,* meaning "God," and the Thracian *nusos,* meaning either "son of" or "tree." Thus, Dionysos can be interpreted either as "Son of God" or "Tree God," the tree perhaps being the winestock, since Dionysos was held to be closely associated with wine, drunkenness, madness, orgies, and ecstasy. "An intoxicated god, a mad god!" remarked historian of religion Walter F. Otto. "Truly an idea which demands our deepest thought."[5]

Myth has it that Dionysos was the child of Zeus, supreme patriarch of the Greek pantheon of deities, and the human female Semele. Semele, pregnant by Zeus, begged the God to make himself fully visible to her. When the God of Thunder and Lightning yielded to her pleas, she was promptly burned to ashes in the resulting conflagration. Zeus rescued the unborn child from her womb, implanting Dionysos into his own thigh and nurturing him there until he was ready to be born.

Two great festivals were held in Dionysos' honor every year: the Lesser Dionysia in December and the Greater Dionysia at the end of March. The latter celebration included dramatic plays, which are the cradle of Greek theater, and they typically deteriorated into wild orgies. In his *Moralia* (953D), Plutarch reported that during one of these winter festivals a group of women who were "out of their senses" wandered off into the hills and had to be rescued lest they should perish in the cold. These women, inspired or "possessed" by their God, would roam about for several days without adequate provisions. They would stop frequently and enact their ritual dances accompanied by rhythmic music. This was their way of throwing off the yoke of the patriarchy of the city for a brief period of time. It was also their way of seeking experiential union with the Divine.

The maenads' ritual, or *orgia,* involved the consumption of wine and raw meat after the animal had been torn apart by the chief priestess—perhaps a substitute for an earlier custom of human sacrifice. This ritual is strongly reminiscent of left-hand Hindu Tantrism, which also involves the consumption of wine and meat as well as fish, normally forbidden to the pious Hindu.[6]

"Wine," speculated Walter F. Otto, "has in it something of the spirit of infinity which brings the primeval world to life again."[7] The wine consumed by the ancient Greeks is likely to have been extremely intoxicating. Since the art of distillation was not yet known, the wine contained only a small percentage of alcohol but a large amount of other intoxicants derived from herbal extracts, some of which were ostensibly hallucinogenic. Drunk undiluted, that wine could kill. Classicist Carl Ruck, who corroborated Wasson's speculations, wrote:

> Thus the wine of Dionysus was the principal medium whereby the classical Greeks continued to partake of the ancient ecstasy resident in all the vegetative forms that were the Earth's child. In social situations, the drinking was regulated by a leader, who determined the degree of inebriation that he would impose upon the revellers as they ceremonially drank a measured sequence of toasts. At sacral events, the wine would be more potent and the express purpose of the drinking was to induce that deeper drunkenness in which the presence of the deity could be felt.[8]

Curiously, while the maenads donned men's clothing, their God has a distinctly feminine constitution. He is not only delicately built, which is why the Greek dramatists satirize him as a sissy, but he also wore garments similar to women's dresses. Transvestism appears to have been a prominent aspect of Greek religious life. The androgynous nature of Dionysos is a feature found also in other deities around the world. Androgyny, as June Singer put it, is a symbol of completeness and the integration of the masculine and feminine aspects of the psyche.[9]

The maenads are often depicted with snakes coiling around their arms—reminiscent of the great Snake Goddess of neolithic times. The *orgia* rite is frequently artistically shown as involving satyrs, who are manifestations of God Dionysos. They are represented as cartoon figures of horny men with oversize genitals. However, their sexual wantonness never leads to rape, as in depictions of love feasts, but only to mischief, and the women use the satyrs' molestations to thoroughly take revenge on them. Thus, the rite symbolizes the stark gender polarization of their society.

Significantly, the role of the satyrs was assumed by the women initiates themselves. The women followers of Dionysos formed ritual circles in which lesbianism was practiced. Such lesbian circles were not unknown in ancient Greece, and the island of Lesbos—whence the term *lesbianism*—was renowned for this practice. However, Eva Keuls has suggested that the maenadic rites "may have developed out of an earlier Dionysiac ritual in which men and women danced together and practiced group copulation."[10] If true, this would be a clear instance of the communal practice of sacred sex. There were also all-male circles of worshippers who, if we can believe Euripides's play *Bacchae,* wore fawnskin hides suggestive of women's apparel.

Finally, we must again note in the complex figure of Dionysos the startling association between ecstasy, or *eros,* and death (*thanatos*). Dionysos, according to some myths, was persecuted and torn to pieces by raving women whom he had cursed. Dionysos himself was not only "the delight of mortals" but was also invoked as "a raging bull." He was not only a harbinger of luminous visions but also a dark, savage deity. As Otto observed:

> This god who is the most delightful of all the gods is at the same time the most frightful. No single Greek god even approaches Dionysus in the horror of his epithets, which bear witness to a

savagery that is absolutely without mercy. . . . Correspondingly we hear not only of human sacrifice in his cult but also of the ghastly ritual in which a man is torn to pieces.[11]

When the Greek cult of Dionysos reached Rome, it was further popularized toward the orgiastic end of the spectrum. Not surprisingly, it was immediately successful among the lower strata of the population, that is, those who did not enjoy citizen status. This success scared the upright citizens of Rome, who were officially respectful of the empire's pantheon of deities but privately rather indifferent to religion. Forgetful of their Etruscan heritage—which knew of a God Fuflun, who was Dionysos's exact equivalent—they protested the wild Dionysian orgies known as the Bacchanalia.

The Bacchanalia were now held several times a month rather than twice annually, and with a great deal more gusto. Historian Reay Tannahill described them vividly thus:

> Men were admitted, and the festivals began to be held under cover of darkness five times a month. All emotional and sexual restraints were thrown off, and the only law was that all the laws of ordinary life should be transgressed. Frenzied women, their hair flying in the wind, ran screaming down to the Tiber to plunge burning torches into the river and bring them out again, miraculously, still alight. The men, raving, incoherent, scarcely in control of their limbs, devoted themselves to the initiates, young men under twenty whom they "forcibly debauched." In this highly charged, orgiastic atmosphere, murder was the natural sequel for any initiate who struggled against his fate.[12]

Here we have a distortion of the archaic ideal of sacred sex, serving merely as an excuse for personal whimsy and sensuality. Not surprisingly, in 186 B.C., the Roman senate banned the celebrations throughout the Italian peninsula. However, Dionysos and his enthusiastic worshippers could not be suppressed for long. In 49 B.C., just five years before his murder at the hands of Brutus and his accomplices, Gaius Julius Caesar lifted the senatorial ban. Suddenly the patrician families developed a faddish interest in the cult and duly transmogrified Dionysos along patriarchal lines into a militaristic deity.

Thus, the Romans, who were far from spiritual geniuses,

succeeded in secularizing the splendid sacred figure of Dionysos, confusing the once genuinely erotic spirituality associated with the God's worship with a life of sybaritic leisure.

In their ecstatic madness, Dionysos and his followers transcend the common world. They live with one foot in the underworld, the realm of death. Dionysos' connection with death and the underworld afforded a convenient bridge to the cult of Orpheus.

THE PHALLIC ORPHEUS

The mystery religion of Orphism emerged some time in the sixth century B.C., and one of its sources was the Dionysian religion. However, the Orphics refined the idea of ecstatic enthusiasm (Greek *enthousiasmos,* literally "being infused with the Divine") and developed a spiritual mysticism that strongly influenced both Neoplatonism and Christianity. They believed that, analogous to the Hindu liberation doctrines, it is possible to identify completely with the Divine and thus escape the endless cycle of reincarnation.

In contrast to the worshippers of Dionysos, the Orphics entertained an ascetic approach to redemption. This is best expressed in their universal ethics of reverence for all life, involving the commendable practice of vegetarianism. Alas, they also shared the paranoid world view of many Eastern traditions inasmuch as they regarded the body as thoroughly polluted.

In its defiled condition, the body was thought to drag down the soul, and hence it was in need of a most thorough purification (*katharsis*) so that the soul might shine forth in its inherent splendor. The Orphic notion that the body (*soma*) is a tomb (*sema*) was later taken over by Gnosticism, which, in turn, detrimentally influenced the theocratic anthropology and anti-sexual ethos of Christianity.

Despite its overall ascetical orientation, Orphism preserved some of the wilder features of its Dionysian tributary. As was pointed out by Arthur Evans in his fine study on Dionysos, the Orphics "continued to see an essential connection between sexuality and religion."[13] This is evidenced by their abundant use of sexual imagery in myth and art, which included homosexual motifs. Evans remarked:

The later Orphics made a prominent use of sexual artifacts in their rituals, the most famous of which was the *likhnon,* a fruit-filled winnowing basket with a large phallus sticking up out of its center. This device was not used here principally as a symbol of the fruitfulness of the earth, but as a symbol of Dionysos' power to provide his followers with a joyous afterlife. . . . In short, the purification that Orphics required in this life did not require abandoning commonly established sexual practices. But sexual imagery was being used less as a celebration of sex itself and more as a metaphorical symbol, as Orphism shed its earlier Dionysian character and moved in the direction of becoming a salvation religion.[14]

The *phallos* as a symbol of post-mortem beatitude represents a *volte-face* transformation of its original agricultural and procreational significance. Only a religion of erotic denial could have conceived of such a radical revision of this ancient fertility symbol. The Orphic *phallos,* like the Christian cross, points beyond the self, beyond life. Thus transcendence is placed above creativity—a vision that influenced and, for many centuries, ruled medieval Christendom.

PAN: THE LUSTY GOAT-GOD

We have seen how satyrs were associated with Dionysos. In Pan we have a satyrlike God, who had his own long independent history.[15] Although he did not have a mystery cult dedicated to him, he nevertheless deserves to be introduced here because of his frequent connection with the Dionysian tradition in classical Greek times. Pan was associated with rural life, hunting, herding, music, dance, and—like his Phrygian counterpart Priapus—not least, eroticism. In his original Arcadian conception, Pan was both shepherd and animal. His head, hooves, furry skin, and genitals were those of a goat, but his trunk and hands were human.

The Athenians remodeled this bucolic deity somewhat to fit better their own theological imagination. Yet Pan remained an intensely sexual character—a restless wanderer who flits from one erotic encounter to the next. Not infrequently he would rape an innocent maiden, an act that Euripides called panic marriage (*panos gamos*). This form of sexual exploit was not unique to Pan, however. According to popular imagination, other deities of the Greek pantheon indulged in the same vice. Pan's steady companions were the nymphs, who were also ever-ready for sexual dalliance with humans and semidivines—hence our word *nymphomaniac* for a woman who is obsessed with sex.

Like his celestial father Hermes, Pan was a master of trick-ery. He was an impish friend to those who loved him but a bringer of disorder and panic to his enemies. To be panic-stricken means to be possessed by God Pan. He was also per-fectly capable of instilling an entire city with such lust that the men walked about with long-lasting painful erections.

Pan's worship was not in temples but in caves or grottoes. The ceremony involved the sacrifice of an uncastrated goat or sheep, offerings of libations of wine, and much boisterous mu-sic and dance, but also a long period of vigil through the night, followed the next morning by erotic play between the cele-brants. While these celebrations may often have retained a sacred character, they just as often degenerated into feasts of fornication.

Pan is a distinctly erotic deity. However, his rampant, cha-otic sexuality departs from the more nurturing sexuality of the Goddess tradition. Gods such as Pan or the Roman Bacchus are associated with a more aggressive sexuality, which is an expres-sion of what we have called the phallic principle. We can almost see in such Gods an attempt on the part of men to create rivals for the more soundly instinctive sexuality associated with the Goddess cults.

CYBELE AND ATTIS

After the Romans had imported more or less the entire Greek pantheon, they looked farther afield for religious inspiration. Thus, the empire witnessed a steady influx of Asian cults. Fore-most among them was the cult of the Great Mother in the form of the Phrygian Goddess Cybele and her divine lover Attis. The youthful God Attis, like his Egyptian counterpart Osiris, died and was revivified.

The cultic worship of Cybele and Attis was accompanied by considerable religious fervor. Mourning the death of Attis at the festival of the vernal equinox, his worshippers whipped and flagellated themselves into a frenzy. The *galli,* as the initiates were known, were eager to draw blood. More than that, not a few postulants would castrate themselves in honor of their God. After all, Attis had done the same for breaking his vow of chastity to Cybele. As George Foot Moore observed:

> The rites were sympathetic means of recalling nature from its winter's death to new life. But, though the original significance did not escape the observation of some of the ancient interpreters, both myth and rite had for those who participated in the mysteries of Attis a wholly different meaning. In the resurrection of Attis they had a convincing demonstration that there was a life after death to which the goddess could raise them as she had raised him. By entering soul and body into the tragedy of the god, by inflicting on themselves the wounds from which he suffered, by becoming Attis in his passion, they became partakers of his risen nature and his immortal life. The hysterical exaltation in which sense, consciousness, and will are paralysed, was for them a divine experience, a foretaste of eternity.[16]

The spring festival consisted of a passion play extending over six days. On the third day, known as the day of blood, the sacred pine tree (under which Attis had castrated and killed himself) was buried like the God's corpse. The following night, the participants celebrated the resurrection of Attis. The more secret ceremonies were performed exclusively by the self-emasculated priests. Sir James George Frazer said about the *galli:*

> These unsexed beings, in their Oriental costume, with little images suspended on their breasts, appear to have been a familiar sight in the streets of Rome, which they traversed in procession, carrying the image of the goddess and chanting their hymns to the music of cymbals and tambourines, flutes and horns, while the people, impressed by the fantastic show and moved by the wild strains, flung alms to them in abundance, and buried the image and its bearers under showers of roses.[17]

The idea of self-mutilation out of extreme religious excitement rings strange to most contemporary ears. Certainly we lack the passion of those men, and our self-image is too closely tied up with our sexual identity defined in physical terms. Beyond this, we can today understand that ecstatic self-transcendence does not need to entail frenzied self-abnegation to the point of destroying our organic wholeness. Nonetheless, in his classic treatment of paganism, Franz Cumont made these cautionary remarks:

> All these excessive and degrading demonstrations of an extreme worship must not cause us to slight the power of the feeling that inspired it. The sacred ecstasy, the voluntary mutilations and the eagerly sought sufferings manifested an ardent longing for deliverance from subjection to carnal instincts, and a fervent desire to free the soul from the bonds of matter.[18]

THE MYSTERY CULT OF ISIS AND OSIRIS

Both the Goddess Isis and her divine brother and lover Osiris were worshipped in Egypt since the earliest pharaonic dynasties. Isis was the Goddess of Fertility, and Osiris was the most popular God of the Egyptian pantheon. It was with him that the pharaohs identified themselves and with reference to him that they justified their divine rule on Earth and in the hereafter. Osiris, who reigned supreme over the Underworld, was a powerful symbol of resurrection for the Egyptians and the later *mystes* of the Hellenistic world.

According to mythology, Osiris was dismembered by his jealous brother Set. Osiris's divine wife, Isis, recovered the scattered parts and breathed life into them again, thus resurrecting her beloved husband. The death and subsequent restoration to life of Osiris, which parallels the myth of Attis, was a central aspect of his cultic worship.

At the beginning of the Christian era, the cult that had sprung up around this divinely incestuous pair became influential in the Greek and Roman worlds. Isis achieved considerable prominence among the mystery seekers in the Roman empire and in part merged with other similar Goddess figures, notably Demeter. Historian of religion George Foot Moore remarked:

> There was much in the cult of Isis that touched the aesthetic sense which lies so close to the religious sentiment, and it was free from savage survivals. Of all the foreign religions which were missioning in the Roman world in those centuries it was the most civilised. The imagination could not fail to be impressed by the immemorial antiquity which renewed itself day by day in the liturgy, and the prestige of old-world wisdom attached to the Egyptian theology.[19]

Some of the mysteries of Isis worship are divulged in the concluding section of Apuleius's *Metamorphoses,* better known as the *Golden Ass,* composed in the second century A.D. Here we encounter Apuleius, who had been transmogrified into an ass, on the beach praying to the great Goddess to unburden him of his ugly nonhuman form. In a spectacular vision, Isis appeared to him out of the ocean instructing him about how he could slough his asinine guise at the imminent procession in honor of the Goddess. Apuleius then describes the procession and how he, an ass, ate the roses held by the head priest and promptly metamorphosed back to his human form.

This part of his entertaining and always thoughtful narrative is clearly an allegory. The ass stands for the unregenerate individual who, through his devotion to the Goddess, is transformed into a real human being. After his spiritual conversion, Apuleius joined the priesthood. At his initiation ceremony, he tells us, in veiled terms, that he "saw the Sun shining in all his glory at midnight."

Apuleius does not mention any sexual ritual, yet we know the Romans were offended by the sexual element of the Isis cult. In 19 A.D., Emperor Tiberius ordered an image of the Goddess to be cast into the Tiber because one of the officiating priests, the Roman *eques* Decius Mundus, had dishonored a patrician woman during the ceremonies. Apparently, when she discovered that her divine lover, who was wearing a jackal's mask during the ritual, was not the embalmer-deity Anubis (a form of Osiris) but a perfectly mortal admirer, she felt utterly betrayed. In her anger, she managed to have the priests of the cult crucified and numerous followers deported.

The noble lady's misunderstanding would never have happened in earlier times, when it was perfectly clear that a mortal man had to play the God's role during the sexual ritual. It was assumed that the man, usually a priest or king-priest, was then acting under the inspiration of the Divine. The human participants were thought to be possessed by the divine players in this drama. We can, however, empathize with the Roman lady's disillusionment. In her era, the original significance of the sacred marriage rite was largely lost.

Because of their anchorage in ancient fertility cults, the Hellenistic mystery traditions retained a varyingly conspicuous sexual element. As has been seen, they suffered from a certain liability to distort the heritage of sacred sexuality, giving rise to corruption and sexular orgies serving no higher purpose. Simultaneously, however, we must note that not all schools succumbed to the popular pressure of vulgarization but preserved their original integrity as vehicles of spiritual transformation. Thus, sexuality was tempered by a call for personal purification through temporary abstinence.

Not all the mystery traditions were as overtly sexual as the religious movement around Dionysos, for instance. But even the Dionysian tradition involved periodic sexual abstinence. "This would stimulate expectations and attentiveness to certain signals," remarked Walter Burkert. "Sexuality becomes a means for breaking through to some uncommon experience, rather than an end in itself."[20]

As will be seen in Chapter 8, abstinence and the build-up of erotic tension played a prominent role in Christianity, for better or worse. But first a survey of the more earthy spirituality of ancient Judaism is in order.

CHAPTER 7

❦

Spiritual Eroticism in Judaism

SEX, POWER, AND THE GODDESS AMONG
THE ANCIENT HEBREWS

Christianity, the dominant religious tradition of the Euramerican world, was originally a radical sect within the fold of Judaism. It is, therefore, not surprising that it incorporated many of the Jewish ideas and customs that were abroad at the time of Jesus of Nazareth. Many of these adopted beliefs and practices had a patriarchal and sex-negative bias.

In the face of this inherited proclivity, we often forget that the ancient Hebrews, or Israelites, had a different attitude toward life—including sexual matters—despite Moses' code. The Jews trace their history back to Abraham, who lived some time around 1800 B.C. Moses lived around 1300 B.C. The federation of Hebrew tribes emerged some time around 1200 B.C. and two centuries later constituted themselves into a kingdom under Saul (d. 1010 B.C.).

Like other Near Eastern peoples, the ancient Hebrews subscribed to polygamy, which was subsequently abolished. Men also had concubines as well as slaves. Thus patriarch Abraham's son Ishmael was the child of Hagar, an Egyptian maid of Abraham's wife, Sarah. Hagar's story has recently been cleverly reconstructed by Savina J. Teubal.[1] The matriarch Sarah thrust her maidservant on Abraham because she herself could bear him no children—not because she was too old, suggested Teubal, but because she was a *naditu,* a Mesopotamian priestess who was not supposed to have children. When the maid gave birth to Ishmael, the relationship between the two women took a wrong turn and ended in Hagar's dismissal from Abraham's household.

Sarah herself got pregnant in due course and gave birth to Isaac, which resolves the whole problem. Teubal has found evidence that Sarah's inpregnation involved a *hieros gamos* rite, probably with King Abimelech, who, in the Genesis story, is merged with Yahweh.

Next the Bible remembers Jacob, who favored Rachel over his second wife, Leah. Then there was the mighty king Solomon, who scandalized his contemporaries by marrying no fewer than 700 foreign women—and surely not merely for the selfless motive of securing the borders of his little kingdom. The Bible records how the wise Solomon got so involved with his non-Hebrew wives that he even started to pray to their pagan gods. Yet from the vantage-point of history we know that his fame far outstripped his sins. His name is, above all, associated with the *Song of Songs*, also known as the *Canticle*.

Before the Hebrew tribes worshipped Yahweh, they worshipped many tribal deities. The most important of these was Baal, a phallic god. This phallic heritage of the Hebrews is still evident in their image of Yahweh, who, like Baal, was called the opener, because he was responsible for the deflowering of virgins such as Rachel. He was also frequently referred to as the Bull of Israel, the bull being an ancient symbol of fertility and sexuality. Baal was, however, not a solitary deity but was closely connected with the Goddess Anat.

Today we associate Judaism with monotheistic worship. But, as Raphael Patai has shown, the Hebrews also knew of the veneration of the Goddess—a tradition that continued into the time of the flowering of Jewish esotericism in the sixteenth century, the Kabbalah.[2] Revivals of Goddess worship occurred repeatedly in the history of Israel. We have knowledge of two Hebrew queens being involved in such a revival. The first is Queen Maacah, the royal spouse of Rehoboam, the king of Israel (the northern kingdom) who ruled between 922 and 915 B.C. Some historians believe that she married her own son Abijam. In the Bible (I Kings 15:2–14), she is recorded to have made a statue of the Goddess Asherah. The second queen is Athaliah, daughter of Jezebel, who ruled Judah (the southern kingdom) from c. 848 B.C. to 842 B.C.—the only woman ever to do so. Under her protection, the paganism of the old Canaanites thrived again, if only for a short while. But we know from the Bible (Hosea 1–4; 2 Kings 15) that even Gomer, the prophet Hosea's

wife, was going off to worship idols. Hosea drew a parallel between his wife's dissolute behavior and Israel's unfaithful relationship to God. Yet he continued to love her, he stated, just as
Yahweh continued to love Israel.

These pagan revivals undoubtedly included the custom of
temple prostitution known throughout the ancient Middle
East. This custom was considered an abomination by the
Hebrews, notably their priestly class, the Levites. "There is no
obvious reason," remarked Reay Tannahill, "why the compilers
of the Old Testament should have hated prostitutes, but at best
their language was intemperate and at worst bordering on the
obscene."[3] However, there is a not-so-obvious reason: The Hebrew priests and prophets hated and warned against prostitutes
because sacred prostitution entailed idolatry, the worship of deities other than Yahweh.

Since the time of Moses, the custodians of the sacred law
insisted on the virginity of unmarried maidens, and trans-
gressors were put to death by stoning or burning. This fate was
shared even by a married woman who had the misfortune of
being raped. This cruel practice can be understood only in the
context of the primacy of the phallic principle in Hebrew society, which is strictly patriarchal and which was opposed to the
Goddess religions of the surrounding older cultures in which
sacred prostitution was an accepted sacrament. In her book
When God Was a Woman, Merlin Stone speculated that the
Hebrew Levites were related to the Indo-European Luvians and
arrived in Canaan as conquerors. She wrote:

> From the point of view of the invading Hebrew tribes, this older
> religion was now to be regarded as an orgiastic, evil, lustful,
> shameful, disgraceful, sinful, base fertility-cult. But may we
> suspect that underlying this *moral* stance was the political ma-
> neuvering for power over land and property accessible to them
> only upon the institution of a patrilineal system, perhaps a sys-
> tem long known to them in the northern lands of the Indo-
> Europeans?[4]

Sex and power have a long intertwined and seldom felicitous history. The patriarchal, phallic spirit reared its head
among the Hebrews at an early age. They were forever trying
to reform the underground impulses of paganism, Goddess

worship, and spontaneous eroticism—a trend that was largely successful. But we also have the evidence of a continuing recrudescence of the feminine principle throughout the early and even the later history of the Jewish people. The *Song of Songs,* discussed below, is an example of a more erotic spirituality that delighted some and horrified others and that to this day elicits a mixed response among both Jews and Christians.

THE HEBREW SEXUAL HERITAGE

The Jewish sexual mores are found codified in the fifth book of the Old Testament, known as Deuteronomy ("Secondary Law"). It is clear from this book that the compiler or compilers regarded the laws as God's rules, which the Hebrews (and modern Jews) must obey to the letter because of the covenant between the chosen people and Yahweh. The most apparent sign of that treaty is the custom of circumcision, which has been described as a "symbolic castration" and a "religious convention which made every man a priest,"[5] or as a means of emphasizing the maleness of the God-worshipping Hebrews as distinct from the femaleness of the Goddess worshippers.[6] In *The Creation of Patriarchy,* Gerda Lerner speculated that "the rite of circumcision demanded as a token of the covenant represents an adaptation of the old Mesopotamian rite, but transmuted as to celebrate the fertility of the One God and His blessing of male procreativity."[7]

For the ancient Hebrews, just as for the modern Jews, marriage and sexual relations between husband and wife were a sacrament, and the delight that they give each other in their intimacy was regarded as a *mitzvah,* or a divinely dispensed law. Adultery is thus not merely a slip in social etiquette but a serious breach of the covenant between God and his elected people. "Drink water from your own cistern, flowing water from your own well" is the advice of Proverbs (15:15).

The husband was seen as the lord or owner (*ba'al*), and a woman became his property by marriage. She was expected to be faithful to him and, not least, to bear him male children, who would ensure the continuation of the husband's lineage. The levirate marriage—in which a man marries the widow of his deceased brother—has the same patriarchal purpose. In this case, if the man was already married, he would enter a polygamous relationship.

Considering the patriarchal orientation of Hebrew society, it may come as a surprise that marital sex is actually looked upon favorably. A man is advised to appreciate his wife's beauty, to be in love with her, and to delight in her body or, as it is stated in the Bible (Hebrews 5:19), "let her breasts satisfy you at all times." No comparable advice is given to the wives, however.

Yet the Hebrew women of yore were not expected to be entirely passive in the sexual relationship, which brings us to Solomon's *Song,* a remarkable lyrical celebration of feminine beauty and love as well as sexual equality. The *Song* is traditionally attributed to King Solomon, David's son. Solomon was responsible for the construction of the famous temple in Jerusalem ("Town of Peace") between 969 and 959 B.C., which stood for 400 years before the Babylonian king Nebuchadnezzar razed it to the ground. Although Solomon's name has long been associated with the *Song of Songs,* it appears that this collection of poems was created many centuries later and was wrongly attributed to that sagacious and lusty ruler. It is not improbable, though, that one or the other song actually dates back to Solomonic time.

When the Hebrew priests put together the scriptural canon, because of *the Song of Songs'* explicit earthy sensuality they debated earnestly whether it was suitable for inclusion. The poems, which tend to be repetitions, are presented as a dialog between two lovers who address each other as "brother" and "sister." Here are some of the verses of this old love song.

> [*She:*]
> O for your kiss! For your love
> More enticing than wine,
> For your scent and sweet name—
> For all this they love you.
>
> Take me away to your room,
> Like a king to his rooms—
> We'll rejoice there with wine.
> No wonder they love you! [1]

• • • • •

Until the king returns
   I lie in fragrance,
Sweet anticipation
   of his entrance.

Between my breasts he'll lie—
   Sachet of spices,
Spray of blossoms plucked
   From the oasis. [5]

   . . . . .

[*He:*]
Of all pleasure, how sweet
Is the taste of love!

There you stand like a palm,
Your breasts clusters of dates.

Shall I climb that palm
And take hold of the boughs?

Your breasts will be tender
As clusters of grapes,

Your breath will be sweet
As the fragrance of quince,

And your mouth will awaken
All sleeping desire

Like wine that entices
The lips of new lovers. [23][8]

We can understand why the compilers of the Hebrew canon had
qualms about including this work. They got around their difficulties by de-eroticizing the poems and interpreting the passion
between these two anonymous lovers as an allegory for the love
between Yahweh and the Jews. Later this was reinterpreted as
the love between God and the human soul. The most remarkable feature of the *Song* is that it expresses a wonderful mutuality and equality between the lovers, who adore each other un-
ashamedly. From everything else we know about the Hebrew
society, this attitude was rather atypical.

Hence scholars have speculated that the *Song* draws on earlier pagan traditions, possibly characterizing the equal relationship between Canaanite Baal and his sister-spouse Anat, who were frequently referred to as brother and sister. In other words, we may see in Solomon's *Song* a fragment of a lyrical myth that celebrates the sacred marriage, or *hieros gamos.* It will shortly be seen how the archaic motif of the sacred marriage surreptitiously persisted even in the Christian tradition in the spiritual union between the Virgin Mary and Christ. But first it is necessary to take a closer look at how Christianity transmuted the Jewish sexual ethics into a powerful world-, body-, and sex-denying ideology.

CHAPTER 8

❧

The Eclipse of Eros in the Christian Tradition

THE CHRISTIAN SEXUAL HERITAGE

The ancient Hebrews offered their sexual passion at the altar of their Gods. After Abraham and Moses, the Jews still viewed sex as a joyous marital sacrament. All this changed with the Jewish splinter group that developed into the independent world religion of Christianity. Now sex became more closely linked with sin and the Devil, probably far more closely than the founder of Christianity himself had in mind.

Jesus, according to Matthew 5:17, came not to change the Mosaic law but to fulfill it. He did change it, however, and the change was radical enough for his small sectarian community to secede from Judaism. In his sexual ethics, for instance, Jesus went beyond the restrictions enshrined in the Torah and beyond the literalism of the rabbis. This is best captured in Jesus' stipulation, as recorded in the Gospel of Matthew (5:28), that "whosoever looketh on a woman to lust after her hath committed adultery with her already in his heart." Christians thus not only had to watch what they were doing but also what they were *thinking*. This represents a major ethical innovation.

It is this same augmentation of the ethical standards of Judaism that we find in Jesus' most famous edict, namely that we should love our enemies, bless those who curse us, do good to those who hate us, and pray for those who exploit and persecute us.[1] This idea of universal forgiveness or love is also prominent in some schools of Hinduism and Buddhism, as is the idea that chastity is first and foremost a matter of a pure mental attitude.

Jesus' stipulation not to lust after women can be interpreted to mean either women other than one's wife or all women, including one's wife. It is clear from the teachings of Jesus that he intended the latter. How, then, did he look upon sexual relations between husband and wife? In his views on marriage, Jesus was thoroughly Jewish. He subscribed to the biblical injunction to "be fruitful and multiply and fill the earth."[2]

Jesus was, however, stricter in his views on divorce, which he considered anathema. In light of this, his followers rightly wondered whether it would not be best to remain unmarried and celibate. He seems to have said that this was indeed a good choice, providing a person was so moved and also truly enabled to practice celibacy.

It is widely assumed that even though Jesus preached about the marital state he himself was unmarried, yet nowhere in the Gospels is it stated that Jesus was *not* married. Some historians have, therefore, speculated that he might well have been married, as was the custom among the Jews. This could explain, for instance, why Jesus was ostensibly not the typical repressed saint but freely mixed with and forgave those he considered sinners—prostitutes, adulteresses, and tax collectors—to the horror of his more conservative contemporaries. For his era, Jesus' attitude toward women was progressive, as Kenneth Maahs acknowledged:

> What is clear to all who survey the Gospels is that Jesus treats women in a manner that can only be described in his day as radical and subversive. He contravenes all cultural and rabbinical restrictions on contact and teaching of women. Attitudes which stand out in the numerous encounters he has with women are always affirmative of their full humanity and the integrity of their moral being.[3]

If, according to Jesus, celibacy was a respectable option for a small minority, his apostle Paul took a more extreme position, arguing that marriage was second best and appropriate only for those who could not completely renounce the lusts of the flesh. St. Paul, a lifelong bachelor, seems to have sublimated his sex drive into missionary zeal and expected his Christian brothers and sisters to follow suit.

As is well known, Paul had considerable difficulty in this regard with his flock in Corinth. Some of them were eager to continue their pagan practice of participating in religious rites involving sexual intercourse; others saw nothing wrong in enjoying the services of prostitutes. Another faction was utterly antisexual, seeking to dull their senses and shunning all earthly delights. So, in one of his famous epistles, Paul berated the fornicators, idolaters, adulterers, and pederasts in the Christian community of Corinth—a harbor town renowned for its abundance of sacred and secular prostitutes.

But Paul also censured the puritans who sought to deny the flesh altogether. Married couples, he advised, should not deprive each other, unless it is for a mutually agreed-upon limited period of time to deepen their spiritual life. Nonetheless, he let it be known that "I desire all men to be as I am myself, but each has his own gift from God: one's gift is celibacy while another's is marriage."[4]

One of Paul's more controversial recommendations contains his reason for marriage: "If they cannot exercise self-control, let them marry, for it is better to marry than to burn [with sexual desire]."[5] This stipulation makes marriage a mere substitute for celibacy. The apostle's preference for the celibate life was directly related to the early Christian belief that the Day of Judgment was near and that, in the face of the imminent Armageddon, it was better to stay single and devote one's life to the worship of God.

Modern critics of Christian sexual ethics have regularly used the apostle Paul as a punching bag. However, as has been seen, his views were in many regards in line with his ancestral Jewish inheritance. Nonetheless, his notion that celibacy was preferable to sexual activity opened the floodgate for the sex-negative teachings of the Church Fathers who based themselves on him—the venerable Ambrose, Jerome, Augustine, John Chrysostom, and a host of other saints. Rosemary Haughton observed:

> The Fathers had to indulge in incredible mental contortions in order to get Paul on their side against sex, but they managed it, and the anti-sex nature of orthodox Christianity has been one of the main tenets of any respectable anti-Christian creed for centuries. . . .[6]

The Christian patriarchs confused holiness with asceticism and celibacy. Their writings ring with a deathly fear of the flesh and of women, who came to be regarded as the source of wickedness and temptation. Madonna Kolbenschlag paraphrased this misogynous view thus:

> To be a Christian one must be desexed—if you are a woman! The flight from sin is equated with the flight from the body and the flight from woman. The path to salvation, toward God, is equated with proximity to, resemblance to, a male archetype.[7]

The fourth-century Byzantine bishop St. John Chrysostom, whose name means "Golden Mouth," maligned women when he announced that all female beauty is but phlegm, bile, and blood. It was, however, St. Augustine who must bear the greatest historical blame for the victory of sex-negativity in Christianity, simply became he was the most influential of the Church Fathers. In his *Confessions* (II.2), he reflected on his profligate youth with much regret thus:

> And what was it that I delighted in, but to love, and be beloved? but I kept not the measure of love . . . but out of the muddy concupiscence of the flesh, and the bubblings of youth, mists fumed up which beclouded and overcast my heart. . . . I boiled over in my fornications.[8]

"Augustine," wrote leading feminist theologian Carter Heyward, "was confused, spiritually and sexually."[9] Heyward elaborated:

> His *spiritual* confusion was, as he knew, a consequence of his failure to take seriously the vast, just, merciful, and mysterious character of the Sacred. What Augustine did not know was that his *sexual* confusion, which increasingly he denied and which, therefore, took up increasingly more space in his life, work, and legacy, was rooted in the same failure to apprehend the same character of the same God.
>
> Rather than embracing sexuality as a dimension of sacred passion, Augustine targeted it as its opposite: the source of sin, setting in theological motion a violent antagonism, which christians (and others) have suffered to this day. Split in his passion,

disintegrated at the root, the converted Augustine (followed by christian men for 1,600 years) made the connections wrong— between sex and God.[10]

As I wrote in another book:

> In his earlier life, Augustine was greatly troubled by temptations of the flesh. He had at least two love affairs, one of which produced a child. His conversion to Christianity had not a little to do with his desire to be finished with sexuality, but it didn't quite turn out that way.
>
> Augustine, a learned man, had imbibed the dualistic metaphysics of Gnosticism, which made up a sharp split between body and spirit. In the light of this "pagan" teaching, he came to consider all forms of sex as sinful. He spoke of the guilt connected with procreation. . . . He firmly believed that Adam's fallen nature is transmitted biologically through sexual procreation. He saw in lust a direct expression of Adam's corruption, which had led to the Fall. We are born corrupt, sinful, and guilty. Augustine's teachings succeeded in souring sex for generations of Christians, who could engage in the sexual act only by piling guilt feelings upon their originally "sinful" nature.[11]

When the saintly Augustine spoke of the corruption of Adam, he did not leave anyone in doubt that it was Eve, not Adam, who was principally responsible for the fiasco in the Garden of Eden. For Augustine and his epigones, man is created in God's image but woman in man's image. She is thus a secondary creation. Only one woman rose beyond this ideology of derivative existence: Mary, the mother of Jesus.

MARY: VIRGINAL MOTHER AND BRIDE OF CHRIST

Given so much negativity and even hatred toward the female gender, the collective psyche of the growing Christian community had to establish a new balance. It did so by creating a powerful and resilient religious symbol—that of the Virgin Mary, the divinized mother of Jesus. Later, Christianity even turned the apotheosized virginal mother of Jesus into the Bride of Christ. This transformation amounts to the conversion of an anti-erotic symbol into a paradoxical image in which virginity and motherhood are juxtaposed with bridal eroticism.

How did this curious transformation occur? To answer this question, we have to unravel over one thousand years of ecclesial and theological history. This has been accomplished with admirable skill by Marina Warner in her accoladed book *Alone of All Her Sex.*[12] The following discussion is largely, though not exclusively, based on Warner's work.

To begin with, we must note that the Gospels say very little about Mary. It is Luke's Gospel that contains the only detailed account of the miraculous events of annunciation (when the archangel Gabriel told Mary that she would soon be pregnant with Jesus), visitation (when Elizabeth recognized the unborn child as her Lord), and nativity (Jesus' birth in Bethlehem). Luke's account served as the scriptural source for the later lore and theological speculation about the Virgin Mary. But only the Gospel of Matthew (1:20) contains any reference to the virginal birth, stating that Jesus was conceived through the Holy Spirit.[13]

What is important to appreciate is that the idea of virgin birth was by no means new. In fact, virgin birth was something of a status symbol for heroes and sages in the classical Mediterranean world. Pythagoras, Plato, and Alexander the Great are said to have entered the world in this fashion. Moreover, the great Goddesses of love—Ishtar, Anat, Astarte, and Venus— were all virgins, although there is an important difference between them and Mary. As has been seen, these Goddesses celebrated the creative powers of sex, whereas the Virgin Mary is pictured as a *virgo intacto* and a paragon of asexuality.

Thus, Christian theologians fashioned the ancient Mother Goddess into a model of ascetic virtue and, as Warner noted, into an effective instrument of female subjugation. Every Christian girl was exhorted to emulate the Divine Mother and remain chaste and virginal until marriage and to continue to cultivate a chaste heart after marriage. In return, these girls were offered equality with men before God, though not in everyday life.

According to some accounts, Mary—like Christ before her—died and was buried only to be resurrected, and she even ascended bodily to heaven. Again this entire notion has its antecedents in the pagan world, for great heroes such as the Greek Herakles or the Hindu Yudhishthira were believed to rise bodily to heaven, where they were glorified. The whole process is known in Greek as *apotheosis.*

At the hands of the pious Church doctors, Jesus' humble human mother was deified; she became the Christian equivalent to the pagan Goddesses. However, unlike those deities, she was separated from the ancient ideal of sacred sexuality. In the middle of the fifth century, the Virgin assumed regal proportions: She became Maria Regina, the heavenly empress seated to the right of God's throne. Medieval artists depicted her crowned and wrapped in splendid robes and majestically holding a cross-staff. "It would be difficult," judged Marina Warner harshly, "to concoct a greater perversion of the Sermon on the Mount than the sovereignty of Mary and its cult, which has been used over the centuries by different princes to stake out their spheres of influence in the temporal realm."[14]

But Mary's transformation from a virtuous human mother to a Goddess did not stop at the symbol of the remote Heavenly Queen. In the twelfth century, Mary was next turned into the Bride of Christ and the ardent object, with Jesus, of the bridal mysticism of St. Bernard of Clairvaux, Ramon Lull, and St. Catherine of Siena. The artistic imagery changed accordingly, now showing Christ and the Virgin lovingly holding hands in conjugal intimacy. Here we have, surely, the final triumph of the pagan tradition of *hieros gamos* between Mother-Goddess and divine Son-Lover.

What was punishable by death on the human level was not experienced as a vile transgression of the moral code but a sublime metaphysical condition that could inspire and uplift the human heart: the union of Mother and Son. This profound change in the symbol of the Virgin Mary met the long-expressed need for a mediator between faltering men and women on the one side and the utterly distant Father-God and the stern and judgmental Christ on the other side.

The Virgin Mary was experienced as the accessible embodiment of divine love, as a benign and clement Mother who could be petitioned through heartfelt prayer. She could be trusted to intercede on behalf of the weak. As the fourteenth-century English mystic Julian of Norwich stated in her *Revelations of Divine Love* (chapter 57), "she who is the Mother of our Saviour is Mother of all who are to be saved in our Saviour."[15]

The conversion of the Divine Queen into the loving Mother, however, did nothing to alter the strife between the sexes in medieval society. Women still faced a rather bleak destiny of suppression, as well as frequent emotional and physical abuse.

Even as the Virgin was made into the most benign symbol, women throughout Europe were widely hunted down, humiliated, raped, and slaughtered. For, with the fifteenth century, the infamous witch hunts began. They represent the ultimate denial and suppression of women and the feminine aspect of existence. Women could not live up to the Madonna image of unsullied purity, nor did men really want them to, yet women were being punished everywhere for failing to be perfect in this imperfect world.

EVE, THE FIRST MAN, AND GUILT

One cannot talk about the Virgin Mary without also talking about Eve, for the Holy Mother has been called the Second Eve, just as St. Paul had introduced Jesus as the Second Adam. If Mary, the mother of Jesus, was elevated into a redeeming symbol that promises life after death, Eve has always been considered as the gateway to death. It was, after all, her weakness that led to her and Adam's expulsion from Paradise in the biblical myth of the Fall.

It has already been seen how the early Christian thinkers changed the age-old pagan belief of virgin birth into a potent sex-negative ideology. With few exceptions, the Church Fathers were obsessed with sex—or, rather, with overcoming the sexual appetite. As Marina Warner put it succinctly:

> Sexuality represented to them the gravest danger and the fatal flaw; they viewed virginity as its opposite and its conqueror, sadly failing to appreciate that renunciation does not banish or overcome desire.[16]

This patriarchal sex-negative ideology is most fittingly epitomized in St. Jerome's notion that the only reason why marriage is at all tolerable is that it leads to the birth of virgins. He apparently did not consider that most of those virgins will one day marry, have sex and lose their hymen, and then become mothers. Surely, if virginity is to have any meaning at all, it must apply to both women *and* men and be primarily a matter of inner purity, which may or may not find expression in physical abstinence from the sex act.

The symbol of Christian sex-negativity is the much-maligned figure of Eve. In the second century A.D., the apologist Tertullian remarked in his Latin work *De virginibus velandis* ("On the Apparel of Women") that it would be appropriate for women to don mourning clothes because they were descendants of Eve, the cause of all human misery. Almost two thousand years later, the female gender is still being treated as if it were responsible for the Fall.

We cannot understand Eve and her abject fate without including Adam in our considerations. *Adam* is not simply a personal name; it is a symbol. The Hebrew word means "man of earth," because, according to the biblical story, the first human being was fashioned by God out of the dust of the Earth (*adamah*). Thus Adam is a generic reference to humankind in the state of Paradise.

According to the myth told in Genesis (2:7–3:24), Yahweh extracted one of Adam's ribs after having put him to sleep. Then he carefully healed the wound and fashioned from the rib a helpmate for Adam. The helper was none other than Eve, the personification of the female gender of the original human race. It was Adam who named her so after the Fall—in Hebrew, *Hawwah*, "Mother of All Living." The word is connected with the Semitic word *hewya*, meaning "serpent," and *hawa*, meaning "to instruct." In the ancient world, the serpent was a symbol for both wisdom and fertility or sexuality.

The agent of the Fall was the serpent, who convinced Eve to eat of the forbidden fruit because it would make her like God. Eve then gave of the fruit to Adam. In that instant, both realized they were naked, and the omniscient Creator knew of their awareness of nudity. He promptly expelled both from Paradise, and history began.

Ancient and modern exegetes have interpreted the Adamic myth in a variety of ways, and their interpretations range from the strictly literal to the purely allegorical. The story has many fascinating aspects, but one of the more interesting and significant is Adam's and Eve's sudden recognition of their nakedness, for here we have a strong connection between "good and evil" and sexuality. Gerda Lerner offered these most insightful comments:

> The consequence of sexual knowledge is to sever female sexuality from procreation. God puts enmity between the snake and the woman (Gen. 3:15). In the historical context of the times of the writing of Genesis, the snake was clearly associated with the fertility goddess and symbolically represented her. Thus, by God's command, the free and open sexuality of the fertility-goddess was to be forbidden to fallen woman. The way her sexuality was to find expression was in motherhood. Her sexuality was so defined as to serve her motherly function, and it was limited by two conditions: she was to be subordinate to her husband, and she would bring forth her children in pain.[17]

As St. Augustine explained, Adam and Eve were by no means born blind;[18] they saw that they were naked. But prior to their consumption of the forbidden fruit, they wore, as he put it, the garment of grace. They were not ashamed of their nudity, because it did not signal to them sexual desire or availability. When God withdrew his grace from them, they became self-conscious and embarrassed. Augustine went on to say that such embarrassment is natural and that "even brothels make provisions for secrecy," because the "parts of shame" (*pudenda*) should be under our conscious control rather than allowed to act independently. Lust, he insisted, is a disgrace.

Adam and Eve felt lust for each other. In order to get their sexual appetite somewhat under control, they made aprons out of fig leaves for themselves. Eve apparently did not cover her breasts, possibly because they were still being associated with motherhood and fertility rather than with sex play—otherwise she would have had to shroud herself from head to toe in the manner of her present-day descendants in some Muslim countries.

The myth of Adam and Eve has informed (and terrorized) the moral and sexual life of generation upon generation of God-fearing men and women, and it still holds sway over the lives of millions of Christians. In the final analysis, this most powerful collective image is responsible for the deeply ingrained feelings of guilt and shame that contribute to the sexual conflict in our own post–Christian society.

Happily, there are hopeful signs that the millennia-long spell of this myth is beginning to be dispelled. A body- and sex-positive spiritual trend is definitely emerging in Christianity, which attempts to heal the breach between man and woman, humankind and the Earth, feeling and thinking, body and mind, and matter and spirit, as well as between patriarchal religion and Goddess worship, the ethics of love and power politics, creativity and transcendence, and ritual and silence. This promising new trend will be discussed in Chapter 13.

The next stop on this voyage through the history of sacred sexuality will be in the late Middle Ages, which witnessed a certain renaissance of erotic spirituality.

CHAPTER 9

❧

The Medieval Love Mystics, East and West

THE RESURGENCE OF EROS IN THE MIDDLE AGES

It is difficult to comprehend how the antisexual millennarian teachings of the Christian Church (rather than of Jesus) could have emerged victorious in a cultural milieu that was so positively sensuous as the far-flung Roman empire. The triumph of a killjoy ideology over the pagan world of Greece and Rome remains something of an enigma. The Christian promise of happiness in the hereafter proved more appealing than the multitude of possible pleasures in the here and now; the principle of hope proved more attractive than the principle of hedonistic fulfillment.

The shift in values introduced by Christianity was purchased at a high price: *Eros,* the life force, was hemmed in and held down. Consequently, the counterprinciple of what Freud called *thanatos*—the death instinct—loomed large. This trend reached its climax in the Middle Ages. Forbidden to express their sexual desires and thus burdened by extreme sexual guilt and shame, our medieval forebears became masters at self-denial, self-blame, and self-punishment. They flagellated themselves literally and emotionally, making a virtual cult out of this practice. The cross to which Jesus of Nazareth was nailed became their favored symbol. In Gordon Rattray Taylor's harsh but substantially correct judgment, "the Church's code of repression produced, throughout Western Europe, over a period of four or five centuries, an outbreak of mass psychosis for which there are few parallels in history."[1]

The most palpable expression of the upsurge of *thanatos* during the Middle Ages is that era's morbid obsession with the image of death. Death was personified as the Grim Reaper and depicted in countless drawings and paintings. However, only in the sixteenth century—the era of the worst witch hunts—was Death portrayed as a rapist, which bears out the close proximity of death and sex, both being threshold events. In the moment of death, we cross the threshold from the known into the unknown or, as some would have it, from existence to nonexistence. In the moment of sexual climax, we yield sobriety and self-control to enter a varyingly intense altered state of consciousness. To this day, the French call the orgasm "the little death."

The witch hunts, crusades, and merciless persecution of so-called heretics are the most concrete and degenerate manifestations of the medieval death impulse, which surged up even as the sexual instinct was crammed down into the dark recesses of the psyche. Sexual repression caused much other neurotic behavior. Thus our medieval forebears were plagued by incubi and succubi, those male and female dream demons specializing in surreptitious sexual intercourse with sleeping humans.

Nuns, who had vowed to live as the brides of Christ, secretly fraternized with visiting monks and then were obliged to murder and bury their illegitimate children. Girls deflowered themselves with wooden dildos in honor of saints such as St. Guerlichon, St. Giles, and St. René—a practice that apparently was often a cover-up for premarital sex, which was strictly forbidden.

In Britain, prayer meetings degenerated into orgies, with phallic representations serving as an anchor-point for the celebrants' excitement. The Gothic churches were embellished with sculptures that would nowadays be considered scandalous, if not blasphemous. Nor did the pagan undercurrent displaced by Christianity ever go completely dry. It was forced underground for long periods at a time, but now and then it bubbled up, revealing itself to be as vital and abundant as ever.

One such moment in European history was the twelfth century—the time of the secular troubadours and heretic Cathars and Waldensians, as well as the love mystics within the Church. As transpersonal theorist John Weir Perry put it, "a new breath of energy did sweep through Europe at this time."[2]

THE TROUBADOURS: EROTIC IDOLATORS

The center of that new energy was the courtly circles of the French Provence, more particularly the troubadours or *trouvères,* as they were known in the south of France. Both designations stem from the same verbal root, meaning "to find." The object of the troubadours' quest was the grail of chaste love, or what their counterparts in Germany, the *Minnesingers,* called *minne.*

The troubadours were courtly poet-musicians who dedicated themselves to, venerated, and loyally served the lady of their choice—a lady who, as a rule, was married to another man. They sought to worship their so-called mistress (*domina*) at a respectful distance, seeing in her the ideal of womanhood, just as pious commoners worshipped the Virgin Mary as the perfectly chaste universal Mother.

Provided they were true to their high idealism, which was not always the case, the troubadours did not want to consummate their love; rather, they wanted to burn with desire for their idealized woman. The troubadour's passionate mood and voluntary suffering is well captured in the following description of Heinrich von Mörungen, a well-known German *Minnesinger* who died in 1222 A.D.:

> His lady is to him as the sun—unattainable and far above him: she inflames him as the fire consumes the tinder, and a kind word from her sends him into a flight of rapture.
>
> His love is shot through with strands of visionary experience and almost religious fervour. . . . His yearning leads him to imagine his own death: his song is like the cry of the dying swan, and . . . he composes his own epitaph, which will proclaim that it is she who was responsible for his death. . . .[3]

Thus, like their entire era, the troubadours too were preoccupied with death. However, they chose passionate love rather than base aggression or dull sensuality as their gate to it. From a strictly Christian point of view, the troubadours' relationship to their mistresses was idolatrous. Yet the clergy, who were under the same spell of mother worship, on the whole tolerated the movement. The women's husbands, usually wealthy noblemen, even sponsored the lovesick troubadours—at least until they grew jealous, with or without good reason.

The troubadour's ideal was not new, of course. Early

Christendom had known comparable relationships in which man and woman were sensuous with each other but abstained from orgasm. The women, who were maidens, were called *agapetae* or *virgines subintroductae*. The practice was, not surprisingly, repressed by the Church Fathers. It appears to have been reintroduced in the Middle Ages by the Cathari sect, which had a still ill-understood connection with the troubadours.

We owe many wonderful literary creations to the troubadours, yet we cannot overlook that their chivalric ideal and romantic gentleness were somewhat self-serving: They related to their mistress more as a fetish than a flesh-and-blood person, and as a fetish she was, finally, a substitute for the Divine. A few troubadours, however, went beyond their secular romanticism and actually donned the monastic habit, thus converting their poetic quest into a full-fledged religious odyssey.

We do not know whether the troubadours, who were by no means all celibate, transferred their lofty idealism to their sexual relationships. This seems doubtful considering the exclusiveness with which they tied themselves emotionally to a single adored woman. Very probably, they did not only pour their passion into poetry and song; they also relieved themselves of the sexual tension created by their painstaking devotion to the *domina* in liaisons with more available women.[4]

Thus, the troubadours can be said to have missed the opportunity to practice sacred sex. While they were clearly cultivating their *eros,* it appears that as a group they did not succeed in integrating *eros* with sex. In this regard, they were still victims of the medieval mentality, which was ambivalent or even negative about sex.

This was also true of the love mystics, though the religious vector of their quest brought at least some of them closer to a solution of the sexual problem: to transcend rather than repress or indulge the assertiveness of the sex hormones. They pursued the unitive force, or *eros,* to its natural completion in the state of mystical oneness. We will turn to them next.

THE LOVER WITHIN: BRIDAL MYSTICISM

If the troubadours turned a real woman into their unreachable ideal, the love mystics of the Middle Ages had their hearts broken by the idealized Divine—generally in the form of the divinized Jesus. The designation *love mystics* generally refers to those Christian mystics, or athletes of the spirit, who made divine love their emotional and intellectual mainstay. Here, the term is applied more generically to include non-Christian mystics as well.

Often, the love mystics used sexual or erotic metaphors to express their spiritual ardor. For them, sacred sex occurred not between man and woman but, on the spiritual plane, between the human soul and the Divine. Nonetheless, their testimony is important to our consideration of the history and nature of sacred sexuality, for the fulfillment of sacred sex, or the cultivation of *eros* through sexual means, lies precisely in the mystic's unitive experience.

Like the troubadours, the love mystics bequeathed to us many remarkable literary works, though of a spiritual nature. In them they express an intensity of passion that easily matches that of the troubadours. Yet that passion was overall less tragic, because the love mystics did believe in the consummation of their love. In fact, it was the prospect of ultimate ecstatic union with the Beloved that saw them through their arid periods and dark nights of the soul. The love mystics knew many such spells of depression and despair, and, as they all confessed, their adopted path was strewn with inner struggle and pain. Their agony was caused primarily by their great longing for the Divine and the fact that only rarely were they granted the grace of union with their Beloved. Like the troubadours, the love mystics loved with an ultimacy that can only be called heroic. They were heroes and heroines of the wounded heart.

One of the first and most significant love mystics was St. Bernard of Clairvaux, who died in 1153 A.D. at the age of sixty-three. He was not only well-educated in theology but also highly skilled in mystical states and visions. Like many of the other love mystics of the twelfth to the seventeenth centuries, he was greatly inspired by the *Song of Songs*. He wrote a learned commentary on it, interpreting it allegorically as the interplay between the soul and the Divine. It is in his sermons on Solomon's *Song* that he elaborated his theology of love. For St. Bernard, God was love, and the path to God was a course of apprenticeship in love.

At the core of St. Bernard's theology is the idea of the intimacy between the Bride (the human soul) and the Bridegroom (Christ); hence this orientation is also known as bridal mysti-

cism or nuptial mysticism. In his commentary he describes in
great detail the process of growth by which the aspiring soul
achieves union with Christ. This process involves not only the
feeling heart but also considerable self-knowledge. "Love is a
great thing," preached St. Bernard, "but there are degrees of
love. The Bride stands at the high point. . . . Love is the very
being of the Bride. She is full of it, and the Bridegroom is
satisfied with it. He asks nothing else. That is why he is the
Bridegroom and she the Bride."[5]

St. Bernard's sermons on the *Song of Songs* show great didactic fervor, and he did not shy away from borrowing the
Song's sensuous imagery. He preached that "if anyone once re-
ceives the spiritual kiss of Christ's mouth he seeks eagerly to
have it again and again."[6] But, true to his conservative nature,
St. Bernard explained that as ordinary mortals we are not qualified for this kiss—we must first prostrate ourselves and become
worthy of kissing Christ's feet and then his hand. Only Christ
was granted the kiss of the Heavenly Father directly; all other
beings would have to content themselves with the "kiss of
the kiss."

St. Bernard did not believe that any creature could experience God as he really is, and that the final realization of God occurred in accordance with each individual soul's capacity. God
was inexhaustible and not confined to the psyche's circum-
ference. "A curious explorer," he remarked about himself, "I
have plumbed my own depths, and he was far deeper than that."[7]

In his tract *On Loving God,* St. Bernard distinguishes four
degrees of love. The first degree is simple self-love; the second is
love of God for selfish ends; the third is love of God for God's
sake; and the fourth is self-love for God's sake, which presup-
poses a life in harmony with, and obedience to, God's will. In
the fourth degree of love, the person is at peace with himself or
herself, capable of enduring the most difficult trials, as did the
martyrs. They participate in God's eternal joy. "Dearest indeed,
who are intoxicated with love," summed up St. Bernard.[8] Alas,
we must note, St. Bernard's ideal of selfless love did not prevent
him from instigating and organizing the Second Crusade to
Jerusalem and from persecuting heretics. Clearly, great wisdom
is needed to refine love and make it open-eyed and universal.

That even the most ardent love for the Divine does not necessarily remove all narrowness is also evident in the case of one

of the great women mystics, Hildegard of Bingen 1098–1179
A.D.). Herself of noble birth, she was adamant that no low-class
person be admitted to the convent in which she later in life
served as prioress. Such elitism notwithstanding, Hildegard
fearlessly spoke out against the persecution of heretics in whom
she saw "forms of the Divine." Here she was one step ahead of
St. Bernard.

St. Hildegard, a contemporary of Bernard of Clairvaux,
was known to her contemporaries as the prophetess of the
Rhine on account of her numerous oracles and revelations,
which caused a great deal of controversy. An accomplished poet
and musician, she left behind a vast literary work of considerable originality. What is particularly outstanding is her theology
of an ensexed universe in which the role of woman is far more
positive than the religious conservatives of her time would con-
cede. This ties in with her conception of God's love as a mater-
nal force. She even boldly compared the trinity to the three components of sexual intercourse: strength, desire, and the act
itself. Hildegard was thus an early, if still very cautious, feminist.

The intermediate position between the saintly Hildegard
and full-fledged bridal mysticism was occupied by the beguine
St. Mechthild of Magdeburg (c. 1207–1297 A.D.). The beguines
were unmarried women who desired to live a spiritual life but
did not become nuns. They lived together in small communities, dedicating themselves to prayer and the active social
work of "caring for the broken." The beguines (there were also
some men in the movement, who were known as beghards)
made poverty, chastity, and service their guiding ideals. The
movement spread from Flanders to Germany and France and
proved an important catalyst between the Church and the
widely felt need for a more practical, mystical spirituality.

Mechthild (also spelled Mechtild) bequeathed to us spiritual poems in which she makes use of the amatory language of
the troubadours. In her only book, entitled *The Flowing Light of
the Godhead,* we see a continuous juxtaposition of the high flight
of love to God and the pain of the soul's quest for union. But her
message is about unexcelled joy rather than suffering—a joy that
is an integral element of the Divine itself. Mechthild comes
across as a sober-headed mystic whose work is free from uncon-
trolled sentimentalism and morbidity.

Love for the Divine is a reflection of the burning desire of
God for the human soul. The passionate attraction between
God and the soul is a constant motif in Mechthild's writings, for
it is this attraction that propels the soul toward ecstatic consummation. With the *Song of Songs* in her mind, she wrote:

> Then the Most Beloved goes toward the Most Beautiful in the
> hidden chambers of the invisible Deity. There she finds the
> couch and the pleasure of Love, and God awaiting her in a super-
> human fashion. This is what Our Lord says:—Stay, Lady
> Soul.—What is your wish, Lord?—That you should be naked.—
> Lord, how can this happen to me?—Lady Soul, you are so "co-
> Lord, how can this happen to me?—Lady Soul, you are so "co-
> natured" in Me that nothing can be interposed between you and
> Me. Never for one single hour was any angel given the honor
> that is bestowed on you for all Eternity. That is why you must
> cast off these two things: fear and shame, as well as all exterior
> virtues. It is only those that you carry within you by nature that
> you must desire to feel eternally: these virtues are your noble de-
> sire and your insatiable hunger which I shall satisfy eternally
> with My infinite superabundance.[9]

Another admirable beguine expounding bridal mysticism
was Hadewijch of Antwerp, who lived in the mid–thirteenth
century. She talked about being swallowed up in her contempla-
tions by an abyss and then being received by the Beloved, with
the Beloved being received in her. She wrote:

> Calm reigns at last,
> When the loved one receives from her Beloved
> The kisses that truly pertain to love.
> When he takes possession of the loved soul in every way,
> Love drinks in these kisses and tastes them to the end.
> As soon as Love thus touches the soul,
> She eats its flesh and drinks its blood.
> Love that thus dissolves the loved soul
> Sweetly leads them both to the indivisible kiss—
> That same kiss which fully unites
> The Three Persons in one sole Being.[10]

A commentator on the *Song of Songs* equal to St. Bernard
of Clairvaux in visionary stature and poetic competence is the
sixteenth–century saint John of the Cross (known in his home-
land as Juan de la Cruz). His thoughts on the *Song of Songs* are

recorded in his *Spiritual Canticle,* which was partly written in prison. St. John's mysticism was frowned upon by the authorities, and his visionary talent was envied by his fellow monastics. For almost a year he was kept in solitary confinement, and he finally had to flee from the inquisitors, forced to live in relative obscurity for the remainder of his life. Even his longtime friend, the famous St. Teresa of Avila, abandoned him, though admittedly after he had warned her that her visions might not all be from God. Much of St. John's exquisite poetry was destroyed, and his prose works remained unfinished.

St. John's *Spiritual Canticle* is filled with subtle discussions of the *Song's* intricacies, rendered possible only because of his own mystical experiences. Even the most sensual metaphor in Solomon's *Song,* which was by no means allegorical in its original intent, is translated into lofty mystical explanation, but the saint is wholly believable in his inspired reinterpretation. He taught that in the mystical consummation between the Bride and the Bridegroom "the soul is divinized through participation in God, to the degree that is possible in this life."[11] He compared this consummation to the light of a star joining that of the sun, which is so strong that it absorbs all other light.

St. John was wrongfully accused of having committed that most heinous of all crimes for a Christian: sexual intercourse with nuns, who were after all the virgin brides of Christ. He responded to all these accusations with awesome stoicism. Unshaken by the assaults on his monastic integrity and faithful to his lifelong passion for chaste but eroticized spirituality, St. John had the *Song of Songs* read to him even in his final hour. In our memories, he lives on as a mystical troubadour of the highest order.

The theme of love and bridal mysticism is present, to one degree or another, in many of the writings of the medieval mystics from the twelfth century onward—from Richard and his brother Hugh St. Victor in the thirteenth century, to Julian of Norwich in the fifteenth century, to Teresa of Avila and Thomas à Kempis in the sixteenth century. Our own era, which suffers from a hypertrophied intellect but atrophied feeling, has produced its own love mystic in the person of social reformer Ernesto Cardenal. Thus, the imagery of sensual love continues to be a part, if only a small part, of the heritage of Christian spirituality.

THE MYSTICAL EROS IN ISLAM AND JUDAISM

What is remarkable about these developments of the twelfth and thirteenth centuries is that they have striking parallels in other religious traditions of roughly the same time. Thus, in medieval Judaism, the *unio mystica* was interpreted by the new kabbalastic movement as the conjunction of two kinds of love (*ahavah* in Hebrew)—the divine intellectual love and the human intellectual love. In his thirteenth-century *Commentary on the Secrets,* Abulafia speaks of the ascending human force, which is met or kissed by the descending divine force, "like a bridegroom actually kisses his bride out of his great and real desire."[12]

Abulafia's work is a commentary on the twelfth-century *Guide to the Perplexed* by Maimonides, who has been called the Second Moses. Maimonides, medieval Judaism's foremost intellectual, was criticized in the fourteenth century by the Spanish Jew Hildai Crescas for downplaying the idea of love. Crescas, by contrast, believed that creation is an overflowing of God's love. Love is also a central value in Hasidism, the mystical reform movement initiated in the eighteenth century.

The Kabbalists breathed new life into the ancient Hebrew concept of the *shekinah* ("indwelling"). Originally signifying the presence of God on earth, the *shekinah* came to be venerated as the "wife of the King," the personification of the feminine power of the Divine, assuming a function analogous to the Holy Spirit in Christianity. The relationship between God and the *shekinah* was seen as the archetype of sexual union between man and woman. According to the thirteenth-century *Zohar,* the classic text of Jewish mysticism, sexual pleasure brings delight to the feminine power of the Divine. Moreover, because of the perfect parallelism or homology between microcosm and macrocosm, a couple's sexual pleasure was thought to even magnify the peace in the world.

Here we have an important instance of sacred sexuality, which echoes the Hebrew's most ancient teachings. True to the prominent asceticism of their tradition, the Christian love mystics sought to sublimate the sexual urge without denying *eros.* By contrast, the much more world-embracing Jewish mystics were not content with cultivating the erotic through allegory and metaphor. Showing perhaps sounder instinct, they embraced their wives while remembering the Divine.

Turning next to Islam, we have such Sufi mystics as Ahmad al-Ghazzali (twelfth century), the most famous of all Muslim writers, who taught that God is Beauty and that beauty is intrinsically lovable; Farid al-Din 'Attar (thirteenth century), who spoke of the torment of love, which makes a lover put the knife to his throat, and of the state in which the self has vanished in the Beloved; and Ibn 'Arabi (thirteenth century), whose practice of love opened his heart so that it became "a pasture for gazelles, a cloister for Christian monks, a temple for idols, the Ka'ba of the pilgrim, the tables of the Torah and the book of the Qur'an."[13] Ibn 'Arabi was forced to write an explanatory commentary on some of his own poems to diffuse the accusation that they celebrated his mistress's charms rather than God's beauty.

Then there was Shams al-Din Hafiz (fourteenth century), known as the Tongue of the Unseen, who looked upon himself as the bondslave of the Divine; and not least that great Sufi lover Jalal al-Din Rumi (thirteenth century). Even such an early Sufi master as Rabi'ah (eighth century) taught in her splendid poetry that the Beloved visited her at dawn when she still lay sleeping. Love (*mahabba*) and Sufism are inextricably linked.

Rumi, who has been hailed as Islam's greatest mystical poet, was born in 1207 A.D. At the age of thirty-seven, he underwent a profound spiritual conversion, which turned him from "the country's sober ascetic" into a formidable ecstatic. He expressed his ardent quest for the Beloved in hundreds of extemporized verses in which he sang of the Beloved who comes like a thief in the night. Rumi was a reluctant poet who cared nothing for poetry itself, yet it kept on pouring forth from him. We can guess at his state of God intoxication when we watch the dervishes perform the famous whirling dance of his invention.

In addition to his poems, we also have, among other didactic works, Rumi's discourses gathered in his famous Persian work *Mathnawi* ("Couplets"), which is an inexhaustible font of colorful anecdotes and parables. A relatively sober work, the *Mathnawi* yet contains incomparable passages, such as the exhortation that "Wherever you are and in whatever circumstances you find yourself, strive always to be a lover, and a passionate lover at that."[14]

According to Koranic law a married man is forbidden to take a vow of celibacy, just as a woman was enjoined to make herself available for sexual intercourse. Since many Sufis were married, we might well ask how they translated their spiritual passion into conjugal bliss. Unfortunately, they did not tell us. We must assume, though, that any serious mystic who is married will not exploit his or her partner sexually. However, such integrity does not necessarily lead to the actual practice of sacred sex. We know that Muhammad, the founder of Islam, was rather lenient toward the male gender in terms of sex, even permitting temporary marriages for sexual convenience. He was not quite so generous toward Moslem women. This preferential treatment of men is suggestive of the fundamental inequality between the genders in the Islamic tradition. Given this built-in tension between men and women, we can understand why sacred sex did not become a recognizable spiritual practice within Islam.

By contrast, the Hindus, though sharing in many respects the Moslems' puritanical disposition, succeeded in articulating sacred sex as a path of self-transcendence. This extraordinary orientation, which will be discussed at length in Chapter 10, was embedded in a much broader tradition of erotic spirituality that is similar to the allegorizing bridal mysticism of medieval Christianity.

ON THE NUPTIAL COUCH WITH KRISHNA: THE HINDU VERSION OF BRIDAL MYSTICISM

India's bridal mysticism is closely associated with the worship of God Krishna, who appeared on earth as an incarnation of the Divine. The Krishna cult is of great antiquity. It made its appearance in the *Bhagavad-Gita* ("Lord's Song"), which is generally attributed to the pre-Christian era. Originally Krishna was a great mystic and charismatic leader who was subsequently venerated as a God-man.

The *Bhagavad-Gita,* considered the New Testament of Hinduism, recommends love (*bhakti*) as the most expedient and highest vehicle of mystical union with God. The Sanskrit word *bhakti* stems from the verbal root *bhaj,* meaning "to participate." Thus *bhakti* is love-participation in the all-encompassing Divine, as well as the ever-flowing love of God.

Already in the eighth and ninth centuries, the troubadours of South India—the Alvars—sang of their passionate yearning and devotion to the Lord. They were true ecstatics, intoxicated by God's love welling up in their hearts. Thus, Namm Alvar burst into song confessing how "this beautiful maid," his own heart brimming with devotion, was yearning for the Beloved. In several poems, he speaks as a heartbroken shepherdess, addressing Krishna.

Another South Indian adept, the female saint Andal of the early ninth century, sings in her poems that only the "nectar of the Lord's mouth" can bring her solace. She calls Krishna a thief, a looting robber and plunderer, threatening to pluck out her breasts that do not bear the marks of his love-play.

In the tenth and eleventh centuries, the north of India also caught on fire with devotion. The *Bhagavata-Purana,* a Sanskrit work of great beauty that recounts Krishna's mythical life story, is a lasting monument to the soaring spiritual aspirations of that age. It contains many passages that describe the mystical path of love in playful erotic terms, but on the whole it remains faithful to the strong ascetic and patriarchal spirit of India.

In the twelfth century, Krishna theology acquired an erotic dimension that invites comparison with medieval Europe's bridal mysticism. This new development is centered on the *Gita-Govinda* ("Govinda's Song"), a mystical poem by the Bengali writer Jayadeva, one of the great poetic geniuses of India. His exquisite Sanskrit work was written to be sung and accompanied by musical instruments. It celebrates in rhymed verse Krishna's love for Radha, the shepherdess who was his favorite during his human incarnation and who was elevated to the status of a Goddess. The poem came to be understood as an allegory of the love between the Divine and the human soul. The *Gita-Govinda* can be regarded as the Hindu counterpart to the Hebrew *Song of Songs.* The imagery in both works is vividly sensuous and plainly erotic.

The *Gita-Govinda* portrays Radha pining for her divine lover. Radha is at peace only when she is in Krishna's arms and smothered by his kisses. According to sacred legend, Krishna in his incarnation as shepherd (*gopa*) enchanted countless shepherdesses (*gopi*), among them Radha. He instilled in them such passion and attachment that they thought about him day and night and willingly left their husbands, children, and homes whenever they heard him play his magical flute in the hills. If Krishna could stir them so deeply it was because he, as the

Divine, resided in their very hearts. They hankered after his sweetness—the honey or delight of the *unio mystica*.

Experiencing Radha's unsurpassed love for him, Krishna himself falls hopelessly in love with her. Whenever they are apart, he suffers as much as she does. She grows weak from pining for him. When Krishna visits her, she turns him away. But Krishna persists in assuring her of his love, and the two make love. Later the love-stricken Radha talks of their sacred tryst to a confidante thus:

> Secretly at night I went to Krishna's hideout in the thicket. While I anxiously glanced around me, he was simply laughing. There was a great longing in his eyes for the delight of sexual union. O my friend, make him love me passionately. I am so enamored of him and am consumed with desires of love. I was shy on our first union. But he was kind toward me, complimenting me in a hundred different ways. I responded through sweet and gentle smiles. Then he unfastened the silk garment around my hips and lowered me onto a bed of tender shoots, and for a long time he rested on my breasts while I caressed and kissed him. He embraced me and drank from my lips. I got so drowsy that I had to close my eyes. The hair on his cheeks bristled from my caresses. My whole body was covered with perspiration, and he was quite restless so great was his intoxication with passion. Filled with pleasure, I cooed like a cuckoo. He is a master of the amatory arts. Blossoms were shrewn all over my tresses from our love-play. My full breasts bore his scratch marks. As he made love to me in various ways, my anklets and my loosened belt jingled. He kissed me and pulled my hair. Languid from tasting the joys of sexual union, my body dropped down limp, while his lotus eyes were slightly closed. Then he declared his love to me.[15]

Jayadeva, a connoisseur of tender emotions and erotic sentiments, managed to find an abundance of ways to describe Krishna and Radha's love-play (*lila*) in explicit terms. Yet the poem is not pornography, or at least not in the accepted sense of the term. Admittedly, the poem is designed to fuel the listeners' (and readers') passion "in the flesh," but only so that the desire thus kindled might bring forth in the human heart the primal response of unconditional love for the Divine.

The *Gita-Govinda* is interspersed with religious exhortations, prayers, and benedictions, almost as if to ensure that the poet's intention is clearly understood: He wants not to evoke a prurient mood but to edify. He employs graphic descriptions of

Krishna and Radha's love-play not to corrupt, degrade, exploit, or dehumanize; rather, he seeks to raise the level of energy in his listeners and readers until they get in touch with their innate yearning for seamless union—the kind of perfect at-oneness that only the mystical merging with the Divine vouchsafes.

Jayadeva's Radha cannot be considered a wanton whore. Her love for Krishna is sensuous and sexual but pure, and no silver changes hands. However, we might see in the figure of Radha echoes of the sacred prostitute of the ancient world, who dedicated her body and sexuality exclusively to the male God and through her complete bodily submission to him partook of his divinity. Radha and Krishna's story, like their relationship, is erotic but not pornographic. The pornographic is always an implicit denial of the erotic, because, as Audre Lorde spelled out, it "represents the suppression of true feeling."[16]

Although Jayadeva wrote for the courtly circles of his time, his work soon became very popular. He inspired generations of poets composing in vernacular languages to try their hand at similar lyrical treatments of the highly popular Radha-Krishna theme. Thus, in the sixteenth century, the saintly princess Mirabai of Jodhpur dedicated her songs to Krishna, whom she called her dark lover. Her simple poems are still sung today in the villages of northern India. After the death of her husband, Mirabai, still a virgin, renounced the world and channeled her passion and devotion entirely into the worship of Krishna. In one of her songs, she addressed her beloved Krishna thus:

> Having beheld Thy beauty
> I am caught and enmeshed.
> My family members repeatedly try to restrain me,
> But attachment to the Dancer with the Peacock Plume
> Has now sunk deep.
> My mind is drowned in the beauty of Shyam [i.e., Krishna],
> And the world says I have gone astray.
> Mira has taken refuge with the Lord
> Who knows the contents of every heart.[17]

In another song, Mirabai confessed:

> I am dyed deep in the love of Shyam.
> I have donned anklets and ornaments
> And danced before Him without shame. . . . [18]

Then, after having roused her passion by his presence, Krishna left again, abandoning Mirabai to mad longing and despair. "My boat has broken,/Hoist the sail quickly/Before it sinks,"[19] we hear her pray. Upon her inner lover's departure, Mirabai became restless and unable to sleep. She left her house plunged in darkness, because her bed seemed uninviting without her lover next to her. In her distress, she compared herself to a night without moon and a pond without lotus flowers. But her faith was vigorous; she believed that Krishna had become inseparable from her. Then the Divine visited her again. We find the poetess bursting into song thus:

> Shri Krishna has entered my heart
> And the clouds have filled the sky.
> Thunder roars, clouds quake
> And the flashes of lightning inspire terror.
> Cloud-banks mount as the east wind blows.
> Frogs croak, the cuckoo sings,
> And the cry of the peacock is heard.
> Says Mira: O my Master, the courtly Giridhara,
> My mind has gone to Thy lotus feet.[20]

For the love-possessed Mirabai, the revelation of the Divine in her heart was an overwhelming event to which the only acceptable response was the surrender of her finite personality to the infinite Being. The metaphor of rain clouds filling the sky is a fitting symbol for the shower of bliss and light that the longed-for union brings. "All my desires are fulfilled," exclaimed Mirabai, "and my sufferings forgotten."[21] She felt healed, restored, and made whole.

Mirabai was considered mad by her peers. She did not mind that label, for she knew she was mad with love for Krishna. Neither do those contemporary male devotees of Radha who so identify with her that they adopt a transvestite lifestyle. They wear what in their imagination are the kind of clothes that Radha would wear, put on makeup, and in every other way assume the demeanor of a woman. Above all, they are in a constant attitude of waiting for their beloved Krishna. The Tantric scholar B. Bhattacharya described such a case of Radha devotion, an old "woman" in her eighties living in what he described as a hovel in the temple courtyard.[22] This man disguised as Radha dropped his/her veil when Bhattacharya approached, giving him the sweetest smile and inviting him into his/her home.

When Bhattacharya was seated, the Radha devotee began to wash the scholar's feet "as a mother would a child's body," ignoring his protests. Then he/she sang to him melodies from the *Gita-Govinda*. Seeing Bhattacharya's persistent feeling of unease, he/she gently reprimanded him: "You seem to resent. Why? Why this ego? Why this sense of ownership when you do not own the body. It is the residence of my beloved. Is it not?" Thus, he/she welcomed Bhattacharya as none other than Lord Krishna himself.

The love mystics of Christianity, Judaism, Islam, and Hinduism by and large maintained that actual physical union between man and woman merely interrupts the longing in the heart. When that yearning is cultivated, however, it becomes a hair-trigger for the transcendence of the mind trapped in the mists of duality. Thus, their erotic mysticism seldom moved beyond the theological and emotional level. The next step—a step that represents not so much an innovation as a revival of very ancient traditions—was taken by some of the adherents of the Hindu and Buddhist tradition of Tantrism. Their incarnate, Dionysian spirituality is the subject of the next chapter.

CHAPTER 10

❦

The Jewel in the Lotus:
The Lessons of Tantrism

THE SECRET CIRCLE: A STORY SET IN INDIA
AROUND 1200 A.D.

Midnight was approaching, yet the air was still oppressively hot
and humid. The monsoon, which would bring relief, was still
weeks away. The large room was dimly lit by oil lamps, and
heavy drapes kept out the light of the new moon and protected
the secret gathering from prying eyes.

They met every fortnight. The house belonged to one of
the wealthiest merchants in town. Unbeknown to most people,
he also happened to be the *guru* of the small group that had come
together for an important celebration; today, a new member
was to be initiated in the Tantric art of sexual union.

There were twelve of them—six men and six women, all
in their early to late twenties, and perfectly nude. They sat in a
circle on a thick carpet. The *guru,* much older, was seated in the
center of the mandala with his own partner, a young girl of exquisite beauty and poise but barely of marriageable age.

The master, an accomplished Tantric adept, had been sitting perfectly still for well over an hour already. In the dim light
he could easily be mistaken for a statue. His partner, seated on
his left, likewise had not stirred for a long time.

This was the third and final day of the *puja,* or ceremony.
Any moment now the master would signal the participants to
begin the ultimate ritual. To prepare themselves for this occasion, they had fasted for twenty-four hours, had chanted sacred
sounds (*mantra*) thousands of times, had invoked and made

offerings to the deities and protective spirits, had consecrated the room, had meditated for many long hours in the graveyard to overcome fear, had bathed and anointed each other's bodies, had duly honored the *guru* and his chosen partner, and, not least, had over many years cultivated their ability to retain the breath for prolonged periods so that they could control the movements of the mind.

Earlier in the evening, they had smoked hemp together in a ritual fashion, and then they had participated in the solemn ceremony of consuming the four forbidden substances—wine, fish, meat, and parched grain, all of which were thought to have an aphrodisiacal effect. Men and women alike felt a heightened sensitivity and alertness, which even the heavy fragrance of sandalwood burning in the bowls at the four corners of the room could not dull. The room, which was the group's temple, was charged with an indescribable energy. The space was filled with a vibrancy that exerted a curious pressure on the body and that would certainly have scared unsuspecting visitors. It was almost as if the air were humming with electricity.

At last the master stirred. Thrice he intoned the precious invocation *Om namah shivaya,* "*Om,* obeisance to the Lord." The signal to begin the final ritual had been given. Careful to avoid any disturbing noises, each man turned to anoint his partner with a reddish paste while muttering holy mantras over her. With great reverence he smeared the paste on her forehead, throat, breasts, abdomen, hands, feet, and, last, the pubic mound. Then each woman did likewise to her partner. Only the *guru* was not anointed in this manner. His young partner was the new initiate. Thus men and women turned themselves into gods and goddesses for the purposes of the climax of the ritual—sexual congress (*maithuna*).

Unused to the mounting energy in the room, the *guru*'s partner made involuntary cooing sounds, and even some of the more seasoned celebrants moaned slightly. Again, the *guru*— now looking utterly transfigured—invoked the Divine. Then he firmly grasped his partner, a virgin, and drew her onto his folded legs. In one swift motion he entered her. There was no pain, or if there was it was swallowed up by the wave of bliss she felt rippling through her, even as her awareness was instantly lifted out of her body into regions of unspeakable luminosity. The girl's eyes rolled back in ecstasy, and her head flopped backward, her tongue protruding slightly.

She was the great Goddess embracing her divine lover. Golden shafts of energy were flowing from her lover into her womb and up into and beyond her head. At an infinite distance, the luminous energy curved and returned, entering her lover's body again, to thus complete circuit after blissful circuit. Both she and the *guru* remained perfectly motionless, as if frozen in time.

Following their teacher's example, the male students now also drew their partners close. In a hush, each woman settled on her partner's lap. There was no need for kissing or other foreplay. The entire ceremony had been sufficient preparation; both men and women were emotionally and physiologically ready for the ritual of congress. The men maintained their erections through visualization and breath control, and the women's precious liquids were oozing liberally merely from the penetration.

But there was no lust between them. There was no thought of possessing the other or of gratifying genital needs. They did not look upon each other as men and women, but as Shiva and Shakti—God and Goddess. The pleasure they felt had been magnified a thousandfold into sheer bliss. Soon they all felt part of a vast space, vibrant with life and consciousness—a huge circle of energy in whose center was the blinding radiance of the *guru,* who embodied the Divine in its absolute transcendence. Most of the participants were only marginally aware of their surroundings, and some were utterly oblivious to them. The peace in the room was awesome, as if heaven had been brought down to Earth.

Suddenly there was a disturbance in this pattern of harmony. One of the couples stirred, then rapidly disengaged. There was a brief whispered exchange. The man hurriedly got up and, covering his erection with his hands, rushed out of the room. The young woman duly prostrated herself to her teacher, and then also quietly left the circle. The others ignored the commotion.

When the young woman stepped into the antechamber, she found the man tearing at his hair. He was disconsolate over having failed his *guru* and his partner. She quickly covered her nudity. He confessed that he had succumbed to feelings of lust for her and some of the other women. He cursed himself. She looked at him in disbelief and shock. Had he not been the longest with his teacher? Everyone had always thought of him as the *guru*'s successor. She had never suspected anything wrong about him in their past unions, nor, she was certain, had any of the other female participants.

He shocked her further by confessing how he had fallen in love with her. How could this be, she wondered? She hardly knew him outside the circle, and each time they were invited to the circle they switched partners precisely in order to avoid the snare of attachment.

Seeing his genuine distress, she told him she forgave him but that she could not reciprocate his love. The feeling he had for her, she reminded him, was not love but passion, which he must learn to overcome. She wrapped her sari around herself and left for the temple. There she could pray and find again the peace that her partner had disrupted.

By the time the teacher emerged from the sanctum, the young man was almost suicidal. Only his long years of spiritual discipline prevented him from storming off and committing an even greater folly. The *guru* knew at once what had happened. He showed no sign of disappointment or anger at the unforgivable interruption during the ceremony. He took his disciple aside and explained to him how even the most advanced practitioners in the art of Tantra must always be on their guard, that even adepts have been known to plummet from their heights through sheer inattention. He explained that desire is built into the human frame; it can never be got rid of entirely but can be transmuted into thirst for the Divine.

Then, breaking into a mischievous smile, he added that sometimes a teacher tests his disciple by sending him thoughts of desire. He promised his disciple that henceforth he would not be plagued by sexual desire. The young man bowed and touched his *guru*'s feet with his forehead. "Get out!" yelled the teacher, in mock anger.

Tantrism: The Historical and Cultural Context

The above story is a fictionalized account of the ritual of sexual congress at the heart of what is called left-hand Tantrism. To understand this ceremony, which involves a complex philosophy and symbolism, we must first understand the meaning of Tantrism.[1]

The designation *Tantrism* applies to the esoteric tradition and distinct cultural style connected with the *tantras,* the books containing the Tantric teachings. The Sanskrit word *tantra* itself means "web" and is explained as "that which expands [*tanyate*] understanding." Tantrism can be defined as a system of beliefs and practices intended to stretch the human mind, to guide its adherents to higher knowledge, or gnosis.

Tantrism emerged on the Indian peninsula as a distinct religious style or movement in the middle of the first post-Christian millennium. Many of its constituent ideas and practices are far more ancient, however. Some of them can even be linked to neolithic sex-and-fertility beliefs and rituals. But whereas the neolithic rites were celebrated for the collective weal, Tantrism had from the outset a decidedly individualistic orientation. Its goal is personal liberation (*mukti*), which is understood as the transcendence of the ego-personality, of the ordinary consciousness. This idea is generally couched in terms of the attainment of unexcelled bliss (*ananda*), or delight.

By the year 1000 A.D., Tantrism had achieved immense popularity in both Hindu and Buddhist religious circles. The reasons for its great success are still only vaguely understood. Undoubtedly one of the attractions of Tantrism, or Tantra, was that it purported to be a new gospel for the dark age (*kali-yuga*). The dark age, a period of moral and spiritual decline, is traditionally thought to have commenced with the God-man Krishna's death on February 18, 3102 B.C., and is expected to reign for another 354,908 years, with conditions getting progressively worse. The masters of Tantrism were marvelous innovators who created a whole new approach and language for communicating spiritual truths.

Tantrism is so comprehensive that it is difficult to characterize succinctly. Almost any assertion that can be made about it is contradicted by one or another of its numerous schools. Most approaches are pronouncedly ritualistic, but some schools emphasize spontaneity (*sahaja*), discarding all formulas and prescriptions for correct living. Common to all Tantric orientations is the idea that the Divine is not, as in monotheistic religions, separated from creation by an unbridgeable gulf; rather, the world is an aspect or manifestation of the Divine.

What is so important about this metaphysical idea is that it is not merely a notion for theologians to toy with, but has served as the cornerstone of a distinctive spiritual discipline. For, so the argument goes, if the Divine is present in and as the cosmos, then God-realization or enlightenment is not a far-off goal but the true condition of every being in this very moment. This revolutionary insight is expressed in the Sanskrit equation "*samsara = nirvana*"—that is, the changeable world is identical with the eternally unchangeable Reality. We are like fish that do not know they are swimming in water and are continuously sustained by it, or like birds that do not know that the air supports their wings and their life. This lack of understanding is our spiritual ignorance.

Tantrism celebrates the divinity *in* and *of* every being and thing. Therefore, the Tantric adepts have not shied away from introducing practices and methods that appear unusual and even sinful and degraded in traditional spiritual contexts. The attitude that best describes their approach is that anything is permissible so long as it leads to the realization of the presence of the Divine here and now. It is in this spirit that some schools of Tantrism have also made use of ritualistic sex (*maithuna*).

We must carefully distinguish between two fundamental forms of Tantrism—the left-hand path (*vama-marga*) and the right-hand path (*dakshina-marga*). On the left-hand path, which has attracted the greater attention in the West, the core ritual of sexual congress is taken literally. By contrast, on the right-hand path it is understood in purely symbolic or allegorical terms, as was the case with the love mystics of Europe and the Middle East, and no sexual contact is involved. Rather, the *maithuna* ritual is celebrated in one's own body-mind, which contains both the masculine cosmic principle, called *shiva,* and the feminine cosmic principle, known as *shakti.*

Both paths exist in Hinduism and in Buddhism, for Tantrism straddles these two great spiritual traditions. The Tantric branch of Buddhism is better known as Vajrayana ("Diamond Vehicle"). The "diamond" or "thunderbolt," as the word *vajra* is translated, can refer either to the penis or to the disciplined mind or, on the highest level of interpretation, to the transcendental Reality as pure Consciousness itself. The union of the *vajra* with the "lotus" (*padma*) is the means to liberation. Again, on one level, the lotus is the vagina; on another level, it is the lotus of the heart, the seat of spiritual intuition; and on the ultimate symbolic level, it is the feminine cosmic principle.

It is also important to understand that Tantrism has from the outset been an esoteric teaching, transmitted from teacher to disciple by word of mouth. However, to our good fortune, early on this secret knowledge was written down in scriptures known in different religious schools as the *Tantras, Agamas,* and *Samhitas,* although the information contained in these writings is only a minute fraction of the total Tantric heritage. Therefore, if we want to understand Tantric practice in depth, we must still seek out a *guru* and hope that he or she will initiate us—a remote possibility, especially if the *guru* is authentic. The Tantrism taught by such New Age *gurus* as the late Bhagwan (Osho) Rajneesh bears little resemblance to genuine Tantrism.

Although Tantrism emerged at a time when, in North Africa, St. Augustine was busy writing his *Confessions,* its roots are far more ancient. We can see a remarkable continuity between some of the central features of Tantrism and the Indus civilization, which flourished peacefully in northern India between 2500 and 1800 B.C.

The Indus civilization has already been mentioned in connection with sacred prostitution. This practice was unquestionably associated with Goddess worship, which appears to have been prevalent in that seedling culture. Numerous terracotta figurines of naked females have been found, which have been taken as depictions of the Great Goddess. Some of the figurines have elaborate headdresses. From their rough modeling, we may conjecture that they were used as cult objects in household shrines.

Among the thousands of steatite stamp-seals found during excavations at the two major cities of Mohenjo Daro and Harappa, one seal has the striking upside-down image of a woman giving birth to a plant, which is clearly the kind of fertility motif associated with the Mother Goddess of the neolithic era. Another seal shows a long-haired female figure standing between two branches of a highly stylized plant, with another figure kneeling before her. Both figures wear horns, suggesting divinity or sacrality.

The *Devi-Mahatmya* ("Glory of the Goddess"), which is a part of the fourth-century *Markandeya-Purana* (92.43–44), includes a verse in which the Goddess says that she supports the whole world with life-sustaining plants growing out of her own body. The widely worshipped Hindu Goddess Annapurna ("Food-Fullness") may well have derived directly from the Mother Goddess of the Indus Valley.

The excavations at the site of Harappa also yielded many

cone-shaped objects, which have been interpreted as representations of the phallus (*linga*). Likewise, ring-shaped stones have
been taken to represent the female organ (*yoni*). If correct, this
would be evidence for the remarkable continuity of the *linga-
yoni* motif in India and its attendant fertility and sexual symbolism.

There are also many connections between later Hinduism
and the tribal culture of the invaders from the Russian steppes
who brought with them their own rich lore, embodied in the
most ancient Sanskrit scriptures—the four *Vedas*. Whereas main-
stream Hinduism tends toward puritanism and life-negating
asceticism, the culture of the Vedic tribes of circa 1500 to 1000
B.C. was clearly life-affirmative and sex-positive. They loved
music, dance, and gambling, were not at all averse to inebria-
tion, and prayed for a hundred years of life on Earth, many children, and plenty of cattle. As one Vedic hymn exhorts, "O men!
Lift, lift up the penis, the bestower of satisfaction! Move it, dig
deep for the acquisition of wealth [in the form of progeny]!"²
While some of the prayers have a symbolic content, many others
are to be taken quite literally.³

The Tantric adepts have always claimed that their new
teachings were really only a restatement of the old Vedic religion. This claim has never sat too well with the brahmins, the
custodians of the Vedic heritage. It is true, however, that an examination of the ancient *Vedas* yields Tantra-like elements. In
fact, the *Vedas* contain a rather elaborate sexual symbolism.

One of the most important Vedic rituals is the ancient
horse sacrifice (*ashva-medha*). At the climax of this fertility ritual, the queen lies with the horse (symbol of the sun) and they
symbolically unite, while officiating priests engage in an obscene dialogue. This curious rite has cosmogonic significance,
because the horse is not only associated with the sun but also
with the primordial waters, the very substance out of which the
universe emerged. It was only when this significance was forgotten that the rite started to be condemned by priestly authorities.

The horse sacrifice appears to be the enactment of an archaic Vedic myth in which the cosmic waters, conceived of as
feminine, have sexual intercourse with the sun, which is referred to as "father." A similar divine but incestuous relationship was believed to exist between Agni, the God of Fire, and

his sister Usha, the Goddess of Dawn. Sadashiv Ambadas Dange, a well-known Vedic researcher, summarized his extensive studies of Vedic sexual symbolism thus:

> To the Vedic people the cosmos was filled with two main elements—male and the female. . . . They saw the whole universe arranged in holy sex-coupling. In fact that was the key to all production and the germination of rain. To activate the cosmic sex when the people needed, or to ensure that the cosmic couples would not fail them, they devised rituals in which sex was imitated in action or as an oral spell.[4]

Dange rightly regards this cosmic eroticism as the source of sacred sexuality. The union of the divine Father and Mother or Daughter was called *mithuna,* which is the original form of the later term *maithuna.* Both words are constructed from the verbal root *mith,* which has the double meaning of "to associate with" and, significantly, "to be in conflict with." Both *mithuna* and *maithuna* mean "coupling" or "pairing" in general and "sexual congress" in particular.

As Dange succeeded in showing, sacred sexuality played an important role already in the ancient Vedic ritualism. Moreover, for the pious brahmin, all sexual contact with his wife was to take the form of a holy rite. A fascinating account of this early sexual ceremony has been preserved in a metaphysical scripture dating back to the eighth or ninth century B.C.[5] The text is too obscure to reproduce here in full, but a paraphrase of the essential content seems appropriate:

> The essence of man (*purusha*) is semen. In order to provide a firm basis for man, the Creator Prajapati fashioned woman. When he had created her, he worshipped her "below." The vagina is a sacrificial altar; the pubic hair is the sacrificial grass by which the fire is lit; the labia are the sacrificial fire. He who knows this secret shares the great world of the Creator. But he who practices sexual intercourse without knowing it loses his semen and his merit to the woman. When even a minute amount of semen is spilled, he should reclaim it and, with it, his strength and glow. He should pick it up with his ring finger and thumb and rub it on his chest or forehead, while reciting, "In me be vigor, power, beauty, wealth, and merit!"
>
> The man should approach a woman after her menstruation. If she refuses his advances, he should first bribe her and,

failing this, beat her with his hands or a stick. Then he should simply overpower her, chanting the magic spell "With power and glory I take away your glory!" However, if she yields to him, he should utter the *mantra* "With power and glory I give you glory!" In this way both become filled with glory.

After penetrating her and "joining mouth with mouth," he should recite a verse so that the woman will be completely distracted by him and nothing else. If the woman is not meant to conceive, he should mutter, "With power, with semen, I reclaim the semen from you!" However, if she is meant to conceive, he should say, "With power, with semen, I deposit semen in you!" In the latter case, he should part her legs, saying, "Spread yourselves apart, heaven and earth!"

The anonymous author of this passages provides detailed magical prescriptions for rendering the womb fertile by invoking different deities. The above ritual illustrates the archaic parallelism between individual and cosmic factors. Needless to say, the passage also bears witness to the patriarchal principle at work: Although the man is willing to share glory (*yashas*) with his woman, her sexual disinterest is regarded as a form of disobedience punishable by physical aggression.

Thus, we find both great insight and ignorance side by side. It took over a millennium of social evolution before, in authentic Tantrism, the woman assumed the role of a voluntary participant in the sacred *maithuna* ritual. This was made possible by the Tantric theology, which conceded to the feminine a place equal to that of the masculine. The woman was then viewed as an incarnation of the ultimate feminine principle, the Goddess, who was far more approachable than God, the masculine principle.

MAITHUNA: THE LOVE-PLAY OF GOD AND GODDESS

The single most significant aspect of Tantrism is Goddess worship. The Divine is envisioned as being polarized into feminine and masculine, respectively called *shakti* and *shiva* (in the Hindu variety of Tantrism). *Shakti* is the dynamic aspect and *shiva* the static aspect of the same all-comprehensive reality. *Shakti* represents creation, matter, nature, and change, whereas *shiva* represents awareness or consciousness. Together they form a

transcendental/immanent continuum, which is inherently su-
praconscious and blissful.

Prior to the arrival of Tantrism as a full-fledged spiritual
approach, the official religious beliefs of India were those of the
Sanskrit-speaking brahmins. Their theology revolved around
the abstract concept of the *brahman,* the Absolute without distinctions. Below the *brahman* were the heavenly realms populated by the deities, most of them of the male gender. The Goddesses of the early Vedic age and the era of the Indus civilization
had long been dethroned by male Gods such as Shiva, Vishnu,
and Krishna. But Tantrism made the Goddess, in the form of
various female deities worshipped all along by the uneducated
masses, respectable again.

In a way, Tantrism is the triumph of India's most ancient
beliefs, reaching back into the neolithic age. Tantrism opened
the doors to anthropomorphic deities such as Kali, Durga,
Candi, Parvati, Radha, Bhavani, Sarasvati, and Lakshmi. Indeed, they were moved into the foreground of worship, ritual,
and iconographic imagination. For the worshipper, these female deities all represent the great Goddess herself.

The devout practitioners of Tantrism experience the Goddess as more approachable than the remote male principle, *shiva.*
For them, she is first and foremost the benign Mother of the
universe who can be petitioned and enlisted in one's spiritual
struggle. Yet, in her form as Kali or Durga, she is also the Force
of change, especially of spiritual transformation and the *destruction* of the ego. The love of the universal Mother is a power to be
reckoned with, which should not be invoked casually.

Shiva and Shakti, as ultimate principles, are also known as
Kameshvara and Kameshvari, respectively. The former designation is composed of the words *kama* ("desire") and *ishvara*
("lord"), whereas the latter ends in *ishvari* ("mistress"). In other
words, they are the principles governing desire, or the universal
impetus for manifestation and change, which gives birth to the
cosmos and is responsible for its final dissolution as well.

On the ultimate level of existence, which we call the Divine, Shiva and Shakti exist in inseparable conjunction. There is
no trace of otherness in this state of wholeness, or *purna.* Without forsaking this primordial wholeness, Shiva and Shakti together initiate the play (*lila*) that leads to the creation of the universe.

That primal state of wholeness or oneness, which the mystics claim to experience, is often depicted in Hindu iconography in the hermaphroditic figure of Ardhanarishvara. The union between the male and the female principle, as the Tantric scriptures affirm, yields or *is* desire and bliss. It is desire when viewed from the level of manifestation, and bliss when realized on the level of absolute Being.

From an ontological perspective, the figure of Ardhanarishvara is a graphic depiction of the reconciliation of opposites aspired to by the mystics of all ages. It is a symbol of the perfect equilibrium that exists on the ultimate level, prior to all form and all space-time. From a psychological perspective, Ardhanarishvara embodies the androgynous reality of the psyche itself.

It is this bisexuality of the psyche, understood as a multi-level system of energies, that underlies the Tantric path (*sadhana*). Without this psychic polarity, the approach of the Yoga of the serpent power, introduced in the next section, would be impossible, for this type of Yoga understands the process leading to the ecstatic union between Shiva and Shakti in purely psychological terms.

Broadly speaking, the goal of Tantrism is to recapture in one's individual case the transcendental fusion between Shiva and Shakti. Finite existence—which, in concrete terms, means human life—is characterized by fission. The Tantric practitioner seeks to achieve a state of bodily and mental harmony that mirrors and attunes him or her to the transcendental equilibrium (*samarasa*), or original wholeness, which is experienced as bliss.

How this psychic balance is to be accomplished is a point of contention among the various schools of Tantrism. Teachers of the Sahajiya school, which espouses the ideal of spontaneity, reject all contrivances and instead claim that we must unlearn the habit of cognizing reality in bits and pieces through the lens of the ego-personality simply by affirming that the Divine is present here and now. Most other schools, however, recommend one or the other technique for realizing the transcendental equilibrium or bliss—from the recitation of words of power (mantras), to complex rituals of worship, to visualization and meditation.

One of these transformative techniques is sexual congress, as taught on the left-hand path of Tantrism. Here it figures as the fifth and concluding aspect of a protracted ceremony. In Tantric parlance, *maithuna* is called the "fifth M" (*panca-makara*), because this Sanskrit term for sexual intercourse begins with the letter *m*, as do the terms for the other four components—*madya* (wine), *mamsa* (meat), *matsya* (fish), and *mudra* (parched grain)—all of which are thought of as having aphrodisiacal properties.[6]

The sexual ritual of *maithuna* is the literal enactment of the fusion that exists on the transcendental plane between Shiva and Shakti. The man represents God; the woman, the Goddess. The purpose of their union is to realize the innate bliss of the Divine.

In some Tantric schools, sexual congress is said to have the specific esoteric function of stimulating the flow of *rajas*. This has often been mistaken for menstrual blood. However, in the present context, *rajas* is the woman's colorless secretion produced during sexual arousal, which corresponds to the man's semen. During the ritual, *rajas* is collected on a leaf and then added to a bowl of water. It is drunk by the man, after having been duly offered to the deity presiding over the ritual.

By contrast, the male participants in the ritual are admonished to retain their semen. Loss of semen is equated with loss of life. Hence if ejaculation could not be prevented, the semen is immediately rubbed into the forehead, the location of what is termed the third eye, the esoteric organ associated with higher intuition and clairvoyance. This curious practice is thought to salvage at least some of the power contained in the semen. It would be interesting to study whether any of the semen's biological properties, such as hormones, can be assimilated through the skin. Only during Tantric rituals of black magic is semen actually consumed.

The practice of stimulating the production of *rajas* for the man's benefit can be looked upon as an objectionable case of exploitation—of vampirism—of the female gender. That there is reason for criticism will become clear when a corresponding Taoist practice is examined in Chapter 11.

Although the Tantric partners ideally remain immobile during intercourse, it is clear from the woman's *rajas* secretion that this ritual has a definite physiological dimension. Yet only in literalist schools are such somatic phenomena given preeminence over the spiritual aspect. Authentic Tantrism is first and foremost a path of moral and spiritual purification and growth, and physiological processes and mental manipulations are secondary. When the Tantric practitioners become overly concerned with the generation of physiological effects, they risk vulgarizing what is essentially a spiritual discipline.

The ritual of sexual congress is also known as the discipline of the creeper (*lata-sadhana*), *lata* ("creeper") being another name for "woman" or "clinging vagina." In her book *The Art of Sexual Ecstasy,* Margo Anand told the story of her own spiritual awakening while making love with her American artist boyfriend in Paris, the city of romance. Her awakening was effectively a spontaneous discovery of the secret of *lata-sadhana.*

Anand was eighteen years old at the time and a beginning student of Yoga. Her partner was a passionate lover, and she described sex between them as "raw, primal, and wild." She found it fulfilling on one level, but on another, she began to wonder how all this excitement connected with the serenity she experienced from her practice of Yoga. In her own words:

> I spoke about my feelings one evening during our lovemaking. We were having sex in the usual energetic way, when I said, "Robert, please slow down; let's try something new." We stopped and simply relaxed, staying bonded together with Robert still inside me. I was lying on top. I felt excited because I had initiated something new, removing his responsibility for making something happen. There was a subtle switch of roles, and I felt him shift into a more feminine, receptive attitude. We remained like that for many minutes, relaxed while at the same time feeling the excitement of sexual arousal in our bodies. I soon felt a kind of warm, glowing energy beginning to diffuse itself through my whole pelvic area.
>
> We wanted to maintain sexual arousal, so when the excitement began to fade, we returned to our usual style of active lovemaking. Then, just before the peak of orgasmic release, we stopped, relaxed, and became still once more. We repeated this pattern several times, and then something totally unexpected happened. Suddenly we both seemed to be floating in an unbounded space filled with warmth and light. The boundaries between our bodies dissolved and, along with them, the distinctions between man and woman. We were one. The experience became timeless, and we seemed to remain like this forever. There was no need to have an orgasm. There was no need even to "make love." There was nothing to do, nothing to achieve. We were in ecstasy.[7]

Neither Anand nor her partner had any idea of Tantrism at the time. On their own they discovered the hidden secret of sexual stimulation without orgasmic release. Later, Anand had a similar experience with a French psychotherapist, a certain Rampal, who had healed himself, by means of Tantric practices, from the devastating effects of a war wound to his lower spine. However, this time no sexual contact was involved. Anand achieved a high-energy experience through relaxation, controlled breathing, and visualization. She wrote:

> The energy was subtle yet so vibrant that it was almost tangible, as if I were being enveloped in a luminous egg that had existed unnoticed within my body and that was expanding and surrounding us as we breathed and gazed into each other's eyes. . . . Now, surrounded by the egg of light, Rampal also seemed luminous. On some level of reality, this man was no longer Rampal and I was no longer Margo. We had become a delicious dance between breath, energy, and light.[8]

Both experiences amounted to a temporary transcendence of what in Christianity is known as lust. One may recall here St. Augustine's ruminations about lust in his monumental *De Civitate Dei* ("On the City of God"), in which he concluded that of the different kinds of lust that may overpower a person, sexual lust was the most sinful of all and was attended with a natural feeling of shame. He remarked:

> This lust assumes power not only over the whole body, and not only from the outside, but also internally; it disturbs the whole man, when the mental emotion combines and mingles with the physical craving, resulting in a pleasure surpassing all physical delights. So intense is the pleasure that when it reaches its climax there is an almost total extinction of mental alertness; the intellectual sentries, as it were, are overwhelmed.[9]

St. Augustine was right when he described lust as a form of craving and a psychic disturbance. Its supposed sinfulness is rooted in the fact that lust is exploitative: Rather than leading to genuine emotional and spiritual union, it reinforces a person's sense of self-dividedness and separateness. Under the sway of lust, orgasm becomes a goal that is pursued with singular drivenness; thus the body's erotic force is dissipated.

In the discipline of the creeper, by contrast, *eros* is carefully harnessed in order to accomplish the difficult task of catapulting awareness into the level of ultimate Reality. When the erotic energy of the body is properly channeled, the body-mind's vibrational rate is augmented to the point where we are bodily attuned to the vibration (*spanda*) of higher levels of existence. During such moments of attunement, genuine spiritual breakthroughs can and do occur.

The vibrational harmonization manifests in the body-mind as a highly energetic state of equipoise. This distinguishes it from more conventional states of balance, such as relaxation or sleep. It is also attendant by an awareness that can be characterized as relational or ecological. This harmonization is not a purely subjective condition but an interpersonal event, involving both Tantric partners and, at its peak, the rest of the cosmos in the experience of *unio mystica*.

THE SERPENT POWER AND THE TRANSMUTATION OF SEXUAL ENERGY

Pivotal to almost all schools of Tantrism is a curious psychosomatic process known as the awakening of the serpent power (*kundalini-shakti*). The kundalini is a specific manifestation of the great Goddess, or Shakti. It is that supreme power as it appears in association with a finite body-mind and is the hidden source that animates the body-mind. In the ordinary individual, the Goddess is said to be asleep, or dormant, maintaining the body by a mere trickle of her total energy.

The practitioners of Tantrism sought to arouse the kundalini force from its state of slumber to full activity, thereby rendering every cell of the body conscious. In order to facilitate this effort, the experts of Tantrism developed a visionary model of the body as a composite of interacting fields of energy. According to this model, there are seven levels of functioning, which are correlated with certain states of awareness. These are referred to as the seven wheels (*cakra*) or lotuses (*padma*).

These centers are focal points of psychosomatic energy aligned along the axis of the body. The lowest center is at the base of the spine; the topmost center is at the crown of the head. The kundalini is imaginatively pictured as a sleeping serpent coiled up at the lowest center. When awakened through different yogic means, notably concentration combined with breath control, the serpent erects itself and shoots up to the thousand-petaled lotus at the crown of the head. This top center is said to be the seat of Shiva, the masculine principle of the Divine, which is pure motionless awareness.

Thus the body is pictured as being polarized. Shiva is traditionally envisioned as static and Shakti as dynamic. Modern interpreters equate the crown center with the negative or minus pole and the base or sacral center with the positive or plus pole. The tension between both poles constitutes the psychic and somatic life as we know it.

When the kundalini, representing Shakti, or the feminine principle, reaches the crown center, she is reunited with her eternal Beloved. This reunion manifests as ego-transcending ecstasy, or *samadhi,* comparable to a powerful implosion.

Apart from the fact that the individual consciousness goes up in light—hence enlightenment—this condition also yields a much-coveted mystical substance. This by-product of the love-embrace between Shiva and Shakti is known as the nectar of immortality (*amrita*), which trickles from the crown center into the body, bringing about its gradual transfiguration and transmutation. This refashioning of the body involves a remarkable process of what I call *superlimation,* as opposed to sublimation. It involves a withdrawal of sexual energy from the lower psychosomatic centers and its deployment for higher spiritual purposes.

The troubadours and love mystics of medieval Europe understood something about the principle of delayed gratification: how love-desire can be kindled by denying it physical fulfillment. However, they appear to have been ignorant of the kundalini process and its attendant process of sexual superlimation. Hence the troubadours' romantic love hardly appeased their sexual appetites, while the love mystics tended to exhibit emotional imbalance or mystical and parapsychological states slanted toward the hysterical.

By contrast, the Tantric adepts, who were masters of Kundalini-Yoga, succeeded in acquiring a detailed understanding of the hidden physiology of sexual abstinence and superlimation. Through extensive experimentation in the laboratory of their own body-mind, they discovered the operational principles of the astounding kundalini phenomenon. Thus they were able to consciously collaborate with what appears to be a natural, if subterranean, process underlying our mental and spiritual life. One of the most remarkable discoveries by the adepts concerns the close connection between the kundalini and sexuality. Their findings are illuminating in understanding the long historical association between sex and spirituality, and, more than that, they are crucial to our modern endeavor to crystallize a body- and sex-positive spirituality.

Gopi Krishna, a Kashmiri pandit who underwent a spontaneous kundalini arousal, acquired firsthand experience of the process of superlimation. As he explained:

> With the awakening of Kundalini, an amazing activity commences in the whole nervous system from the crown of the head to the toes. . . . In the Chinese documents this phenomenon is described as the "circulation of light" and in the Indian manuals as the "uprising of Shakti (life energy)." The nerves in all parts of the body, whose existence is never felt by the normal consciousness, are now forced by some invisible power to a new type of activity. . . . Through all their innumerable endings, they begin to extract a nectar-like essence from the surrounding tissues, which, traveling in two distinct forms, one as radiation and the other as a subtle essence, streams into the spinal cord. A portion of the essence floods the reproductive organs which, too, become abnormally active as if to keep pace with the activity of the entire nervous system. The radiation, appearing as a luminous cloud in the head, streams into the brain and at the same time courses through the nerves, stimulating all the vital organs, especially the organs of digestion, to adjust their functions to the new life introduced into the system.[10]

As the renowned German scientist-philosopher Carl Friedrich von Weizsäcker noted in his introduction to the above-quoted book by Gopi Krishna, this yogic transmutation of semen is on the surface similar to Freud's notion of sublimation. Yet, von Weizsäcker continued, whereas Freud's model is reductionistic and abstract, Gopi Krishna's description purports to be descriptive and realistic. Moreover, the pandit turned Freud upside down when he proposed that the sexual substance feeds the higher centers.

Von Weizsäcker highlighted some of the difficulties inherent in Gopi Krishna's model, though he proffered no solution for them. In Gopi Krishna's view, his model simply accounts for his own experience of kundalini awakening and the subtle observations he was able to make about his inner environment over many years.

The subtle nerve energy described by Gopi Krishna is known as *ojas* in the Sanskrit scriptures of Tantrism and Yoga, as well as in Hindu naturopathic medicine. The term is derived from the verbal root *vaj,* meaning "to be strong." Thus, ojas is strength or vitality. In Hindu naturopathy, it is said to be the quintessence of the constituent elements of the body. Some modern interpreters see in it albumen or glycogen, but for the Tantric practitioners it is something far more insubstantial or subtle. Perhaps we can interpret it as that aspect of the universal life-force that sustains the somatic structures (called *dhatu* in Sanskrit), such as the intra- and extracellular fluid, blood, or skeletal, muscular, and nervous tissue. Ojas is thought to be present to a particularly high degree in semen.

Hence the preservation of semen has the force of a re-ligious commandment for Hindus, and ejaculation has long been surrounded with feelings of fear and guilt. While such negative feelings are clearly detrimental to our psychic health, the Hindu injunction to preserve the semen is not without wisdom, as any longtime meditator skilled in introspection can vouchsafe, because seminal discharge tends to lower the energy level of the body, which affects meditation.

Just as by stopping all thought in meditation a state of withdrawal from the external world is achieved, so the denial of ejaculation brings about a seeming reversal of the semen. The mysterious energy that would otherwise have been dissipated is now salvaged and, beyond that, amplified. It thus becomes available for the spiritual transformation of the person.

Since women are correctly credited with a counterpart to semen, the secretion from inside and at the top of the vaginal entrance, we must assume that this occult process of reversal is also possible for the female gender. However, we do not yet have a woman's description that is equivalent to the elaborate obser-vations made by Gopi Krishna. The Tantric scriptures remain silent on this point, having been written by, and mainly for, male initiates.

The technical Sanskrit term for the upsurge of transmuted sexual vitality into the brain center is *urdhva-retas,* meaning "up-ward semen." It is widely praised in the Hindu scriptures as the fruit of prolonged chastity. Medical science, of course, knows nothing whatsoever about this matter, which is not surprising, since some authorities still deny even the existence of a female secretion corresponding to the male semen. However, we may confidently assert that the kundalini process, obscure as it is, is not one of the phantasms of esoteric lore. It corresponds to a set of real phenomena that have been experienced by people of widely different cultural backgrounds, including men and woman who had not the slightest inkling of its existence.

To summarize, Kundalini-Yoga is internalized sacred intercourse. Everything that happens in left-hand Tantrism between male and female occurs here in the subjective space of consciousness. This is thought possible because the divine masculine and feminine principles are not only macrocosmic but also microcosmic realities. In the language of modern psychology, our body-mind is androgynous.

TANTRIC EROTICISM AND FREUDIAN SUBLIMATION

Authentic Tantrism offers us a vista of possibilities for which there are no equivalents in our modern secular society. Tantrism, or Tantra, shows that the sexual drive cannot merely be deployed in orgasm or sublimated in philosophy and art but also transmuted to the point where the whole body-mind becomes simultaneously eroticized *and* transcended.

One might recall here that the term *sublimation,* first used by Sigmund Freud, means "rendering sublime." The word *sublime,* again, probably stems from the Latin prefix *sub* ("up to, under") and *limen* ("lintel"), denoting "up to the lintel"—that is, up to the highest limit. In Freudian psychology, sublimation is the deflection of libido (sexual energy) from what is considered its normal goal, which is sexual gratification. It is deflected into channels that are culturally more acceptable, such as artistic creativity, a romantic ideal, selfless action, or even mystical experience, which are all deemed more sublime than mere sexual fulfillment. From Freud's perspective, of course, philosophy, religion, and mystical experience, however lofty, are in the final analysis only forms of deception, even though they can be helpful.[11]

Because of the established Freudian meaning of *sublimation,* we might do well to coin a different term for the central task accomplished in Tantrism and other similar traditions. I have already suggested the term *superlimation,* "going beyond the lintel (of the Freudian world view)"—that is, transcending all boundaries or limits—for the crowning accomplishment of Tantrism is the transcendence of the mind and thus human culture itself. The ultimate realization of Being, which is inherently blissful, does not deny, negate, or even deflect the sexual drive.

As B. Bhattacharya's mysterious female teacher remarked, "In order to train the tiger one must remain close to the tiger."[12] From a Tantric perspective, the Freudian libido is only a specific manifestation of the universal life-force. Sexual desire is merely a particular instance of the cosmic *eros,* of the ever-present bliss, the universal mating dance.

Under the influence of nineteenth-century scientism, Freud stood the traditional religious understanding of sexuality on its head. He saw in the sex urge the very foundation of human culture. It took the psychological reform movement instigated in the 1960s by such farsighted researchers as Abraham Maslow to begin to correct Freud's mistake. However, we are still awaiting a full-blooded psychology/spirituality of the body. The current dialogue with teachings such as Tantrism may prove constructive in our endeavor to create such a new understanding.

That dialogue began in the opening decades of the twentieth century, which saw not only the publication of the first English translations of Tantric scriptures and scholarly monographs on Tantrism but also the emergence of the first Western schools of that ancient tradition. These schools of Neo-Tantrism are, by and large, popularizations of the Tantric teachings, and consequently misunderstandings abound.

What is most misleading is that many Neo-Tantric teachings espouse a hedonism that is absent from original Tantrism. Thus, not a few Neo-Tantric teachers instruct their students to arouse each other until they are close to orgasm, or expect them to achieve one or more orgasms during each session. Some even encourage their students to find relief in orgasm after having stimulated each other for the purpose of achieving an altered state of awareness. The *maithuna* ritual itself is thus turned into a hunt for pleasurable experience.

This approach is far removed from the love-play of the divine couple, which serves as an archetypal model in traditional

Tantrism. Orgasm is not part of the original Tantric repertoire.
Orgasm, it is said, generally does not lead to bliss, merely to
pleasurable sensations in the genitals. Instead, the emphasis in
most traditional schools of Tantrism is on awakening the body's
erotic potential without risking orgasm. At its best, the Neo-
Tantric approach leads to what psychiatrist Stanislav Grof labeled oceanic sex. As Grof explained:

> In oceanic sex, the basic model for sexual interaction with an-
> other organism is not that of a liberating discharge and release
> after a period of strenuous effort and struggle, but that of a play-
> ful and mutually nourishing flow and exchange of energies re-
> sembling a dance. The aim is to experience the loss of one's own
> boundaries, a sense of fusion and melting with the partner into a
> state of blissful unity. The genital union and orgasmic discharge,
> although powerfuly experienced, are here considered secondary
> to the ultimate goal, which is reaching a transcendental state of
> union of the male and female principles. . . . Some of the sub-
> jects who have reached this form of sexuality, when asked what
> function the genital orgasm has in it, would respond that it
> serves the purpose of "removing biological noise from a spir-
> itual system."[13]

Grof rightly distinguished oceanic sex from Tantric sexuality,
where genital sexuality is merely a vehicle for a higher realization. The traditional maithuna is a sacred occasion celebrating
the transcendence of experience, for the ecstatic condition of
bliss is not an experience at all, since the experiencer is one with
the experienced. In the state of ecstasy, the division between
subject and object is left behind together with the conceptual
mind and the ego–identity that could revel in that bliss.

In Neo-Tantric circles, however, the native bliss of Reality
is all too often confused with a heightened state of sensory pleasure, whether or not genital orgasm is involved. While pleasure
has its place in the scheme of things, according to authentic Tantrism it cannot alleviate our fundamental alienation from the
cosmos or help us overcome our basic fear of death, nor can it
bring us permanent spiritual fulfillment. Pleasure, like pain,
pertains to the nervous system. Genital orgasms or even so-
called whole-body orgasms are psychosomatic phenomena, not
spiritual manifestations. Bliss is the everlasting orgasm of God
and Goddess in divine embrace.

The psychotechnology of left-hand Tantrism is the ancient world's most sophisticated endeavor to utilize the great reservoir of sexual energy locked into our bodies for spiritual purposes. The mysterious process of sexual superlimation connected with the kundalini arousal deserves close study in the future.

CHAPTER 11

❧

The Sexual Tao: The Chinese Way of Circulating Life-Energy

TAO: THE NAMELESS WAY BEYOND GOD AND GODDESS

India, as has been seen, has produced the remarkable esoteric teachings of Tantrism and Kundalini-Yoga. The Chinese have elaborated their own unique equivalents, which are subsumed under the heading of Taoism. Taoism is the Western term for those many Chinese schools that speak of the ultimate Reality as the *tao,* or "Way." Like the adepts of Hindu and Buddhist Tantrism, the ancient Taoist masters were experts in manipulating the life-energy of the human body, and they also applied their consummate mastery to the sexual process. But before the Taoist contribution to sacred sexuality is studied in more detail, it is only fitting that the philosophical foundations of that long-lived tradition first be examined.

The Chinese character for the word *tao* is composed of a symbol for "head" and a symbol for "going." Originally a third component was placed beneath these two characters, which signified "standing still." Thus the original meaning of *tao* was "a track which, though fixed itself, leads from a beginning directly to the goal."[1] The idea expressed here is that the *tao,* though itself perfectly still and stable, is yet the source of all movement, of creation. It is the principle behind all creativity and thus also behind the procreative process. It is the great Mystery in which all beings and things participate and to which the sages attune themselves to realize wholeness, happiness, health, and even longevity.

155

Lao Tzu, the semilegendary founder of Taoism who probably lived in the sixth century B.C., opens his famous *Tao Te
Ching* with this verse:

> Tao that can be spoken of,
> Is not the Everlasting Tao.
> Name that can be named,
> Is not the Everlasting name.[2]

The *tao* is the ultimate Reality, which is conceived of as im-
personal and all–comprehensive. It is said to be beyond the male
God (*ti*) of most ancient times, and it is celebrated as being
beyond that which from the third or fourth century on was
known as Heaven. The eternal *tao* is the universal ground of all
visible and invisible things, and it is the most authentic core of
the human personality.

Hence Lao Tzu recommends that the wise person should
drop the notion of being an independent agent. Instead, the
sage should allow the *tao* to perform all necessary actions by
using his (or, indeed, her) body-mind as an instrument:

> Therefore the sage manages affairs without action,
> Carries out teaching without speech.
> Ten thousand things arise and he does not initiate them,
> They come to be and he claims no possession of them,
> He works without holding on,
> Accomplishes without claiming merit.
> Because he does not claim merit,
> His merit does not go away.[3]

The sage is like water. He flows with the current of life, not
presenting any obstruction to the flux. He is empty of himself.
Thus he is filled with the *tao,* and his actions are purely spontaneous. This is the grand Taoist ideal of *wu-wei* ("no-action").
The principle of spontaneity (*tzu-jan*) is axial to all schools of
Taoism, regardless of their metaphysical and practical differ-
ences. It also underlies Taoist sexual practice.

Generally, two streams of Taoism are distinguished: philosophical Taoism and religious Taoism. The former, crystallizing
around the teachings of the *Tao Te Ching,* consists primarily in
the cultivation of spontaneity. Religious Taoism (*tao chiao*) emphasizes more the pursuit of psychological wholeness and phys-

ical well-being through a wide range of magical practices, including a versatile sex technology.

In later times, philosophical Taoism tended toward abstract speculation, whereas religious Taoism showed an increasing concern for personal longevity and even bodily immortality. In this respect, both orientations suffer from a one-sidedness that is absent from early Taoism, as embedded in Lao Tzu's work. As is evident from his *Tao Te Ching,* the path of the sage is not merely a personal quest but his salvation is for the good of all.

It is significant that of all the ancient Chinese works known to us, the *Tao Te Ching* alone emphasizes the feminine principle. As Ellen Chen observed, the *tao* is the "womb of nonbeing." In Chapter 28 of Lao Tzu's work, the opening verse reads cryptically: "To know the male/But to abide by the female. . . ." Just as all creatures have sprung forth from the *tao,* they also return to it. Thus, the *tao* is the universal Mother—an idea that furnishes a connection to our earlier consideration of erotic spirituality in the paleolithic and neolithic eras.

The single most important premise of Taoism is that in the dimension of the everlasting *tao* there is a primordial harmony between the feminine and the masculine. These two polar principles are known as the forces of *yin* and *yang,* which are the diastole and systole of the cosmic heart. The dynamic equilibrium between them is beautifully represented in the familiar image of *t'ai chi,* the circle composed of a descending white drop with a black "eye" and an ascending black drop with a white "eye," respectively standing for the forces of *yang* and *yin.*

The image corresponds to the Hindu notion of *shiva* (cosmic masculine principle) and *shakti* (cosmic feminine principle) in eternal embrace. This bipolar equilibrium must become an experiential reality for the spiritual practitioner. He or she must live immersed in that balance, and this is possible only because the microcosm faithfully mirrors the macrocosm.

According to Lao Tzu, death is the inescapable consequence of the separation of the male from the female principle. In the infant, male and female principles are still unsevered. The infant is filled with life-force (*ch'i*) and is also replete with undiminished reproductive force (*ching*); hence the young child is considered as being deathless, like the *tao.*

In Chapter 55 of his work, Lao Tzu compares the accomplished sage to the infant who enjoys "perfect adaption" (*te*).

Unlike adulthood, thought does not complicate the infant's existence. The infant suckles and cries and grasps firmly—all in perfect harmony with its inner nature. Unselfconscious, without interfering mind (*hsin*), the infant lives out the fullness of the *tao*. The Taoist practitioner aspires to realize that same innocent and balanced condition in all matters.

The vehicle by which this inner harmonization can be achieved is itself a manifestation of the cosmic polar play of *yin* and *yang,* namely the life-breath or *ch'i*. Like the idea of spontaneity, the notion of *ch'i* is fundamental to all forms of Taoism. *Ch'i* is the Chinese name for what the Hindus and Buddhists call *prana* and the ancient Greeks knew as *pneuma*. Without this vital force, the animated body would be a corpse.

The regulation of the breath of life consequently plays an eminent role in the schools of religious Taoism. They have elaborated a variety of aids to living—from alchemy, to herbalism, to sexual disciplines. The practice of controlling *ch'i* is known as *tao-yin,* or "circulating the *tao*," a technique referred to already in the *Chuang Tzu* (Chapter 15), a work in part authored by a sage of the same name.

> To huff and puff, exhale and inhale, blow out the old and draw in the new, do the "bear-hang" and the "bird-stretch," interested only in long life—such are the tastes of the practitioners of "guide-and-pull" exercises, the nurturers of the body, Grandfather P'eng's ripe-old-agers.[4]

Grandfather P'eng Tsu is the Chinese counterpart of the Hebrew Methuselah. He is said to have lived to the age of eight hundred and has inspired countless generations of religious Taoists in their search for longevity and immortality. Indeed, the great masters of Taoism are known as the immortals. Their quest for the Golden Elixir of Life, known as the golden pill (*chin-tan*), has prompted them to study very attentively the connection between life, breath, and sexuality.

THE TAO OF SEX: WHITE TIGER AND GREEN DRAGON

According to Chinese mythology, both Taoist spirituality and the sexual arts were invented by the resourceful, if legendary, Yellow Emperor (Huang-ti) and his three immortal ladies, who are thought to have lived nearly five thousand years ago. The Yellow Emperor had twelve hundred women in his harem and would have died prematurely had he not known the secret of seminal control. However, since he was a master of making love to his women without forfeiting his precious life-sustaining liquid, he succeeded in perfecting his body to a degree at which he rose bodily into the heavenly domain.

Certainly the *ars amatoria* are very ancient in China, and the Chinese sex manuals are the oldest and most detailed in the premodern world. Eight such manuals were in circulation by the end of the first millennium B.C. Their Indian equivalents are several centuries younger: The famous *Kama-Sutra* of Vatsyayana was composed at the end of the third century A.D., though its author seems to have based his work on earlier but no longer extant writings. The *Kama-Sutra* was intended as a guide for the well-to-do urbanite who wanted to take the boredom out of his love life. We can almost regard it as a playboy's manual with a superficial moral tinge. As a sexological work, however, the *Kama-Sutra* is rather disappointing and lags behind its Chinese counterparts. The same holds true of the other Hindu manuals on sexuality, which merely tend to echo Vatsyayana. They all tend toward the scholastic, and there is good reason to doubt that any of the writers had firsthand experience of what they were writing about.

The situation is refreshingly different with the Chinese sex manuals, which brim with technical details that are undoubtedly the fruit of long personal experimentation. What is more, they are informed by the occult philosophy of religious Taoism, which makes them more than sexological treatises and relevant to our consideration of erotic spirituality. In addition, they treat sexuality as part of a holistic system of personal hygiene and medicine.

While none of these ancient works appears to be extant today, many partially survive in the form of quotations in the Japanese medical encyclopedia titled *Ishimpo*, which cites over two hundred of the old scriptures. This is a tenth-century work compiled by a Chinese physician living in Japan. It includes a long section on the bedroom arts, which has been translated into English by Howard S. Levy together with the late physician and historian Akira Ishihara.[5] In the thirty chapters of that section of the *Ishimpo*, various Taoist and medical authorities make their appearance.

Apart from the Yellow Emperor himself, we also encounter in these chapters the long-lived P'eng Tsu and the emperor's three immortal ladies, Woman Plain, Woman Selective (also called Woman Mysterious), and Woman Profound (also called Rainbow Woman)—all of them experts on the *ars amatoria*. On the connection between Taoism and medicine, Levy and Ishihara noted:

> The Taoist adepts of ancient China revered the Yellow Emperor and adopted what they believed to be his medical theories. Many of them became physicians, and in this curative capacity they were received by emperors and aristocratic courtiers as honored guests. They gave instructions in boudoir practices to men who were surfeited with female companions; this was especially true of the T'ang (seventh to tenth century), which was characterized by vast numbers of prostitutes, female entertainers, and concubines. In a practical way, therefore, the sex handbooks of the Taoists served as first-aid kits for the Chinese gentleman of leisure, whose well-being was threatened by unending amorous play and unrepressed profligation. The Emperor had thousands of women in his harem, and he was on intimate terms with at least several dozen. To him, advice on how to conserve was advice on how to survive.[6]

The emperor's secret, we are freely told, lay in the proper harnessing of his semen; for the Taoist—as with the Tantric—semen spells life, and loss of semen signals loss of life. The underlying idea is that our reproductive system is the secret powerhouse that generates the very stuff of bodily existence, ensuring not only health but also longevity and even immortality. Again we note the iron link between sex and death.[7] Alexis Carrel, a Nobel laureate in medicine, commented on the connection between the sex drive and vitality as follows:

> The sexual glands have other functions than that of impelling man to the gesture which, in primitive life, perpetuated the race. They also intensify all physiological, mental, and spiritual activities. No eunuch has ever become a great philosopher, a great scientist, or even a great criminal.[8]

Carrel went on to say:

> The testicle, more than any other gland, exerts a profound influence upon the strength and quality of the mind. In general, great

poets, artists, and saints, as well as conquerors, are strongly sexed. The removal of the genital glands, even in adult individuals, produces some modifications of the mental state. After extirpation of the ovaries, women become apathetic and lose part of their intellectual activity or moral sense. The personality of men who have undergone castration is altered in a more or less marked way. The historical cowardice of Abelard in face of the passionate love and sacrifice of Heloise was probably due to the brutal mutilation imposed upon him. Almost all great artists were great lovers. Inspiration seems to depend on a certain condition of the sexual glands. . . . It is well known that sexual excesses impede intellectual activity. In order to reach its full power, intelligence seems to require both the presence of well-developed sexual glands and the temporary repression of the sexual appetite.[9]

The nineteenth-century Taoist master Chao Pi Ch'en believed that life-force, as stored in the sexual organs, is quantifiable. In his treatise *The Secrets of Cultivation of Essential Nature and Eternal Life,* he observed:

A practiser should regard his body as a country and the generative force as its population. Unstirred generative force ensures security for the population, and the fullness of spirit and (vital) breath increases the prosperity of the country.[10]

Thus, the preservation of semen leads to inner peace and physical well-being, whereas the loss of semen throws the country into rebellion and chaos. The adept Chao Pi Ch'en explained the benefits of seminal control thus:

If the generative force is gathered for a hundred (successive) days, sixty-four chu [measures] of vitality are gained and a unit of positive principle is produced; this is like "adding fuel" to feed and prolong life.

With the same determination, if the generative force is gathered for another hundred days an additional sixty-four chu [measures] of vitality are gained while the positive principle is increased to two units; the body now becomes very strong and all ailments vanish.

If the gathering of generative force continues for another hundred days an additional sixty-four chu [measures] of vitality are gained with the positive increased to three units; all cavities in

the body are cleared for rejuvenation, and the practiser's steps are
light and quick with clear and good hearing.[11]

Master Chao went on to describe the different effects for
successive increments of practice. Thus, after one hundred more
days, the practitioner's skin becomes lustrous and his white hair
turns black again; subsequently, he becomes high-spirited and
grows a new set of teeth; next he regains the circle of *t'ai chi,* the
ultimate Reality, thereby restoring his bodily energies to the
fullness and wholeness that a baby enjoys.

Taoists measure the vitality of the body in terms of units of
chu. The healthy, balanced body is thought to have a total of 384
chu. One *chu* is the twenty-fourth part of one-and-one-third
ounces. As Master Chao explained, vitality increases by sixty-
four *chu* every thirty-two months until the full amount is
reached at the age of sixteen. After that, a person who does not
consciously conserve his or her vitality progressively loses energy—sixty-four units every eight years.

How is seminal mastery to be accomplished? The Taoist
texts are full of advice and descriptions of useful exercises. First
of all, the Taoists, believing as they do in naturalness rather than
repression, do not consider an active sexual life an impediment
to spirituality. If anything, they encourage sex as a means of
augmenting the life-force of the body and thus as a transformative agent in the spiritual process.

According to Taoism, the sexual relationship between
woman and man is a manifestation of the dance between the
cosmic principles of *yin* and *yang.* In other words, for the Taoist
the question is not whether or not to have sex but how to engage
in it. Long ago, they noted that there is a very important difference between the male and the female orgasm. Whereas the
woman's secretions mostly remain within her body, the man
ejaculates the semen—and, as the Taoists see it—dies a little
every time. In their view, every seminal discharge is another
step toward the grave.

The rationale behind this belief is that the semen is a life-
carrying force and that every man is endowed with a limited
supply of reproductive energy during his lifetime. This notion
will not seem quite as fantastic when we recall that one ejaculation, composed of between two hundred and five hundred
million wriggling spermatozoa, apparently has the nutritional

value of two steaks and ten eggs. It is true that men, as we are told in a popular book on sexual chemistry, "can produce in half a second more sperm, the smallest cells in their body, than the eggs a woman can produce in her whole lifetime."[12] However, when the authors of that volume comment that "sperm is a cheap and easily renewable resource," they completely contradict the position of Taoism. As the Taoist masters insist, the constant production of semen in a sexually active male who equates sex with orgasm can have terrible hidden costs: degenerative disease and premature death.

According to the Taoist teachings, the man gets depleted from his seminal emissions, whereas the woman, whose body reabsorbs her orgasmic secretions, gets stronger through sex. Daniel P. Reid, a Western student of Taoism, put it this way:

> The contrasting nature of male and female orgasm has important implications for two types of sexual activity that have aroused a lot of controversy over the ages and appear to be gaining in popularity today: masturbation and homosexuality. Viewed from the angle of Yin and Yang, the results of these two activities are very different indeed for men and women. For men, masturbation represents an irretrievable and uncompensated loss of Yang semen-essence. While healthy males between the ages of 16 and 21 are veritable "fountains of semen" for whom masturbation is relatively harmless, by the time they reach 25 or so, all the old shibboleths regarding male masturbation come true: weakness in thighs and knees, numbness in lumbar region, loss of vitality, depression, etc. By the time they reach 30, men should entirely give up this self-defeating habit and start conserving semen exclusively for intercourse with women. Men who continue masturbating habitually into their 30s, 40s and 50s rob themselves of the very essence and energy that fuel their lives and protect their health.
>
> A woman, by contrast, may masturbate to her heart's content without damaging her stores of essence and energy.[13]

Reid made the further observation that, for the same reasons, homosexuality is damaging to men but harmless for women. He noted that the ancient Taoist physicians even diagnosed a homosexual syndrome, which they called "dragon yang" (*lung-yang*). This ailment includes fatigue, skin ulcers, impotence, and low immunity. The mixture of *yin* with *yin* in most lesbian relationships amounts to little more than what the ancient Chinese called "polishing the mirror," a rather harmless activity. However, the juxtaposition of *yang* and *yang* in male homosexual relationships is, according to traditional Taoist wisdom, intrinsically antagonistic. As Reid pointed out, this antagonism can be demonstrated under the microscope when the semen of two different men is mixed; there is war!

Another writer on Taoist sexuality, Stephen T. Chang, commented that since *yin* and *yang* are both present in every man and woman, Taoism neither condones nor condemns homosexuality.[14] However, he pointed out various drawbacks that homosexuals, particularly those who wish to engage in sex as a transformative and rejuvenating practice, ought to know. On balance, therefore, he too regards homosexuality as tending to create a psychoenergetic imbalance that could prove hazardous to a person's health.

Mantak Chia, a Thai-born contemporary master of Taoism teaching in America, advised homosexual men and women to balance their *yin* and *yang* energies themselves regularly to either the earth or the sky, combined with conscious breathing.[15] Whereas the earth is predominantly *yin,* the sky is the carrier of *yang* energy.

The teachings of Taoism, like those of Tantra and other similar sexo-yogic schools, are designed for heterosexual partners. The Taoist bedroom arts (*fang-shu*) revolve around what is called dual cultivation, which corresponds to the Tantric rite of *maithuna*. However, in contrast to the adherents of Tantrism, the Taoists encourage variety and playfulness in lovemaking. Whereas in Tantrism the focus is more directly on transcending the body-mind through solemn rituals, the Taoists are perennially concerned with accumulating psychosexual energy, which is then utilized to rejuvenate and immortalize the body.

Not surprisingly, Taoism has developed a most elaborate sexual technology, entailing complex notions of the energy currents in the body, a highly evolved understanding of nutrition and diet, numerous breathing exercises, and as many positions for lovemaking. The positions have very colorful names, such as Tiger's Tread, Cicada Affixed, Cranes with Necks Intertwined, Silkworm Reeling Silk, Sky-Soaring Butterfly, and so forth. Apart from affording delight, these positions are thought to have different health benefits.

Taoist writers also bestowed very colorful designations

upon the various anatomical parts. For instance, the penis is frequently called "jade stalk" or "male vanguard," and the vagina is named "jade gate," "cinnabar hole," or "hidden place," while the clitoris is spoken of as "jade terrace" or "mouse in the empty boat." Finally, the "white tiger" is the semen that must be carefully guarded, and the "green dragon" is the female secretion rich in *yin* force. On the nonsexual level of alchemy, these cryptic terms refer to lead and cinnabar (a sulphide of mercury), respectively.

For the Taoist practitioner, the objective of intercourse is to absorb the partner's psychosexual energy. Thus, the man seeks to acquire the woman's *yin* energy and the woman the man's *yang* energy. Regrettably, in some schools this was viewed as a form of combat between the sexes, with the woman trying to deplete her male partner and the man desperately struggling to avoid ejaculation while soaking up as much of the woman's *yin* energy as possible. This attitude has, not without justification, led to accusations of vampirism.

For the most part, it was the gentlemen of leisure who exploited women, especially virgins, for their inner alchemical quest. But, on occasion, a woman got the better of the male gender. Thus, Chinese history recalls the sexual vampirism of Empress Wu Tze-tien, who lived in the seventh century A.D. She is remembered as ancient China's foremost dragon lady. Starting out as a chambermaid, she fought her way to the imperial throne through her sexual skills and inexhaustible appetites. In her long life, she is said to have drained thousands of men of their *yang* energy, thereby ruining their health and killing them before their time.

Through the preservation and indeed augmentation of his or her primary energy (*ching*), which corresponds to *shakti* in Hinduism, the Taoist practitioner enriches his or her store of vital energy (*ch'i*) and thus becomes capable of more profound spiritual work. For through the recycling and transmutation of *ch'i* energy, the spiritual energy known as *shen* is nourished. The *shen* energy, corresponding to the Tantric *shiva*, is associated with the so-called cavity in the head. *Cavity* is the Taoist term for the yogic *cakra*, or subtle energy center.

The Taoist practitioner stokes the furnace of his or her sex glands to create the heat necessary for the inner alchemical process of transmutation. This process is explained in two ways. According to one explanation, the augmented energy rises to the head, where it stored, which is represented in art by the strangely domed skulls of the immortals. According to another explanation, the pent-up *ch'i* energy is used to create what is termed the immortal embryo in the cauldron in the abdominal center. As Master Chao Pi Ch'en explained:

> The union of spirit and vitality produces the immortal seed as revealed by the white light in the heart, lights flashing in the head, the dragon's hum and the tiger's roar in the ears. . . . If the immortal seed is fully developed the golden light will manifest. [16]

Careful nurturing of this immortal seed produces what is known as the immortal fetus, which is a shapeless spiritual field associated with a golden light. One late Taoist text, translated by Richard Wilhelm and made famous by C. G. Jung's commentary, speaks of this burgeoning spiritual reality as the "golden flower." [17] This flower blooms when the inner light, or energy, is consciously circulated. Put differently, through proper cultivation, the immortal fetus grows until it is mature enough to be externalized—that is, released through the crown of the head. Then it can be seen outside the body.

Further practice will enable the Taoist practitioner to integrate this new spiritual body with the physical body, whereby the latter is rendered increasingly insubstantial. Thus the practitioner gains at long last the elixir of immortality.

The idea of a metamorphosed body is of course not unique to Taoism. It is a common notion in Tantrism as well, and it is also reflected in the doctrine of the spiritualized body of Jesus. Before Jesus, Enoch is said to have walked with God and to have lived on earth a full 365 years before he ascended bodily into heaven. The great ninth-century Hebrew prophet and miracle-worker Elijah likewise is believed to have been physically lifted into the divine domain, which we may understand as a metaphor of transubstantiation.

Adepts of the stature of the great Taoist immortals are few and far between. Most practitioners of sexual Taoism, it appears, fall far short of the grand ideal. In fact, the sexual path can be a trap of its own, through which the ego-personality falls into the bottomless pit of self-indulgence and self-glorification. In his still readable work *Pain, Sex and Time,* Gerald Heard, a prominent spokesman for Hindu nondualist metaphysics during the first half of our century, expressed his fears about Tantric Yoga, which apply to Taoism with equal force. He said:

> It is hard not to conclude that in all these attempts to use the primal energy as it manifests itself through the sexual channels so that it raises consciousness to a higher level, we have a technique of extreme precariousness. Indeed, it may be said to be comparable with drug-taking for the same purpose. In both cases the individual consciousness is apt to be distracted and dissipated by the medium employed, so that, forgetting the purpose, the means becomes the end.[18]

Clearly, we cannot divorce sexual techniques from their spiritual and moral bedrock without running the risk of corrupting the tradition we have chosen to follow and without debasing our own life. In other words, we must tread the razor's edge of spontaneity without egoic motivation or attachment. As the wise Lao Tzu admonished:

> Those who keep this Tao,
> Do not want to be filled to the full.
> Because they are not full,
> They can renew themselves before being worn out.[19]

As will be appreciated, Taoism has made a unique contribution to our understanding of the play of psychosexual energy in the body. It has also furnished us with a wonderfully dynamic concept of reality, which meshes neatly with contemporary notions of the world as process rather than static object. Most important, we can expect the Taoist tradition to continue to fertilize our endeavors to articulate a body- and sex-positive spirituality. For, whereas Tantrism has nowadays very few qualified representatives, there are a number of fine Taoist masters who are accessible to inquisitive Westerners.

CHAPTER 12

❧

Sexual Magic and Neo-Paganism

SEX MAGIC AND THE MAGIC OF SEX

Human sexuality and magic have a long joint history, which, as has been seen in an earlier chapter, extends back to the Stone Age. For millennia, the sex act was surrounded by magical beliefs and practices; in traditional societies it still is. Even our postmodern civilization has its own taboos, myths, and superstitions about sexuality. Thus, despite scientific research to the contrary, many people believe that a small penis is functionally inadequate; that it is harmful for a woman to swallow the man's sperm; that there is a clitoral and a vaginal orgasm and that, psychoanalytically speaking, the former is inferior to the latter; that anything is permissible so long as nobody is hurt; that orgasm is essential to one's health; that ejaculation is always associated with orgasmic pleasure; or, indeed, that sex is something to be ashamed about.[1]

What our civilization at large has definitely lost, to all our misfortune, is the age-old sense that sex is imbued with the numinous, that it is part of the larger mystery of existence, and that it can be a window onto the sacred Reality. But perhaps we have not entirely lost that sense, because now and then people in love still speak of the magic of sex. They refer to moments in their lovemaking when they experience a sense of enchantment, of profound connectedness with each other, when their bodies and inner beings hum in harmony with the web of life itself. In such moments, we exceed our hormonal impulses and genital compulsions; we may even catch a glimpse of the workings of magic.

Magic envisions the world as a web of powerful forces that

169

influence our individual lives. In the magical world view, sex is a particularly potent means of intermingling magical forces between people, because of the intimate bodily and emotional contact of the sex act. Magic is about applying the will to those invisible forces and making them useful to one's goals, whether moral or immoral. The word *sex* is thought to derive from the Latin verb *secare,* meaning "to cut" or "to sever." Yet, paradoxically, sex is about joining, uniting, and overcoming the separation between genders. It is thus essentially a magical act through which distinctions are lifted. This is the other side of the magical world view: the experience of mystical participation in each other's life, or what the French anthropologist Lucien Levy-Bruhl called *participation mystique.*

On the assumption that all things are interconnected, magic turns everything into a subject of one's personal will. All magical action is intended to incorporate the world, including other living beings, and to bring it under one's subjective influence. The act of sexual love is an act of literal incorporation whereby lovers permit the partner's body (penis, tongue, or finger) to enter into their body (vagina, mouth, or anus). The body boundaries between lovers are deliberately blurred so that they can participate more fully in each other's life and life-force. Lovers cast a magical spell on each other that draws them into a rare mutuality of experience, which can create such a degree of consonance between them that they lose their sense of personal identity. Writer George Leonard's experience, as related in the first chapter of this book, offers a poignant example of the sexual participation mystique.

The erotic nature of magic was clearly understood by the fifteenth-century philosopher and practitioner of magic Marsilio Ficino. In his book on love, entitled *Amore* (VI. 1), he observed that "the whole power of Magic is founded on Eros."[2] As historian of religion Ioan Couliano pointed out in his landmark study on the connection between Renaissance magic and eroticism:

> At its greatest degree of development, reached in the work of Giordano Bruno, magic is a means of control over the individual and the masses based on deep knowledge of personal and collective erotic impulses. . . . Magic is merely eroticism applied, directed, and aroused by its performer. But there are other aspects of the manipulation of phantasms, one of them being the mirac-

ulous Art of Memory. The bond between eroticism, mnemonics, and magic is indissoluble to such an extent that it is impossible to understand the third without first having studied the principles and mechanisms of the first two.[3]

What Couliano called the Art of Memory (*ars memoriae*) was a highly developed Yoga-type technology during the medieval age. Demanding utmost concentration in the deployment of one's imaginative powers, it served both intellectuals and meditators to comprehend reality through the exercise of memory. This medieval mnemotechnology also proved of great importance to those wishing to master the principles of magic. For visualization, or imagination (*imago* meaning "picture") lies at the heart of the magical arts.

The visual, imaginistic nature of magic can be clearly seen in the cave paintings of the Stone Age. One particularly striking instance of magic connectivity, involving sexuality, is found in a paleolithic stone drawing from Algeria that was reproduced by psychoanalyst Erich Neumann in his acclaimed work *The Great Mother*.[4] This drawing shows, in outline, a female figure with upraised arms and a male figure, turned sideways, holding a bow, as well as three animals. Both human figures appear to be nude. The most remarkable aspect is that the female's genitals and the male's penis are connected by what appears to be an unbroken power line.

One may speculate that this drawing suggests a ritual empowerment of the man at hunt. The woman invokes the invisible, or sacred, and her genitals are the power-transforming station, linked to the man's penis by a transmission line. This drawing captures the essence of paleolithic humanity's magical relationship to the world and to sexuality. It also epitomizes the quintessence of magic itself, which consists in the energetic connectivity between beings and things that transcends the discrete boundaries of space and time. The woman's invocation or prayerful absorption of numinous energy did not necessarily coincide with the time of the man's hunt, nor was it in the same location, yet woman and man were connected by an invisible cord of power—and that power was, in essence, erotic.

The image is, moreover, a faithful representation of an archetypal reality, namely the fact that the female is a vessel of life. Erich Neumann proffered the following very important insight:

Woman as body-vessel is the natural expression of the human experience of woman bearing the child "within" her and of man entering "into" her in the sexual act. Because the identity of the female personality with the encompassing body-vessel in which the child is sheltered belongs to the foundation of feminine existence, woman is not only the vessel that like every body contains something within itself, but, both for herself and the male, is the "life-vessel as such," in which life forms, and which bears all living things and discharges them out of itself and into the world.[5]

That is to say, woman is the container of magical power and potency—the biological prototype of the alchemical cauldron. She is the life-bearing goddess of most ancient times. Symbolically speaking, woman is the world itself. As Neumann tried to show, this is a psychological archetype that is still very much alive in us—men and women alike. He further observed that the mental and physical health of a man depends on whether he can live at peace with this archetypal reality in himself or whether he fights it. If he cannot accept it, he will inevitably experience woman as a vessel of doom, which swallows and devours the phallus, which emasculates, and which usurps the man's virility. From this negative perception, the Goddess in her terrible form as the Hindu Kali, the Near-Eastern Lilith, or the Aztec Xochipilli-Cinteotl was born.

Neumann made the further important comment that magic began as what may be termed food magic, associated with fertility, and was originally governed by the feminine.[6] Fertility, both literal and metaphorical, is indeed a recurrent motif in magical thought and practice.

THE MAGICAL POWER OF SEMEN

Giordano Bruno is remembered in our schoolbooks as a pioneer cosmologist who, in the year 1600, was burned at the stake for his heretical ideas. What is seldom mentioned is that he was also a veteran practitioner and theoretician of magic. Bruno firmly believed that "phantasy," or the imagination, "can really influence the object."[7] According to Bruno, *eros* rules the world, and it is the magician's special task to achieve control over *eros* and its diverse manifestations. *Eros* is responsible for the attraction between people and, consequently, for their "enchainment."

Magic, for Bruno, required both ardent desire and abstinence. One way in which the magus could hope to escape enchainment to the object of his passion was by means of the esoteric practice of *coitus reservatus,* or prolonged intercourse without ejaculation. Bruno apparently did not teach this technique, though we should not exclude this possibility from the magical agenda of his time. After all, *coitus reservatus* was, as we have seen, known already to the early Christian community but was condemned by the ecclesial authorities. This practice surfaced again with the Cathars, who formed what can be described as a counter-Church, seriously challenging the supremacy of Roman Catholicism at one time.

We thus have here a striking European parallel to the spiritual practices of Indian Tantrism and Chinese Taoism. The former tradition promises its followers both liberation (*mukti*) and enjoyment (*bhukti*)—a combination that has been wholeheartedly rejected by the Hindu orthodoxy. It is based entirely on a magical attitude toward the world, which does not harp on a rigid compartmentalization of spirit and matter, good and evil. Very likely this practice was one of the esoteric exports of India and the Far East.

One modern writer on magic, Louis T. Culling, seems to think that so-called sex magic stems from the Sufis and was transmitted through the secret society of the Templars and through alchemy.[8] Culling also maintained that these esoteric Sufi teachings survived, in modified form, the Inquisition and that they are found scattered in the works of Eliphas Levi, Gerard Encausse (Papus), and others. The most complete transmission is allegedly to be found in the Order of Oriental Templars (*Ordo Templi Orientis*), whose British branch was headed by Aleister Crowley. Crowley, who was described by the media as "the wickedest man alive" and by his mother as "the Beast," was one of the most original representatives of modern occultism. He was also one of the first to dabble in Tantric sex practices.

According to Culling, the practice of withholding ejaculation and thereby preserving one's vital energy is part of what he called Dianism, leaving the word itself unexplained. Dianism is apparently the second degree of the sexual magic taught by Crowley. In his curious book *Sex Magick,* Culling emphasizes that sexual magic must not be confused with *karezza,* as practiced by the short-lived Oneida Community founded by John

Humphrey Noyes in the mid-nineteenth century. In this com-
mune, every male member was married to every female member. It was incumbent on the men to practice what was termed
male continence, that is, *coitus reservatus. Karezza,* Culling observed, had "no psychologically effective method for prevent-
ing frustration because of the no climax rule."[9]

It is evident from Culling's description of Dianism that
this approach owes much to Tantrism.[10] The Tantric provenance
of sexual magic, as taught in more recent times, is completely
evident to readers of Aleister Crowley's works. However, Crowley himself can hardly be said to have observed the wisdom of
the Tantras. By his own description, he was a sexual obsessive
with a prodigious carnal appetite. The possibility of using sex
for magical purposes suggested itself to Crowley in a decisive
event in his life as a magician. It was in December of 1909 that
he experienced a vision that empowered him as a master in his
own right. The vision was triggered, as Colin Wilson revealed
in his excellent biography of Crowley, by an act of sodomy, in
which Crowley assumed the passive role.

From then on, Crowley appears to have channeled his sexual obsession into magical rituals with women and men alike.
When no suitable disciples or prostitutes were available, he
would not hesitate to engage in solitary masturbation. Strangely, Wilson remarked that these magical rituals were "not some
kind of excuse for sex."[11]

One of Crowley's magical sex rites is particularly telling as
a misguided effort to exploit the sex drive to achieve an altered
state of consciousness, which Donald Michael Kraig labeled
"eroto–comatose lucidity."[12] The ritual in question involves a
practitioner and several aides, usually of the opposite gender.
The function of these aides is to exhaust the practitioner's sexual
capacity "by every known means." If any of the aides tires, he or
she is at once replaced. Before long, the practitioner falls into a
sleep of exhaustion, which, however, he or she is not permitted
to continue. Instead, the aides continue to stimulate the practitioner sexually to arouse him or her from sleep, but they cease
their activities the moment he or she has returned to the waking
state. In due course, the magical practitioner will find himself
or herself in a semiconscious condition that is conducive to
clairvoyance and other psychic phenomena.

From a Taoist or a Tantric point of view, the price paid for
eroto–comatose lucidity is exorbitant, and the end result is

hardly worth the ordeal. The practice is said to have been invented by one of Crowley's students, but perhaps only a man of Crowley's sexual stamina and obsessiveness could have deemed it suitable as a magical device. In contrast to his tireless sexual exploits, Crowley's experiment in celibacy was a travesty. He was, however, bold enough to disclaim its merit as a spiritual orientation in its own right, whether as a permanent or as a periodic voluntary practice.

Even if Crowley lived and breathed magic, we can hardly overlook his sexual neurosis, whatever his ultimate goals and motivations may have been. Crowley is an example of an individual who should have steered clear of left-hand Tantrism. He tended to bring out the worst in his associates and is known to have exploited and devastated the lives of many of them.

THE REAWAKENING OF THE SEXUAL GODDESS IN NEO-PAGANISM

Sex and fertility rites as well as magical beliefs have been the backbone of the archaic cult of the *magna mater,* the ancestral Goddess. They are also an inalienable part of the religious movement of Neo-Paganism, which frequently revolves around the celebration of the Goddess.

Neo-Paganism has been an aspect of twentieth-century culture since the early 1960s. It is a motley movement comprising animistic, pantheistic, and polytheistic beliefs, as well as magical and religious practices that owe much to pre-Christian, so-called pagan sources, such as witchcraft and Druidism. As Margot Adler, one of the movement's widely respected spokeswomen, put it:

> Most Neo-Pagans sense an aliveness and "presence" in nature. . . . They share the goal of living in harmony with nature and they tend to view humanity's "advancement" and separation from nature as the prime source of alienation. They see *ritual* as a tool to end that alienation. [13]

While not all Neo-Pagans are Goddess-worshippers, many are. Those whose celebrations and worship revolve around the Horned God of antiquity acknowledge that he is the consort of the Great Goddess. All share in an earth-centered spirituality, which means a spirituality that pays reverence to embodiment and sexuality. This is commendable as far as it goes. However, there are those in the Neo-Pagan movement who criticize it for being too buttoned-down.[14]

Could it be that its participants are simply too self-conscious because they cannot shake their sexual and emotional inhibitions? Certainly as far as the women of the movement are concerned, this failure to fully embody the Dionysian spirit appears to be historically atypical. As Robert Lawlor wrote, not without some justification:

> Feminine sexuality, as it existed before the centuries of repression, is almost opposite to what modern women are programmed to experience in terms of their sexuality. It is recorded, even in European history prior to the Medieval witchhunts, that women express a boundless, lusty sexuality, one that far exceeds that of men.[15]

In his book *Earth Honoring,* from which the above quote is taken, Lawlor also referred to a recent sex survey that showed that men think about sex quite frequently—but, according to a complementary survey, not as frequently as women. This statistical finding is certainly not paralleled by any pronounced orgiastic trend in Neo-Paganism. In this respect, the Neo-Pagan movement is paradigmatic of most contemporary spiritual groups. Nor should we blame the AIDS scare alone for this state of affairs. Deeper cultural factors, involving massive repression, are unquestionably in operation here.

Still, Neo-Pagans are affirmative of sexuality, and not a few groups have incorporated sexual rituals. As Starhawk, a popular writer and lecturer on the subject, explained about the Goddess, who is a central image of Neo-Paganism:

> The law of the Goddess is love: passionate sexual love, the warm affection of friends, the fierce protective love of mother for child, the deep comradeship of the coven.[16]

To put Starhawk's remarks differently, the love of the Goddess is both *agape* and *eros.* Therefore the pagan worshipper does not, in theory at least, fear sensuousness. She or he is ready to approach the altar stripped of all masks, including garments concealing what are commonly considered the shameful parts.

As Starhawk noted, "the 'ecstasy of the spirit' is not separate from 'joy on earth.'"[17] This is again the Tantric ideal of the coessentiality of the bliss of liberation (*mukti*) and enjoyment (*bhukti*).

We have come full circle in our consideration of sexuality and spirituality. We began with the Great Goddess, the looming symbol for the numinous in the dim past of humanity, and conclude with modern pagan efforts to end our patriarchal civilization's repression of the feminine and to construct a new order in which heaven and earth, intellect and genitals are acknowledged as co-creative forces in our life. Some of these contemporary efforts appear as fumbling and as bizarre as those of earlier generations and cultures. Others, however, are clearly integrative and healing for individual and collectivity, thus deserving not only our full attention but our dedication.

CHAPTER 13

-❦-

The New Erotic Christianity

ALAN WATTS AND INCARNATIONAL THEOLOGY

Today, after almost 2,000 years of repression of what has been referred to as the lower human nature, Christianity is trying to return to a more wholesome, integrated viewpoint. Among the first to announce the new spirit was Alan W. Watts, an ex-Anglican priest, who became one of the most influential popularizers and promoters of the cultural encounter between East and West in the 1960s. One of the chapters of his book *Nature, Man and Woman* is entitled "Spirituality and Sexuality." It is a brief examination of the Christian dichotomy between Spirit and Nature and its alternative—a body-positive spirituality. Writing in 1958, Watts made the important (and humbling) observation that we simply do not know what the human being is, and that therefore we are likewise ignorant of human sexuality. He also remarked that man is a mystery to woman, just as woman is a mystery to man.[1]

In an earlier work, written when Watts was still a priest, he tried to find and revive the mystical spirit in Christianity. Understandably somewhat more cautious than in his later writings, he sought to develop a *philosophia perennis* out of Christian and non-Christian materials. In doing so, he avowed with great eloquence the kind of nondualist metaphysics that is characteristic of many mystics around the world. "Full of mysterious and infinite life," he wrote, "the Eternal Now lies beyond every concept and image, but is yet the source of all images. The very idea, the very word 'God' may indeed distract us in the process of realization because it is still a symbol, a concept, standing between us and the Reality—Now!"[2] In the context of such a philosophy, guilt has little or no place. Consequently we find Watts state rather boldly:

> The point which modern Church religion seems so far from under-standing is that a full and mature Christian morality can never be based on the sense of guilt; to far too great an extent organized Christianity thrives on the exploitation of this sense, appealing simply to man's pride and fear. . . . Real repentance, however, is not a self-regarding action; it is turning away from self and towards God.[3]

Watts went on to say that a new incarnational morality was needed that would seek to transform the world and the flesh rather than to deny either. The mystical realization of union with God was to be inclusive of all the normal human functions—from eating and drinking to having sexual inter-course. These functions, Watts explained, should be elevated, or "beautified." He wisely added that "those who expect religion to effect a complete spiritualization of body, mind, and emotion on the space-time level are indulging an absurd spiritual pride."[4]

Toward a Nonpuritan Christianity

As has been seen in an earlier chapter, our impulse toward sex-ual union enshrines the desire for transcendental union, the col-lapse of all opposites (*coincidentia oppositorum*), as mystics expe-rience it. This point was made by sociologist and priest Andrew M. Greeley in his popular book *Sexual Intimacy*. He wrote, "When a husband and wife . . . seek unity with one another, they are attempting to achieve in their union a perfection which exists permanently in God."[5] He added:

> . . . sexual hunger is not merely a hunger for the Absolute and the Real; it is also a hunger for union between the Male and the Female, which union exists permanently in God. In such a per-spective, it becomes possible to say that when a husband and wife who are deeply in love with each other reach the climax of their sexual orgasm, they have achieved something that is, in the strict sense of the word, "godlike," because they have temporarily fused the Male and the Female.[6]

How serious Greeley is about his erotic spirituality is made clear in the test case of the man and the woman who meet in an elevator and feel electrified by the possibility of sexual intercourse between them. Rather than dismissing this encounter as perverse and immoral and a springboard for sin, Greeley asserted that "they are in fact experiencing a touch of the divine unity." We can make sense of Greeley's theology and the above quotation only when we know that he understands the mystery of God as including the mystery of his/her androgyny.

In a subsequent book, entitled *Love and Play*, Greeley reiterated and consolidated his life-affirmative position. He tackled the mystery of sexuality from the angle of play and playfulness. Borrowing theologian Hugo Rahner's notion of the "playing God" (*Deus ludens*), Greeley stated:

> I take it as axiomatic that a sexual relationship from which all imagination and celebration has been removed is not a Christian relationship. It may very well be an admirable, praiseworthy, responsible, sensible way to live; the religion that underpins it— stoicism—has always been impressive, but it is not Christianity. Stoic sexuality—puritanism—is not Christian sexuality no matter how much it may claim to be.[7]

Lest he should still be misunderstood, he added:

> We may continue to be dull, but to the extent that we are dull we are false to the belief we profess.[8]

To back up his nonpuritan, joyous Christianity, Greeley referred to the theological concept of the spirit. He vividly characterized the spirit as a "whirling, twirling, dancing, darting poltergeist Deity, who flits and leaps, spins, and dives, dashes in madcap movement through the cosmos, flicking out sparks of creativity and vitality wherever he goes."[9] Indeed, the spirit embodies the principle of life, diversity, and overflowing richness. Given the spirit's playful presence in the universe, asked Greeley, how can Christians possibly believe that sex must be dead serious or, worse, sinful?

To be sure, Greeley did not equate playfulness with mere

hedonism. He acknowledged that for playful sex to be appropriate, it must occur in the context of a sustained complete human relationship based on the conviction that love is possible.

Such a full relationship necessarily includes an awareness that each person is, psychologically speaking, androgynous. As Carl Jung taught us, each man contains a feminine psychic component and each woman a masculine psychic component, though one or the other aspect may be obscured by ignorance and repression. The significance of this intrapsychic complementarity was explored by the British writer John Moore in his book *Sexuality and Spirituality,* which he opened with the observation that "the relationship between sexuality and spirituality is surely one of the strangest of all mazes."[10]

Moore took a developmental approach to his subject. He based his consideration on the fact that the human brain is lateralized into a left and a right hemisphere, each with its own characteristic functions. Idealizing somewhat those functions, he equated the left hemisphere with what are traditionally considered feminine and the right with masculine traits. He then furnished a catalog of characteristics for both feminine and masculine expressions.

We find such traits as *procreative, concrete, centrifugal, horizontal, divisive, imitative,* and *gregarious* on the feminine side and *creative/destructive, discrete, centripetal, vertical, integrative, original,* and *solitary* on the masculine side. Some of Moore's attributions make sense while others seem farfetched, and some may well offend feminist sensibilities.

Jeanne Block, a professor of human development at the University of California, found the labels *masculine* and *feminine* too loaded. She proposed to replace them with *agency* and *communion,* respectively. Thus, a woman who is ambitious or practical should not be considered masculine but "high in 'agency' characteristics." Block's innovative way of thinking was cited approvingly by theologian Dody H. Donnelly in her book *Radical Love.*[11] As Donnelly insisted, ridding our language of the baggage of exclusivist male words is not simply a feminist fad but an essential program for healing the rift between the genders. She sees such a course of action as integral to developing a sound spirituality.

It is clear from Donnelly's book that, for her, a sound spirituality must of necessity also be fully erotic:

Spirituality must be sexual if it is to be *human* spirituality. We love God either as ensexed and embodied creatures or not at all. We love God as humans who are men and women all the time in everything we do.

Why do some people want to keep the Spirit (God) in the parlor while making love in the bedroom? The best sources seem to suggest that God likes bedrooms, too. In fact—can we possibly emphasize it enough?—God *invented* the bedroom's activity. So making love can celebrate God's creativity in our own design as human lovers.[12]

A good portion of Donnelly's book is dedicated to spelling out just what erotic spirituality means. Here is another passage climaxing in a mystical exuberance that is rare among theologians:

God not only loves us in and through our sexuality but, of course, delights in our own human lovemaking. That love of beauty, union, and creativity is the sexual drive itself and God's gift. Sexuality is an aspect of our deeply human yearning for fulfillment and meaning, for God. In its total pervasion of our lives, *eros* is the source of life and fuels all our loves—including our love for God!

Through our unique personalities we're called to shine back to God the joyful experience of loving and being loved sexually and spiritually. That response may be simply our daily amazement, wondering, yearning, expectation, and stunned delight at nature's wondrous bounty of dazzling color, scent, and sound—God's daily wooing of our hearts. We know the Beloved is near, indeed, resident within us always. We see his blood upon the rose, in the diamond eye and flashing wing of bluebird, while the white night awes our timid, quivering souls.[13]

The indwelling of the Divine has traditionally often been conceived as an immaterial, even ethereal, presence. However, in terms of erotic mysticism, the notion of divine immanence makes sense only when it is understood as a concrete, bodily event. Peter Campbell and Edwin McMahon, two Catholic priests, succeeded in grounding theology by applying Eugene T. Gendlin's therapeutic method of focusing to the spiritual process. "There is support within our bodies for unitary consciousness,"[14] they stated in epitomizing their orientation, which they call bio-spirituality. They explained:

Theology speaks *about* God. But in order to appreciate the rich *humanistic* impact of such truths, one must draw on more experience than one can think in the mind. Body-knowing, then, when integrated with mind-knowing becomes a Rosetta Stone with which to unlock the hidden evolutionary significance of latent bio-spiritual clues hidden within the Judaeo-Christian tradition and, no doubt, within other religious traditions as well.[15]

Focusing is the art of bodily knowing, of employing feeling in appreciating real-life situations. The body carries felt meanings that go beyond the conceptual mind, and focusing means living *in* and *as* the whole body, not merely in the head and as the mind. Focusing requires that we allow our body to speak to us, that we become receptive to its messages. Since most of us are not truly happy, enlightened, or in communion with the Divine, we must assume that something is blocking out our happiness, enlightenment, or transcendental communion.

Through focusing, we can discover our fears and the other, largely unconscious, feeling preoccupations that prevent us from total organismic integration. Bodily integration manifests in the ability to accept one's present condition, to love oneself. All too often, those practicing Christian *caritas* and *agape* are incapable of self-love. As theologian Paul Tillich remarked:

> An *agape* in which there is no *eros* has no warmth. *Eros* without *agape* lacks discrimination. They belong together and cannot be severed.[16]

In a similar vein, Campbell and McMahon said:

> Christian spirituality has yet to resolve this split between loving one's neighbor and loving one's self. Churches still do not understand that all the preaching and teaching of theological truths and ideals will not make this problem go away. The neglect of body consciousness is an enormous obstacle both to human maturing as well as to spiritual growth. . . . Any new paradigm for Western spirituality must actually take a leap into body consciousness rather than simply talking about it theologically.[17]

Bio-spirituality, then, is about the discovery of the Mystery not only as it awes us outside ourselves but also as it reveals itself *as* ourselves. Since the mystery of existence is larger than our preconceived notions of reality, our experience of it is apt to be full of surprises. Campbell and McMahon therefore regard the availability for surprise as a necessary disposition for spiritual growth. This availability goes hand in hand with the ability to laugh at oneself and at life. As they commented:

> Humor and playfulness are somehow part of transcendence. They are one more way the human person says "Yes" to being within some greater reality. They are an unrationalized, organismic admission that the limited center and sense of self are *not* the total picture.[18]

MATTHEW FOX AND THE EROTIC CHRIST

The importance of the concept and experience of Mystery and its connection with humor and play was recently acknowledged by Matthew Fox, a Catholic priest and spokesman for creation spirituality. In his controversial book *The Coming of the Cosmic Christ,* Fox made the point that ritual worship must be playful and joyful to have a transformational effect on the celebrant. "If not at worship," he dared to ask, "where else in our culture is there space ample enough and relaxed enough to invite the divine child out to play?"[19] In his view, playfulness is an integral part of *eros,* and *eros* "belongs at the heart of worship."

Fox, who agreed to a year of silence under pressure from his superiors, has proven a strong advocate of an erotic spirituality within Christianity. He made these astute observations:

> When religion is anthropocentric and lacks a cosmology, it has very little to tell us that is good news about sexuality, which is so special a gift of the cosmos. When this happens, culture secularizes sexuality and misuses it. Pornography substitutes for mysticism. (In America today we are spending seven billion dollars yearly on pornography.) . . .
>
> If I were asked to name in one word the message I have received from my religion regarding sexuality over the forty-five years of my life I would answer: *regret.* I believe that the Western church, following in the spirit of St. Augustine, basically regrets the fact that we are sexual, sensual creatures. . . . But there is another tradition besides St. Augustine's regarding our bodiliness and deep sexual natures—the tradition of *praise.* It is time that the

voice of the churches joined the voices of the other creatures to praise the Creator for the surprising and imaginative gift of our sexuality.[20]

Fox availed himself of the erotic imagery of Solomon's *Song* to develop his ideas about the Cosmic Christ—the Being who "can be both female and male, heterosexual and homosexual," and who "rejoices and is intimately at work and play when lovers make love."[21] The Cosmic Christ, in Fox's vision, is also the Being who "is wounded when people are victims of rape, impotence, sterility, or sexual scapegoating" or "saddened when the mystery and mysticism of sexuality is reduced to moralizing about sexual acts."[22]

With good reason, Fox proposed that Solomon's *Song* "may well contain within its profound treatment of sexual love as divine love an entire spirituality of sexuality that could offer a new starting point . . . for a theology for sexuality today."[23] It has been noted in an earlier chapter how strongly the *Song of Songs* influenced the love mystics of medieval Christianity. Yet even though the love mystics made use of erotic metaphors and sensuous language, their spirituality followed the ascetic ideal of chastity. Fox has a more embodied, sexual spirituality in mind—a sacred sexuality that would mirror more faithfully the quite earthy spirituality of Solomon's *Song.*

While one may not agree with Fox's visionary theology on all points, his positive orientation toward sexuality and creativity is to be wholeheartedly applauded. It is courageous and imaginative efforts of this kind that, in the long run, will restore Christians and those influenced by the Christian heritage to a sounder way of relating to their body, their genitals, and their sexual and erotic relationships—in fact, to all their relationships.

III

The Challenge of Sacred Sex Today

❧

CHAPTER 14

Sex As Energy and Communion

THE SEXUAL THRESHOLD BETWEEN THE SECULAR
AND THE SACRED

The preceding chapters have covered some of the countless manifestations of erotic spirituality. Invariably a key element in the diverse traditions that were surveyed has proven to be the notion of sex as energy. This is the important idea that sex involves more than the solid physical body, which is capable of producing pleasure through nervous stimulation. Thus, in the earliest periods of human history, sexuality was linked with the power of the Goddess and was considered to have magical potency. Later, sexuality was understood as the play between God and Goddess on the human level—again implying an encounter extending beyond the flesh.

This archaic belief, originally associated with neolithic fertility rites, survived in Chinese Taoism and Indian Tantrism, where it acquired primarily a psychological significance. In these later philosophies sexuality was viewed as an expression of the larger power animating the mortal frame. The same fundamental belief has been discovered in other religious traditions. In medieval Europe, the troubadours and love mystics aspired to translate the native sexual drive into a psychological potency of the highest order. This led the troubadours to a chivalric idealization helping them to transcend the compulsions of the flesh, and it kindled in the love mystics an emotional upliftment that, in the state of mystical ecstasy, enabled them to transcend the body itself.

To speak of sex as energy means to acknowledge that the

human body is arising within the vast dimension of psycho-somatic energy, which makes up the quantum reality of physical existence. According to the animistic world view, which we in-herited from the Stone Age, everything is ensouled, or alive with energy. Traditional concepts such as *prana, ch'i, od, mana, orenda, manito, tirawa, imunu, ntum,* and *megbe* all imply that there is a dimension to life that is dynamic or energetic and that has primacy over the material realm.

That energy is characteristically equated with the psyche, or an aspect of it—hence the term *animism,* which is derived from the Latin word *anima,* meaning "soul" or "spirit." The world is thus ensouled, filled with mysterious life-force. From the legends and art of so-called primitives we can gather that they not merely believed in, but actually saw, this universal energy.

There is no place for such a notion in modern science, whether hard or soft. Ideas such as *prana* or *ch'i* are judged pre-scientific mumbo-jumbo by most scientists. Yet, luckily, there are a few intrepid researchers who beg to differ. Since the advent of quantum physics, which tells us that our apparently solid body is mostly empty but energy-filled space, they have more of a chance of being heard.

THE EROTIC IMPLICATIONS OF EINSTEIN'S THEOREM

Einstein's famous formula $E = mc^2$ has far-reaching implica-tions, which we as yet barely acknowledge in our day-to-day ex-istence. His theorem that unbelievable amounts of energy are packed into matter should have long revolutionized the very way we think about ourselves and human life as a whole. Unfor-tunately, because the implications are so profound and require such a total reorientation, we have been slow in accepting them both as a culture and on the personal level.

Einstein's formula vindicates the crucial doctrine of the an-cient spiritual traditions, namely that what we perceive as our solid body is nothing but structured *energy.* Consider, for exam-ple, how when we clap our hands or pinch our arms, there is sound and pain. Are these effects merely an illusion? Do we not walk on *terra firma* rather than fall right through the ground on which we stand? Is our everyday experience all wrong? Or was

Einstein out of his mind? None of these is the case, but our customary view of things is definitely limited. Beyond that, it has assumed the power of an insidious ideology that effectively keeps us shut out from the hidden energetic dimension of reality.

Einstein published his revolutionary findings about the nature of space and time in 1905, laying the foundations for modern quantum physics. As futurologist David Loye stated in his book *The Spinx and the Rainbow,* the new physics is a psychophysics, and its first fundamental tenet is that *everything* is energy, that all material forms are simply coagulated energy waves.[1] Loye also specified the new psychophysics' second tenet, namely that this principal energy is the common bond between all things, however varied they may be. A third tenet, he noted, is that the human mind is the bridge between the world of material multiplicity and energetic unity.

There is a rare neurological condition in which the person has lost his or her proprioceptive sense of the body. In other words, he or she is unable to sense the presence of the body, experiencing it instead as though it were dead wood. Many people in our modern Western society are in a condition that approximates that neurological disease: They are largely unaware that they are bodily presences. They dwell in the mind, in their thoughts and intentions, but not in their kinesthetic sensations.

For instance, a friend confided to me recently that during her first few rolfing sessions it became utterly clear to her how, most of the time, she was completely unaware of her feet.[2] To one degree or another this obliviousness to our physicality is true of most of us. We are trained to place our attention outside our bodily environment. Even in sports we seldom come to enjoy the actual sensations in our body; we instead compete, which is a social event requiring us to project our attention outside. When people first learn to relax they find it very difficult to feel, or sense, certain parts of their body.

We need to reach a here-and-now experience of the presence of the body in order to experience its energetic nature. In deep relaxation, we may experience vibrations, streamings, and all kinds of other unusual energetic processes, which may even frighten us at first.

Our civilization encourages us to neglect the *lived* body, even to ignore and deprecate it. This dovetails with the inherited

Christian ideology that the flesh is corrupt and that we must therefore place our attention on the Eternal, the paradise beyond the finite human body and its concerns. Even those who dismiss Christian theology and religion are frequently still under the spell of the vanished body, or what philosopher Drew Leder called the "dys-appearing body."[3] We are alienated from our own bodies, and in fact many of us deliberately disown them.

In his brilliant book *Coming to Our Senses,* Morris Berman exposed the historical roots of our society's pathological attitude toward the body.[4] One of his most penetrating observations concerns the relationship between this attitude and our neurotic attachment to ideology. He remarked:

> When you've lost your body, you need an ism. From there it is a short step to seeing other isms as life-threatening, and to seeing the Other as an enemy.[5]

To paraphrase Berman, when we no longer feel the body's pulsating reality, we rely on the mind to create intellectual certainties for us. In this sense, ideologies are substitutes for our primary experience of somatic aliveness. By contrast, when we consciously dwell *in* and *as* our body, we experience the body differently, and this radically transforms our relationship to the world, which is our larger body. Then we cease to rely exclusively on ideological crutches and trust more the innate wisdom of the body.

What also happens is that we begin to experience the energetic dimension of corporeal existence and find that the body is not an inert lump after all. This becomes especially obvious in our sexual life, which tends to be where energy is expressed most directly. Then we experience concretely what psychoanalysis conceives in rather abstract terms as *libido*.

PSYCHIATRIC INTERLUDE: FROM FREUDIAN LIBIDO TO REICHIAN ORGONE

Freud borrowed the term *libido* and its underlying idea that sex is energy from a fellow sexologist. The word stems from the Latin and means "desire," "passion," or "lust." This pivotal psychoanalytical concept was from the outset one of the more problematic aspects of Freud's theories. He defined *libido* as "a variable quantitative force, by which processes and transformations of sexual excitation could be measured."[6] He further understood it as being separate from psychic energy in general and as having a distinct chemistry of its own. Sexual excitation, he noted, is supplied by all bodily parts, not merely the famous erogenous zones.

Freud made a distinction between a *somatic* and a *psychic* manifestation of the libido, speculating that the one can be transformed into the other. He also held apart an *object* libido from an *ego* libido. The former is libido flowing out to an object (one's lover or a substitute); the latter is directed toward oneself and is narcissistic, as experienced by the infant who is entirely focused on his or her own pleasure.

When libido cannot be converted into pleasurable experience, it flips over into anxiety and, if this becomes a pattern, neuroses and psychoses occur through the act of repression. This is a simplified view of what amounts to a fairly complex theory, which, moreover, underwent a number of modifications in the course of Freud's long professional life and, later, at the hands of his students.

The libido concept was modeled on nineteenth-century mechanistic ideology. For Freud, the libido runs like liquid through a system of pipes. Through traumas it gets fixated, which is analogous to a kink in a pipe cutting off the supply. The libido is a current that charges or discharges neurons, yet Freud and his collaborators never identified the precise physiological correlates of this notion.

The Freudian libido is a heuristic construct, not a living reality. The same holds true of Carl Gustav Jung's extended use of the concept: He understood the libido not merely as sexual energy but as psychic energy in general.[7] It was another of Freud's students, the ingenious Wilhelm Reich, who sought to give the libido notion the empirical anchorage it lacked. He greatly elaborated Freud's ideas on the dynamics of sexual energy, maintaining that the repression of trauma is kept alive in the suppression of sexual feelings, the psychological armoring of the body, and the blocking of orgasm.

Reich was very interested in—some critics say obsessed with—orgasm, which he studied in depth long before Masters and Johnson. He insisted that orgasm normally produces only

an incomplete discharge of psychosexual energy. This then
leads to a progressive congestion and, in due course, pathological manifestations such as neuroses and sadomasochism. Reich
sought to prevent these blockages and their unsavory consequences through total orgasm.

For Reich the libido was an analytical abstraction of an actual biophysical reality, which he called the orgone.[8] This neo-
logism is a composite of the words *organism* and *orgasm*. The
orgone, in Reich's definition, is a universal fluid that is not only
present, in varying concentration, in the organism but in the
cosmos as a whole. He believed that orgone is in constant motion, is nonentropic and responsible for the creation of matter,
and serves as the medium for electromagnetic and gravitational
phenomena. Reich further believed that orgone energy can be
made visible under certain conditions and measured with oscil-
lographs.

Beyond that, Reich believed that orgone could be accumulated by means of certain devices, such as his infamous orgone
box. He spent several hours with Einstein, demonstrating his
accumulator, but his hope of winning Einstein's support was
soon dashed. The great physicist, like so many others, could not
accept Reich's explanations of the demonstrated effects. Reich's
work became increasingly eccentric and threatening to the medical establishment, finally unleashing the fury of the Food and
Drug Administration. Like so many true visionaries, Reich was
misunderstood, maligned, and persecuted. He died in prison,
having defied the powerful Food and Drug Administration.

In presenting his orgone idea, Reich unwittingly reiterated
an ancient teaching that sees the universe filled by a superfluid,
called *prana* in Sanskrit and *ch'i* in Chinese. However, unlike
Jung, Reich had no spiritual interests and so did not pursue these
traditional connections. Doing so might have prevented him
from making some of his more extreme claims, such as those in
his later thinking in which orgone became almost a God substitute. Today, new findings on life-energy at least partly vali-
date Reich's research.[9] Taken together, investigations of this
principle—including Reich's research—have yielded an impressive body of data that seems to confirm that there is indeed such
a thing as a field constituted of bio-energy. This goes a long way
toward corroborating the energy concepts of such erotic-
spiritual teachings as Taoism and Tantrism.

Where Reich and the Eastern sex-positive traditions part

company is in his overevaluation of orgasm. An apostle of total orgasm, he failed to appreciate that the psychosexual energy can be harnessed for a purpose that exceeds bodily and psychological well-being. It is one thing to be able to experience full orgasm and the free flow of sexual energy in one's body and quite another to marshal that freely flowing energy for the spiritual process.

SEX AND EVOLUTIONARY ENERGY

From time immemorial, the human race has been preoccupied with sex. This peculiar preoccupation has by no means been purely physiological, as a means of ensuring the survival of our species. On the contrary, reproduction has become an almost secondary facet of a much broader symbolic concern with sex. The fact that our body's anatomy manifests either male or female characteristics (and very rarely is hermaphroditic) has served as a model for structuring our world both socially and cosmologically in an almost bewildering diversity of binary combinations. Furthermore, the relatively accessible experience of orgasmic oblivion has served as an encouragement for rich speculations about, and a surfeit of techniques for, the ecstatic transcendence of those binary biological and cultural patterns.

Today, in daily practice, sex is frequently divorced from reproduction, irrespective of the antediluvian position in which religious fundamentalism has entrenched itself. The formula that sex is intended solely for reproduction has lost credibility for most of us. We are obliged to ask: What is the purpose of sex? Does it have a purpose beyond reproduction? Is there a higher evolutionary agenda into which it fits? These questions were posed half a century ago by the writer and social critic Gerald Heard.

Heard dismissed the mechanistic view of scientism, which takes sex as the end product of evolution (procreation securing the survival of a species). Instead he argued very ably that the phenomena of pain and of sexual lust are signs that evolution has not used up all its energy. According to Heard, our heightened sensitivity to pain and our seemingly insatiable sexual appetite suggest a huge reservoir of evolutionary energy stored in our bodies.

Orgasm was, for Heard, a counter-evolutionary habit. He

understood it as "an uprush of primary energy which over-
charges and so dissipates or divides consciousness."[10] Addressing our addiction to orgasm, he commented:

> Modern man's incessant sexuality is not bestial: rather it is a psy-
> chic hemorrhage. He bleeds himself constantly because he fears
> mental apoplexy if he can find no way of releasing his huge
> charge of nervous energy. Meanwhile the entertainment indus-
> try is largely devised with the express purpose of keeping his
> veins open; a hot bath in which he may die painlessly. The trag-
> edy of our education is that today it tells us nothing of the
> methods whereby creative catharsis might be attained. This
> tragedy is all the more serious because at the very time that edu-
> cation has become completely ignorant of such knowledge, our
> species for lack of it is in danger of staggering down into extinc-
> tion. For, without that knowledge, we must oscillate between
> the *tedium vitae* of sex exhaustion and the frantic destructiveness
> of the Puritan repression which ends in the monomaniac mili-
> tarists.[11]

In order to restore individual and social sanity, Heard saw it
as essential that we carefully harness the evolutionary energy
that is otherwise squandered in orgasmic release.[12] He proposed
that a synthesis of Yoga, Vedanta, and Quakerism might prove
viable in this radical reorientation. Today we would want to see
the inclusion of one or the other form of body therapy, which
involves the invisible dimension of energy.

While Heard's evolutionary speculations about sexuality
are germane, his opinion that orgasm is necessarily dissipative is
too one-sided. As has been noted in earlier chapters, orgasm can
also prove a portal through which we can slip into the wondrous
realm of bliss, or ecstatic self-transcendence.

SPIRITUAL WORK WITH THE PSYCHOCOSMIC ENERGY

A considerable part of any practical spirituality relates to the invisible or energetic dimension of existence. In our society, with
its emphasis on visual proof, the invisible—insofar as it is not
quantifiable—is widely decried and denied. Thus too many of
us live a truncated life, cut off from our invisible roots, including our own unconscious and the whole realm of the spiritual or
sacred. Hence the signal importance of inner work, whether it

takes the form of a traditional discipline such as Taoism or Tantrism or some contemporary therapy.

Working with the psychosomatic energy—by means of visualization, meditation, or controlled breathing—can put us more directly in touch with the mystery of our own larger embodiment. Psychosomatic energy is the bridge between the visible and the sacred, between microcosm and macrocosm, as well as between sexuality and spirituality, for it is a field that extends far beyond our bodies and connects us to the cosmos at large. By becoming more fully aware of the dynamics of that energy, our consciousness is supplied with the charge that is necessary to break through the confining walls of ordinary perception. It can help us become conscious of our larger environment or "body"—the hidden reality celebrated in all the esoteric traditions.

Psychiatrist Gerald G. May warned, however, that such energy work is not only difficult but potentially very dangerous, if undertaken without expert guidance.[13] There is much truth in this. Nevertheless, it is vitally important that we become aware of the existence of this form of energy and the possibility of working with it.

Basically, the challenge confronting us is to unlearn our ingrained ways of thinking and feeling about the world as if it were a distant place from which we were isolated, as well as to learn new responses—namely, to experience reality not as a conglomerate of spatial solids but as an infinite web of energy that manifests the miracle of our familiar space–time world. This view is not only more commensurate with actual reality but also far more exciting. It opens up countless new possibilities of relating to the world and to other beings, for we can now take into account their hidden depths. Far from becoming more anonymous, other beings assume uniqueness. While we see more of them, we can also see beyond their individuality to the all-comprehensive glorious Mystery in which they emerge and into which they ultimately disappear again.

By consistently working with the psychosomatic energy as it is accessible to us through the body, we are able to literally, not merely metaphorically, see beyond the visible spectrum of light. This is the art of clairvoyance, which has very ancient roots. As the Swiss cultural philosopher Jean Gebser hypothesized, it is quite likely that our earliest forebears were naturally psychic, capable of clairvoyance and clairaudience.[14]

With the rise of the rational consciousness, which is the characteristic cognitive mode of our contemporary Western civilization, these psychic abilities gradually became submerged. Today only a few individuals are born with these gifts, though in emergency situations many people discover to their amazement that they are capable of astonishing psychic feats. [15] As we reclaim our connection to the invisible, we also recover our ability to function consciously on levels other than the material realm. Above all, we give ourselves the opportunity to rediscover the sacred and, ultimately, our spiritual identity beyond space–time.

SEXUAL COMMUNION

An obvious way of working with the psychosomatic energy is through the energy mobilized in sexual play. As we have seen, this was in fact precisely the approach espoused by the esoteric traditions of Tantrism and Taoism. However, their orientation has frequently been misunderstood. In those schools of thought, psychosomatic energy is not accumulated or manipulated merely to serve the programs of the ego-personality; rather, the primary purpose of traditional paths is to use that energy in order to transcend the divisive ego.

Thus, sacred sexuality is not about energy play or sexual intercourse per se but about communing or identifying with the ultimate Reality, the Divine. This is a decisive distinction. For the spiritual practitioner, sexual intercourse is an opportunity to encounter the sacred dimension, which surpasses the individual man or woman just as it surpasses all other manifest forms. The bliss arising from the sexual union is not orgasmic pleasure but the innate delight of the primordial Androgyne, the ultimate Male/Female, the God/Goddess.

Almost three thousand years ago, the Indian sage Yajnavalkya instructed his wife Maitreyi that the wife is dear to the husband not because of external attributes but because of the Self, the *atman*. [16] In other words, love that wells up from the depth of one's being reaches to the depth of another's being. Like a rainbow, it has no graspable beginning or terminal point, but we can see and enjoy it. Such love is an expression of the bliss of Reality itself.

Because that original bliss is not dependent on any external or internal factors but is the eternal condition of the universe, it can be realized with or without sexual intercourse. According to the *Gospel of Thomas,* an early gnostic text, Jesus is said to have taught that one enters the Kingdom of God "when you make the inner as the outer, and the outer as the inner, and the upper as the lower, and when you make male and female into a single one, so that the male shall not be male and the female [shall not] be female."[17]

When erotic spirituality, or sacramental sexuality, is successful the gender distinctions on which it is based are suspended, for when there is ecstasy, all opposites coincide. There is no "I" and "Thou," no male and female. The original Reality is a symbiotic whole. The person who has awakened to that Reality is thereby rendered whole. Sexual communion is a way of celebrating that wholeness.

Of course, the ensexed body does not cease to exist in ecstasy. To transcend does not mean to evaporate; rather, our body image is widened to include all other bodies. We become the magnificent body of the universe itself, the total field of existence. It is the mind-made categories that vanish to make room for that direct realization of what there really *is.*

Thus, spiritual realization is somatic to the highest degree. It is ultimate embodiment, not a ghostly state of being. But the perceived body of the great ecstatics is no longer knowable by any ordinary or even extraordinary means. The mind is too puny and its technical extensions are too feeble to capture the splendor of the cosmic body in its entirety. There remains only mystical identification, awe, and compassion.

CHAPTER 15

❧

Toward an Erotic Spirituality for Today

COMING DOWN TO EARTH

Sex as sacramental transcendence, as has been seen, has an impressively long history. It is a history of rare collective insights and personal accomplishments as well as experiential cul-de-sacs and outright failures. Sacramental sex, as the Tantras tell us, is a path riddled with dangers. It calls for a "heroic" (*vira*) person, who is not only virile but also self-disciplined. All too often, what is ostensibly sacred sex turns out to be little more than concupiscence, without a trace of holiness.

The greatest pitfall associated with sacred sexuality is that ecstasy is made into a goal of the ego-personality, which is then pursued with an exploitive insensitivity that violates the personhood of others and, ultimately, of oneself. This error is understandable enough. After all, well-intentioned neophytes, willing as they are to forgo the flimsy pleasure of orgasm, need something to look forward to. But this utilitarian attitude is self-defeating, because it fortifies the ego that is to be transcended. The realization of bliss (*ananda*), which is the promised bloom of sacred sexuality, cannot arise while the ego principle is firmly ensconced in the body-mind. The desire for transcendence must not be propelled by egoic motivations. Rather, it must be guided by the ideal of surrendering everything we *seem* to be so that, paradoxically, we can become what we truly *are*.

All too often, especially in the West, sacred sex—like meditation—is used as a means of self-fulfillment rather than

self-transcendence. The brief orgasmic thrill is renounced in
favor of a more subtle hedonism, but hedonism nonetheless. It
is easy enough to get addicted to the good bodily sensations and
heightened feeling states generated by Tantra-like sexual practices. However, if we are honest with ourselves, we will admit
that they are not the great bliss spoken of in the traditional
scriptures.

An excellent thought experiment, which proves this point
very quickly, is to picture yourself as experiencing those de-
lightful sensations—and *nothing but* those sensations—on and
on and on, until the end of time and beyond. Would you choose
this state over any other experience, or would you suspect even-
tually succumbing to boredom? Even the slightest hesitation in
your response would be telling. Only authentic bliss, which occurs already at the end of time and beyond, is utterly desirable;
from within it, anything else is simply an unthinkable option.

The Canadian historian Morris Berman made some comments that are pertinent to our present consideration. He wrote:

> The real goal of a spiritual tradition should not be ascent, but
> openness, vulnerability, and this does not require great experi-
> ences but, on the contrary, very ordinary ones. Charisma is *easy;*
> presence, self-remembering, is terribly difficult, and where the
> real work lies.[1]

Spirituality, then, is not primarily about altered states of
consciousness, however lofty and personally desirable they may
be. It is about embodiment and grounding, or, as some theologians would put it, the incarnation of the spirit. The challenge is
not to go out of the body but to realize that it is the temple of the
sacred. This realization can be understood in psychological
terms as the pursuit of what Abraham Maslow called meta-
values in the fully embodied condition.[2] These higher values revolve around the enhancement of our being, as embodied in
such ideals as wholeness, unselfish love, creativity, and spontaneity.

The Hindu tradition knows of superhuman types called
descents, or *avataras,* who are deemed incarnations of the Divine. They are very special beings who, like Jesus the Christ,
come down to earth to purify the world. The Hindus are awaiting the coming of the *avatara* Kalki; the Buddhists are expecting

the Buddha Maitreya; the Jews are yearning for the prophesied Messiah; some Moslems are praying for the coming of the *mahdi;* and the Christian world is hoping for the return of the Christ.

Without wishing to affirm or deny any of these millennarian beliefs, today the real challenge is that we must *all* become *avataras.* There is nothing sacrilegious about this notion. After all, the great adepts of Hinduism, Buddhism, Judaism, Islam, and Christianity all exhort us to follow their example: to transcend space-time and become the universal Body and to be present in the world as a benign influence. So long as we place our faith in a single individual to save this world from itself, we can always justify our moral and spiritual inertia. Salvation psychology has dominated our Western civilization for two millennia. Meanwhile the clock of our personal destiny and of our collective fate is ticking away.

The question is: How do we relate to our own inevitable death, and how do we relate to the growing threat to our species and our home planet? Waiting without taking action is clearly not the answer. We are today called to take practical steps toward our own spiritual transformation and the transformation of our society. This task begins with the ordinary.

The belief that spirituality is about extraordinary feats stems from the ascetic tradition, which characteristically defined itself in opposition to ordinary life. We no longer need to subscribe to this one-sided perspective, which is rooted in the patriarchal world view. Heaven is not separated from Earth by an impermeable membrane. Reality—or the Divine or the Self— is not miles apart from our ordinary state. It is what the Swiss philosopher Jean Gebser called the ever-present origin, the *tao,* which underlies all the psychic states of our waxing and waning consciousness.[3] We merely need to switch our inner focus to consciously sense ourselves immersed in that condition to the point where we *become* it. This is as simple as turning a key. A friend of mine, who spent many years with a spiritual teacher, discovered this point for herself in 1967, at the age of forty-four:

> At the time I was enormously busy and having all kinds of responsibilities. In addition, I was doing a spiritual exercise that I found very difficult indeed. It involved seven voluntary actions

that had to be performed simultaneously. I was to repeat this exercise seven times but never managed to do it more than twice without faltering. I got very frustrated with myself. One night I went to bed very late. I was quite exhausted. Everything seemed just too much. In desperation I prayed, saying that if there was any part of me that knew more and was more capable than I, this was the moment to take over. I had reached the limits of my abilities.

That night I woke around 2 o'clock. I found myself in another state. There was no conscious passage from my ordinary waking consciousness to that condition of fullness or wholeness, which may have lasted for thirty minutes to an hour. In that condition, everything seemed so simple and easy, and my previous struggle and inner conflict seemed like a joke to me. I felt the strong impulse to run out into the streets and tell everyone that life was in reality quite uncomplicated and joyous. I resisted the temptation to wake my husband, who peacefully slept next to me.

Then, as suddenly and imperceptibly as I had entered into that condition, I slipped out of it again. I continued to feel a certain fullness but I also felt helpless. I had no idea how the transition had occurred. I thought there must be a key to it all. In fact, I was so convinced that there must be a simple explanation for this switch that I even started looking for a physical key in and around my bed! As I collected myself more, I realized the absurdity of my search. All day long, however, I kept on asking myself the same question: How am I connected to that condition?

The next night I awoke again at the same time, and once more I found myself in that state of fullness from which nothing was absent. This time I slightly touched my husband, and he woke up. As I was tracing the contour of his hand with my finger, I *knew* his hand. It was the hand of all my past lovers and all the lovers I would know in the future. I felt I *knew* my husband completely. We spontaneously made love. It was very passionate.

When I orgasmed, I found that the orgasmic sensation was not a localized point but a line that continued evenly for a long time. I realized that our lovemaking was so wonderful because I was feeling free and happy within myself. I understood that ordinarily our love life is so impoverished because we are not in that state of fullness. But, as was also clear to me, we could always be in that condition because it is our true condition.

Later that day, my husband and I discussed some ridiculous

problems and, before I knew it, I had lost that state of fullness. This experience made me realize how the key has to do with psychic balance and harmony and, of course, the transcendence of the ego.

FINDING THE SACRED IN THE ORDINARY

The Kingdom of God is indeed near. It is the turn of a key away. We do not need to go anywhere—especially not up—to open that hidden portal; rather, we must be willing to be fully present *in* and *as* our body. We must also be prepared to acknowledge and demonstrate, through compassionate action, that we share our somatic reality with countless other beings with whom we are interconnected and interdependent. Contemporary spirituality is, then, meaningful only to the degree that it is ecological in the broadest sense of the term. The connecting link between each individual's body-mind and the multitude of others is *eros,* love-desire.

The ecological spirituality called for today is founded in a deep recognition of the unity of life—a unity that is celebrated in the act of love, whether sexual or erotic in the larger sense. *Eros* is connective energy par excellence. Through erotic passion we overcome our habitual egoic insularity and reach out into the core of other beings. Blazing *eros* recognizes no barriers; it is the organic impulse toward wholeness. That wholeness is the holy, the sacred. The word *holy* is etymologically related to "whole," both of which refer to a condition of completeness or fullness. Psychotherapist and contemplative Bruce Davis put it beautifully thus:

> Holiness is present at every dawn and at every sunset. . . . Holiness is in the rain, the snow, every season for the person who embraces his or her own seasons . . . . Holiness is in the smile we wear and the tears we shed. Holiness is in the smile we appreciate on others and their tears that we care for.[4]

We have become accustomed to thinking of the sacred as something that is *apart,* or wholly other. We have banished sexuality to the bedroom and, in a similar compartmentalizing fashion, treat sacredness as a matter for the church or the temple.

Both attitudes are the product of our stark rationalistic intelligence, which strains at squeezing the ultimately incomprehensible universe into airtight categories. Yet the universe keeps bulging out, upsetting all our individual pet beliefs and the models of science. We can always ignore or explain away the abundantly existing anomalies, but we can do so only at a loss. Thus, we have for over a century tried to systematically demythologize and profanize the world, thereby depriving ourselves of the very marrow of human life.

The priesthood of scientism has declared the demise of God (not merely the male projection but the idea of the Divine itself), and it has likewise ousted the notions of consciousness, psyche, and soul, throwing generations into confusion and existential despair. Scientistic ideologues, technocrats, and commercial manipulators have even subverted our reverence for the planet that feeds us, indoctrinating us into believing that the Earth is an inexhaustible resource to be exploited at will.

We have forgotten how to sense and respond to the sacred within and around us. Some 2,600 years ago, Thales of Milet said that the world is chockfull of divinity. We are hardly able to imagine such a possibility. Yet Thales' idea, which undoubtedly reflected his daily experience, has the support of many religious traditions. It is even underpinned by certain interpretations of modern quantum physics. As physicist–philosopher Fred Alan Wolf writes:

> Quantum mechanics, perhaps more clearly than any religion, points to the unity of the world. It also points to something beyond the physical world. It matters little which interpretation you choose—parallel universes, Feynman paths of action, qwiffs [quantum wave functions] that flow and pop, or consciousness as the creator. All of these interpretations point to the mystery of the physical world from a nonphysical perspective.
>
> We might say that God's will is exercised in the world of the qwiff, the quantum wave function. . . . It is a world of paradox and utter confusion for human, limited intelligence. For it is a world where a thing both occupies a single place at a single time and occupies an infinite number of places at the same time.[5]

Fortunately, our present era is trying to correct the ideological absurdities we inherited from nineteenth-century scientific materialism. Nowadays many endeavors are afoot to restore the sacred to postmodern life. Of course, their success depends largely on what we as individuals are willing to do about our moral and spiritual life and whether we can realize the sacred in the midst of the most ordinary circumstances: washing dishes; eating dinner; commuting to work; tending our children; recycling paper, glass, and plastic; saving water, electricity, and gasoline; making love; and accepting and expressing our feelings.

Jungian analyst June Singer calls these practices "sweeping the temple." In her book *Seeing Through the Visible World,* she explains that we do not need to go on an external pilgrimage to find the sacred. We can stay in place, for there is sacred space within and all around us, but we need to do some excavation work to gain access to it. As Singer puts it:

> This involves clearing away the overwhelming trash and debris of self-imposed concerns, petty resentments and angers, the need to prove oneself right, mean competitiveness, little lies, taking advantage of people who are weaker and more defenseless, piling up money for its own sake, and all the other aids devised to puff up the ego. Practicing dying would be a method that leads to recognizing the futility of such efforts. The first step, however, is to clean house, inside and out.[6]

"Inner work," emphasizes June Singer, "begins with the body, whether we recognize this fact or not."[7] This seems like a platitude, yet how many spiritual seekers have struggled in vain to realize truth, God, or higher knowledge by escaping from what they termed the prison of the body! In treating the body as an enemy, the antagonist of the spirit, they doomed themselves to experiences of an amputated God. They failed to see that the body is part of the great Mystery. We can learn from their mistake.

In body-positive spirituality, body and world are rendered transparent. They become like glass, pervious to the ordinary light. The body reveals itself to be a hologram in which the universe is captured—a vision that is at once playful and humorous. We are the Home we seek—chockfull with divinity.

GOD, GODDESS, AND INTIMACY

We are witnessing an astonishing revival of interest in esotericism and mythology. Psychology, which was previously disfigured by its denial of the existence of consciousness, is proving instrumental in this development. We owe an enormous debt to C. G. Jung, who paved the way for the largely felicitous wedding of psychology to mythology. Jung was the first of Freud's disciples to distance himself from Freudian mechanistic ideology.

In his endeavor to break away from the limiting causal explanations, Jung formulated the concept of the collective unconscious that is populated by what he called archetypes. These are immensely powerful symbols, such as God, Heaven, Evil, Savior, Hero, and "Wise Person," which all precede our individual life experiences and help shape them, largely without our conscious knowledge. These primordial images can be considered organs of the collective unconscious, of whose hidden workings we can catch valuable glimpses in our dreams and the world's mythologies. Jung commented at length on Eastern spirituality, Gnosticism, and medieval alchemy, and through his many works opened up for us the realm of religious symbolism as a psychological factor.

Building on the momentum created by Jung, historian of religion Joseph Campbell brought psychomythology, or myth-opsychology, to the larger educated public. His best-known book, *Hero with a Thousand Faces,* which reads like a compelling detective novel, proved tremendously influential.[8] In this work and his other writings, Campbell persuasively argued that mythology is the key to self-understanding and planetary unity. After his death in 1988, the media cleverly inflated Campbell's already popular image to almost messianic proportions. While we may find Campbell's eclectic approach unconvincing as philosophy, his legacy is undeniably a formidable force in today's efforts at spiritual reconstruction.

Campbell's approach lends potency particularly to the feminist consciousness-raising movement, which emphasizes the exploration of our personal myths in terms of the traditional myths woven around God and Goddess figures. These figures from classical Greek mythology are thought to represent different archetypes in the male or female psyche.[9] Such archetypal myths can indeed help us understand our own psychological patterns better. However, we must guard against taking them too seriously, lest—as with astrological signs—we begin stereotyping ourselves and others.

Psychomythology of this type, which explains psychic life along mythological, or metaphoric, lines, offers a strong connecting point to the polytheistic beliefs of Neo-Paganism. In the latter tradition the Gods and Goddesses are seen as actual realities with whom the practitioner of wicca can interact and even identify.

In Neo-Tantric circles, again, God and Goddess step down from their mythological canvas to become flesh-and-blood realities in the form of the ritual male and female celebrants. This is indeed how the ancient Tantrics looked upon each other during the sacred rite of *maithuna*. They were merely following an even older tradition, in which priest and priestess were ritually transformed into embodiments of the Divine in its male and female aspects. The ritual intercourse was like a well-staged sacred drama, designed to ensure the fertility and prosperity of the community at large. Unquestionably, a certain amount of play-acting happened during those occasions, but when successful, these sacred rites led to the actual transfiguration of the participants.

Similarly, in Tantrism the *maithuna* ritual was never intended merely as a titillating pastime, a game for bored middle-class citizens. In genuine Tantric groups, sacramental coitus was always a powerful occasion, charged with numinous energy and orchestrated with awesome punctiliousness by a qualified teacher who was present during the ceremony and participated in it with his own partner. It was never merely fun but a form of yoga demanding a concentration that few of us today could hope to muster.

The Tantric ritual was not about some humanistic ideal of personal growth but about the radical transcendence of the self, or ego-personality, so that the Divine could irradiate the body and lift the mind beyond itself in ecstasy. As highly self-conscious moderns, we find this a terrifying prospect. There is little of this awe and dedication in Neo-Tantrism. Playing at being God and Goddess is not tantamount to being in touch with, or possessed by, the cosmic Male and Female.

Moreover, traditional Tantrism concerns the transcendence of what we would regard as characteristically human. The Tantric partners barely know each other as individuals. Individuality is, after all, the illusion from which they seek to escape. The personality is looked upon as an unimportant,

arbitrary pattern in Nature. There is no room for intimacy in the
Tantric ritual; the participants are anonymous, seemingly face-
less. Their relationship is strictly defined by the consensual purpose, which is to invoke, worship, and identify with the transcendental Reality in the form of God (*shiva*) and Goddess
(*shakti*).

Yet what most of us today are crying out for is precisely
intimacy and respect for our individuality. Our postmodern
civilization is strangulated by a lack of intimacy. Ever since the
breakdown of the extended family, people have suffered enormous loneliness and alienation. How many marriage partners
are unable to talk to each other, and how many parents are unable to talk to their children?

Few of us could handle the cool eroticism of a traditional
Tantric *maithuna* ceremony. We clearly must find our own spiritual approach, which does not deny intimacy but goes through
it to the level of mutual transcendence. There is certainly something alluring about seeing one's partner as God or Goddess, as
it is nowadays advocated in Neo-Tantric circles. However, so
long as this is not our actual experience of each other but merely
an exercise in mind expansion, we do little more than massage
our ego. Beyond that, there is the added liability of reducing the
other person to a sign or a symbol to be exploited for our personal growth. In other words, instead of acknowledging the
personhood of our partner, we indulge yet again in the kind of
narcissistic pseudorelationship that is rampant in our society.

Intimacy is conditional on our acceptance of embodiment.
We must be intimate with ourselves before we can be intimate
with another person. This means we must be able to hear our
hidden voices or messages from our psyche, our mind, and our
body. First and foremost, it means that we must be present in
our feelings: to notice, acknowledge, and be present with our
fear, anger, frustration, sadness, greed, lust, envy, or jealousy.
Only then can we learn to be present, in a feeling way, with the
feelings of another person, and only then can we sense the
numinous, or sacred, enlivening and shining through the other.

From being present with our own and other people's feelings, we move to being present spiritually. The practice of spiritual presence is the conscious disposition of embodying all-
inclusive love, or *eros*. In her novel *A Wind in the Door*,

Madeleine L'Engle referred to this practice as kything.[10] The verb *to kythe* stems from the Scottish dialect and means "to be manifest"—but also "to appear without disguise." Availing themselves of this salvaged word, a theologian and a psychologist, Louis M. Savary and Patricia H. Berne, coauthored a marvelous book on the art of kything. They offer the following definition:

> Kything is the practice of spiritual presence, and its purpose is to bring about a loving spiritual connection, union or communion between two or more persons or living things. It is not to be confused with a number of other mental states, spiritual experiences or psychological processes, including: unanimity, consensus, symbiosis, participation mystique, identification, projection, falling in love, empathy, telepathy, mind-reading, channeling, psychological pathology, occult phenomena, a mystic state, a religious experience or an imaginary playmate.[11]

Savary and Berne regard kything as a natural human ability, since we all participate in the spiritual dimension. However, by intention and in the appropriate context, kything can assume a sacred function. Kything clearly is ecological in the extended sense of the word. The word itself is related to *kith* and *kin,* suggesting deep connectedness, or intimacy.

Intimacy is the erotic imperative exercised in the arena of interpersonal feelings. Transcendence without feeling, or what we might call cold fusion, is exclusive of the world and other beings. Erotic transcendence, or hot fusion, is the path of passion and creativity. Feminist theologian Rita Nakashima Brock observed:

> Erotic power is the power of our primal interrelatedness. Erotic power, as it creates and connects hearts, involves the whole person in relationships of self-awareness, vulnerability, openness, and caring.[12]

Erotic power is not about overwhelming or dominating the other person. It is, rather, about empowering and the sharing of life-energy. The unifying symbol of erotic power is not the head, the thumb, or the penis but the heart—anciently eulogized as the very center of the universe.

RITUAL BEYOND NEUROSIS

Twenty years ago, anthropologist Mary Douglas spoke of a "world-wide revolt against ritualism."[13] By this she meant the widespread rejection of traditional forms of ritual and ritualism. Her observation is in principle correct. However, when we look around us we quickly discover that we have substituted our own secular or quasi-religious rituals for the jettisoned sacred ways. The Saturday football game is one example, so is the daily catching up with news, and the so-called quality time we periodically allocate to our children or spouse is another.

Ritual provides structure. However, when deprived of all sacred content, it can easily degenerate into mere stereotypical action, repetitive behavior that adds nothing to our being. We then speak of empty ritual. Rituals of this type are generally a symptom of neurosis. They are engaged in to limit rather than foster spontaneity and creativity, which are experienced as threatening. Through empty ritualism we can conform without having to think, feel, and make decisions on our own.

As Lewis Yablonsky has shown in his book *Robopaths,* this style of behavior is, unfortunately, epidemic in our contemporary Western civilization.[14] We live life at a blurring pace, bombarded by information and rushing from activity to activity, without adequate time for intellectual and emotional—as well as physiological—digestion. Time seems to fly at a rate that leaves no time for simply being.

Those who feel the need to slow down or even stand still in the midst of this giddying pace sooner or later feel moved to reintroduce ritual into their lives—ritual as sacramental performance, as a way of acknowledging and celebrating the presence of the sacred. They carve out for themselves a slice of sacred space and sacred time so as to punctuate their days with a deeper meaning.

If done consciously and in communion with the sacred reality, any activity can become a meaningful and life-enhancing ritual. This is true also of our sexual life. The historical chapters of this book have illustrated how other cultures and eras have approached this subject. Although their answers may not necessarily dovetail with our contemporary needs and competences, I believe we can always learn from, and even be inspired by, them.

I also believe that we need to articulate a distinct spiritual-

ity that involves guidance but not intrusive authority; disciple-
ship and the willingness to learn from anyone but not mindless
submission to a master; self-discipline but not excessive self-
mortification; self-knowledge but not obsessive self-watching;
and constancy but not dogmatic adherence to principles or practices. Above all, the new spirituality should overcome the dualistic opposition between heart and brain, body and mind, Heaven
and Earth, God and creature, and one person and another. It
should appreciate that life is a palette splashed with colors: Reality, or the numinous, irrevocably inheres in and *is* all things.

❧

Notes

Chapter 1

1. V. Packard, *The Sexual Wilderness: The Contemporary Upheaval in Male-Female Relationships* (New York: Van Rees Press, 1968), p. 17.
2. A. Ellis, *The American Sexual Tragedy* (New York: Black Cat Editions, rev. ed. 1962), p. 293.
3. *See* A. Toffler, *Future Shock* (New York: Bantam Books, 1971).
4. *See* M. Friedman, *Doesn't Anyone Blush Anymore: Reclaiming Intimacy, Modesty and Sexuality* (San Francisco: HarperSanFrancisco, 1990).
5. *See* Diagram Group, *Sex: A User's Manual* (New York: G. P. Putnam's Sons, 1981).
6. *See* R. Eisler, *The Chalice and the Blade* (San Francisco: Harper & Row, 1987). While I can commend this work for its social vision, Eisler's reading of neolithic history is not entirely convincing. She appears to project our modern concerns into archaic cultures.
7. A. C. Kinsey, W. B. Pomeroy, and C. E. Martin, *Sexual Behavior in the Human Male* (Philadelphia and London: W. B. Saunders Company, 1948), p. 224.
8. A. C. Kinsey et al., *Sexual Behavior in the Human Female* (Philadelphia and London: W. B. Saunders, 1953), p. 17.
9. S. Hite, *The Hite Report* (New York: Dell Publishing, 1976), p. 480.
10. *See* R. May, *Love and Will* (London: Collins, 1972); H. Lyon, *Tenderness Is Strength: From Machismo to Manhood* (New York: Harper & Row, 1977); H. Goldberg, *The New Male: From Self-Destruction to Self-Care* (New York: New American Library, 1979); S. Keen, *The Passionate Life: Stages of Loving* (New York: Harper & Row, 1983); G. Leonard, *Adventures in Monogamy: Exploring the Creative Possibilities of Love, Sexuality and Commitment* (Los Angeles: J. P. Tarcher, 1988; first published 1983).
11. R. Bly, *The Pillow & The Key: Commentary on the Fairy Tale Iron John* (St. Paul, MN: Ally Press, 1987), p. 5.
12. A. Greeley, *Love and Play* (New York: Seabury Press, 1977), p. 47.

CHAPTER 2

1. W. W. Dyer, *Your Erroneous Zones* (New York: Funk & Wagnalls, 1976), p. 91.
2. R. Potter-Efron and P. Potter-Efron, *Letting Go of Shame: Understanding How Shame Affects Your Life* (San Francisco: Harper & Row, 1989), pp. 3–4.
3. *See* the unpublished study by David Ogren "Sexual Guilt, Behavior, Attitudes, and Information," doctoral dissertation, University of Houston, 1974.
4. A. Comfort, *Sex in Society* (Secaucus, NJ: Citadel Press, 1975), p. 65.
5. Ibid., p. 54.
6. K. Leech, *Experiencing God: Theology as Spirituality* (San Francisco: Harper & Row, 1989), pp. 250–51.
7. M. Berman, *Coming to Our Senses: Body and Spirit in the Hidden History of the West* (New York: Simon & Schuster, 1989), p. 22.
8. *See* D. Leder, *The Absent Body* (Chicago: University of Chicago Press, 1990).
9. *See* A. Maslow, *The Further Reaches of Human Nature* (New York: Viking Press, 1971).
10. E. Fromm, *The Art of Loving* (London: Unwin Books, 1962), p. 14. This passage is in italics in the original.
11. A. M. Greeley, *Sexual Intimacy* (New York: Crossroad Books/Seabury Press, 1973), pp. 86–87.
12. Ibid., p. 87.
13. V. J. Seidler, *Rediscovering Masculinity: Reason, Language and Sexuality* (London and New York: Routledge, 1989), p. 102.
14. *See* S. Freud, *Civilization and Its Discontents* (New York: W. W. Norton, 1961).
15. A. Lowen, *Pleasure: A Creative Approach to Life* (Harmondsworth, England: Penguin Books, 1975), p. 19.
16. J. Henry, *Culture Against Man* (New York: Random House, 1963), p. 43.
17. Ibid., p. 43.
18. Lowen, *Pleasure*, p. 74.
19. *See* W. Reich, *The Sexual Revolution: Toward a Self-Governing Character Structure* (New York: Farrar, Straus & Giroux, 1969).
20. K. Dychtwald, *Bodymind* (Los Angeles: J. P. Tarcher, 1986), p. 117. Emphasis in italics is mine.
21. R. A. Johnson, *Ecstasy: Understanding the Psychology of Joy* (San Francisco: Harper & Row, 1987), p. vi.
22. H. Steiner and J. Gebser, *Anxiety: A Condition of Modern Man* (New York: Dell Publishing, 1962), p. 65.
23. A. Wilson-Schaef, *Escape From Intimacy: The Pseudo-Relationship Addictions* (San Francisco: Harper & Row, 1989).
24. K. Wilber, *The Atman Project: A Transpersonal View of Human Development* (Wheaton, IL: Theosophical Publishing House, 1980), p. 100.
25. Ibid., p. 101.

CHAPTER 3

1. *See* A. M. Greeley and W. C. McCready, "Are We a Nation of Mystics?" in *New York Times Magazine,* January 26, 1975.
2. *See* A. Maslow, *The Farther Reaches of Human Nature* (New York: Viking Press, 1971).
3. *See* J. C. Pearce, *The Crack in the Cosmic Egg: Challenging Constructs of Mind and Reality* (New York: Pocket Books, 1977).
4. A. M. Greeley, *Ecstasy: A Way of Knowing* (Englewood Cliffs, NJ: Prentice-Hall, 1974), p. 93.
5. M. Laski, *Ecstasy in Secular and Religious Experiences* (Los Angeles: Jeremy P. Tarcher, 1990), p. 145. This is a reprint of the 1961 edition.
6. Sir A. Hardy, *The Spiritual Nature of Man: A Study of Contemporary Religious Experience* (Oxford: Clarendon Press, 1979).
7. H. C. Lyon, *Tenderness Is Strength: From Machismo to Manhood* (New York: Harper & Row, 1977), pp. 152–53.
8. *See* R. M. Bucke, *Cosmic Consciousness: A Study in the Evolution of the Human Mind* (New Hyde Park, NY: University Books, 1961).
9. G. B. Leonard, *The Transformation: A Guide to the Inevitable Changes in Humankind* (New York: Dell, 1972), p. 21.
10. *See* A. Huxley, *The Doors of Perception/Heaven and Hell* (Harmondsworth, England: Penguin Books, 1959).

CHAPTER 4

1. *See* J. G. H. Clark, *From Savagery to Civilization* (London: Cobbett, 1946), p. 56.
2. R. Lewinsohn, *A History of Sexual Customs: From Earliest Times to the Present* (New York: Perennial Library/Harper & Row, 1971), p. 12.
3. M. Stone, *When God Was a Woman* (New York: Harcourt Brace Jovanovich, 1976), p. 13.
4. *See* E. W. Gadon, *The Once and Future Goddess* (San Francisco: Harper & Row, 1989).
5. *See* A. Leroi-Gourhan, *Treasures of Prehistoric Art* (New York: Harry N. Abrams, n.d.). Leroi-Gourhan's view has been endorsed by James Mallaart and Alexander Marshak. *See* J. Mellaart, *The Neolithic of the Near East* (New York: Scribner, 1975) and A. Marshak, *The Roots of Civilization: The Cognitive Beginnings of Man's First Art, Symbols and Notation* (New York: McGraw-Hill, 1972).
6. *See* R. Eisler, *The Chalice and the Blade: Our History, Our Future* (San Francisco: Harper & Row, 1987), p. 28.
7. N. Smart, *The Religious Experience of Mankind* (London: Collins, 1970), p. 48.
8. *See* G. Lerner, *The Creation of Patriarchy* (Oxford: Oxford University Press, 1986).

9. W. A. Fairservis, *The Threshold of Civilization: An Experiment in Prehistory* (New York: Charles Scribner's Sons, 1975), p. 195.

CHAPTER 5

1. D. Wolkstein and S. N. Kramer, *Inanna: Queen of Heaven and Earth* (New York: Harper & Row, 1983), p. 37.
2. Ibid., p. 44.
3. M. E. Harding, *Woman's Mysteries: Ancient and Modern* (New York: Harper & Row, 1971), p. 152.
4. R. Tannahill, *Sex in History* (New York: Stein and Day, 1980), p. 48.
5. C. G. Berger, *Our Phallic Heritage* (New York: Greenwich Book Publishers, 1966), p. 12.
6. G. R. Scott, *Phallic Worship: A History of Sex and Sex Rites in Relation to the Religions of All Races from Antiquity to the Present Day* (New Delhi: Amarko Book Agency, 1975), p. 266.
7. E. C. Keuls, *The Reign of the Phallus: Sexual Politics in Ancient Athens* (New York: Harper & Row, 1985), p. 1.
8. N. Qualls-Corbett, *The Sacred Prostitute: Eternal Aspect of the Feminine* (Toronto: Inner City Books, 1988), pp. 21–23.
9. The quotation is from Aristophanes' last comedy, *Plutus* (149ff.), which was produced in 188 B.C.
10. Qualls-Corbett, *The Sacred Prostitute*, p. 39.
11. N. Stone, *When God Was a Woman* (New York: Harcourt Brace Jovanovich, 1976), p. 157.
12. R. Tannahill, *Sex in History*, p. 81.
13. F. Henriques, *The Pretence of Love: Prostitution and Society*, vol. 1: *Primitive, Classical & Oriental* (London: Panther Books, 1965), p. 330.
14. The Sanskrit word *deva* is derived from the verbal root *div*, meaning "to shine."
15. *See*, e.g., D. Metzger, "Re-Vamping the World: On the Return of the Holy Prostitute," in G. Feuerstein, ed., *Enlightened Sexuality: Essays on Body-Positive Spirituality* (Freedom, CA: Crossing Press, 1989), pp. 71–77.
16. Ibid., p. 72.
17. Ibid., p. 73.
18. Ibid., pp. 74–77. Metzger's position has caused difficulty in some Christian quarters. Yet, remarkably and significantly enough, temple prostitution was known even within the hallowed halls of the Christian Church. We know that there was a very active and no doubt lucrative Church brothel in Avignon, which inspired the early sixteenth-century Pope Julius II to found its counterpart in Rome. Admittedly, this happened in one of the darkest eras in the history of the Vatican. What we have here, then, is not so much sacred sexuality but the economic and sexual exploitation of girls and women.

Chapter 6

1. S. Angus, *The Mystery-Religions* (New York: Dover Publications, 1975), p. 42. This is an unaltered republication of the second edition of this work, published in 1928.
2. This quote is according to Plutarch, the influential Greek philosopher and biographer, who lived in the first century A.D. *See* W. K. C. Guthrie, *The Greeks and Their Gods* (Boston, MA: Beacon Press, 1955), p. 293.
3. J. Godwin, *Mystery Religions in the Ancient World* (San Francisco: Harper & Row, 1981), p. 9.
4. R. G. Wasson, A. Hofmann, and C. A. P. Ruck, *The Road to Eleusis: Unveiling the Secret of the Mysteries* (New York: Harcourt Brace Jovanovich, 1978), pp. 80–81.
5. W. F. Otto, *Dionysus: Myth and Cult* (Bloomington: Indiana University Press, 1965), p. 50.
6. Tantrism will be discussed in Chapter 10.
7. Otto, *Dionysus: Myth and Cult*, p. 101.
8. R. G. Wasson et al., *The Road to Eleusis*, p. 42.
9. J. Singer, *Androgyny: The Opposites Within* (Boston, MA: Sigo Press, 1989). The first edition of this work was published in 1976.
10. E. Keuls, *The Reign of the Phallus: Sexual Politics in Ancient Athens* (New York: Harper & Row, 1985), p. 362.
11. W. F. Otto, *Dionysus*, p. 113.
12. R. Tannahill, *Sex in History* (New York: Stein and Day, 1980), p. 118.
13. A. Evans, *The God of Ecstasy* (New York: St. Martin's Press, 1988), p. 160.
14. Ibid.
15. *See* the excellent study by P. Borgeaud, *The Cult of Pan in Ancient Greece* (Chicago, IL: University of Chicago Press, 1988).
16. G. F. Moore, *History of Religions*, vol. 1 (Edinburgh: T. & T. Clark, 1914), pp. 582–83.
17. J. G. Frazer, *The Golden Bough: A Study in Magic and Religion* (New York: Collier Books, 1963), p. 405. This one-volume abridged edition of Frazer's monumental study was first published in 1922.
18. F. Cumont, *Oriental Religions in Roman Paganism* (New York: Dover Publications, 1956), pp. 50–51. The original French edition of this work was published in 1906.
19. G. F. Moore, *History of Religions*, p. 588.
20. W. Burkert, *Ancient Mystery Cults* (Cambridge, MA: Harvard University Press, 1987), p. 108.

Chapter 7

1. S. J. Teubal, *Hagar the Egyptian: The Lost Tradition of the Matriarchs* (San Francisco: Harper & Row, 1990). Teubal also wrote a work on Sarah entitled *Sarah the Priestess* (Athens, OH: Swallow Press, 1984).

2. R. Patai, *The Hebrew Goddess* (New York: KTAV, 1967).

3. R. Tannahill, *Sex in History* (New York: Scarborough Books, 1982), p. 82.

4. M. Stone, *When God Was a Woman* (New York: Harcourt Brace Jovanovich, 1978), p. 162.

5. G. R. Taylor, *Sex in History*, p. 255.

6. M. Stone, *When God Was a Woman*, p. 150.

7. G. Lerner, *The Creation of Patriarchy* (Oxford and New York: Oxford University Press, 1986), p. 192.

8. M. Falk, *The Song of Songs: A New Translation and Interpretation* (San Francisco: HarperSanFrancisco, 1990), unnumbered pages.

Chapter 8

1. *See* Matthew 5:44.

2. Genesis 1:28.

3. K. H. Maahs, "Male & Female in Pauline Perspective: A Study in Biblical Ambivalence," *Dialogue & Alliance,* vol. 2, no. 3 (Fall 1988), p. 20.

4. 1 Corinthians 7:6.

5. 1 Corinthians 7:9.

6. R. Haughton, *Love* (Baltimore, MD: Penguin Books, 1971), p. 82.

7. M. Kolbenschlag, *Kiss Sleeping Beauty Good-Bye: Breaking the Spell of Feminine Myths and Models* (San Francisco: Harper & Row, 1988), p. 184.

8. E. B. Pusey, trans., *Confessions* (London: Everyman Editions, 1907), pp. 21–22.

9. C. Heyward, *Touching Our Strength: The Erotic as Power and the Love of God* (San Francisco: Harper & Row, 1989), p. 90.

10. Ibid.

11. G. Feuerstein, "Sexuality as Sacrament: The Options of Spiritual Eroticism and Celibacy," in G. Feuerstein, ed., *Enlightened Sexuality* (Freedom, CA: Crossing Press, 1989), p. 89.

12. M. Warner, *Alone of All Her Sex: The Myth and the Cult of the Virgin Mary* (New York: Pocket Books, 1978).

13. The scripture that was most influential on the cult of Mary and Mariology, however, was the apocryphal Book of James, which may have been written in the early second century A.D. James was Jesus' brother. The book is a pious fabrication and, although some Church Fathers swore by it, was never incorporated into the scriptural canon and was later even condemned.

14. Warner, *Alone of All Her Sex,* p. 117.

15. C. Wolters, trans., *Julian of Norwich: Revelations of Divine Love* (Harmondsworth, England: Penguin Books, 1966), p. 164.

16. Warner, *Alone of All Her Sex,* p. 50.

17. G. Lerner, *The Creation of Patriarchy* (New York/Oxford, England: Oxford University Press, 1986), p. 196.

18. Augustine, *De Civitate Dei* XIV, chapter 17. See the translation by H. Bettenson, *Augustine: Concerning the City of God Against the Pagans* (Harmondsworth, England: Penguin Books, 1972), p. 578.

CHAPTER 9

1. G. R. Taylor, *Sex in History* (New York: Vanguard Press, 1954), p. 49.
2. J. W. Perry, *The Heart of History: Individuality in Evolution* (New York: SUNY Press, 1987), p. 143.
3. F. Ranke, "Courtly Literature (1160–1250)," in Bruno Boesch, ed., *German Literature: A Critical Survey* (London: Methuen, 1973), p. 54.
4. Duke Guillem IX, the earliest troubadour on record, was a well-known womanizer, and his *chansons* were often quite lewd. *See* P. Blackburn and G. Economou, *Proensa: An Anthology of Troubadour Poetry* (New York: Paragon House, 1986).
5. G. R. Evans, trans., *Bernard of Clairvaux: Selected Works* (Mahwah, NJ: Paulist Press, 1987), p. 273.
6. Ibid., p. 221.
7. Ibid., p. 255.
8. Ibid., p. 199.
9. E. Zum Brunn and G. Epiney-Burgard, *Women Mystics in Medieval Europe* (New York: Paragon House, 1989), pp. 59–60.
10. Cited in V. M. Lagorio, "The Medieval Continental Women Mystics," in P. E. Szarmach, ed., *An Introduction to the Medieval Mystics of Europe* (New York: SUNY Press, 1984), p. 177.
11. A. T. de Nicolas, *St. John of the Cross: Alchemist of the Soul* (New York: Paragon House, 1989), p. 215.
12. Cited in M. Idel, *Studies in Ecstatic Kabbalah* (New York: SUNY Press, 1988), p. 8.
13. Cited in W. Stoddart, *Sufism: The Mystical Doctrines and Methods of Islam* (New York: Paragon House, 1986), p. 51.
14. A. J. Arberry, *Discourses of Rumi* (London: John Murray, 1961), p. 178.
15. This passage is a paraphrase rather than a literal translation of verses II.11–17.
16. *See* A. Lorde, "Uses of the Erotic: The Erotic as Power," *Weaving the Visions: New Patterns in Feminist Spirituality,* ed. J. Plaskow and C. P. Christ (San Francisco: Harper & Row, 1989), p. 209.
17. A. J. Alston, *The Devotional Poems of Mirabai* (Delhi: Motilal Banarsidass, 1980), p. 36.
18. Ibid., p. 40.
19. Ibid., p. 60.
20. Ibid., pp. 92–93.
21. Ibid., p. 93.
22. *See* B. Bhattacharya, *The World of Tantra* (New Delhi: Munshiram Manoharlal, 1988), pp. 267–68.

CHAPTER 10

1. For a fuller treatment of Tantrism, *see* my *Yoga: The Technology of Ecstasy* (Los Angeles: Jeremy P. Tarcher, 1989).
2. *Rig-Veda* (V. 12).

3. The profound symbolism of the Vedas has been explored by the British Vedicist Jeanine Miller in her books *The Vedas: Harmony, Meditation and Fulfillment* (London: Rider, 1974) and *The Vision of Cosmic Order in the Vedas* (London: Routledge & Kegan Paul, 1985).

4. S. A. Dange, *Sexual Symbolism From the Vedic Ritual* (Delhi: Ajanta Publications, 1979), pp. 29–30.

5. See *Brihad-Aranyaka-Upanishad* (VI. 4. 1ff.). This is the oldest known work on Vedanta, or Hindu nondualist metaphysics.

6. To confuse matters, the female partner in the sexual ritual is also known as *mudra* ("seal"). The obvious symbolism behind this usage is that the female is comparable to wax and the male to the stamp that leaves an imprint on the wax. They belong together and have no usefulness apart from each other.

    There are, as one might expect, other far more esoteric meanings. One is that the *mudra* seals off the outside world so that awareness is raised to higher levels of inner experience. It also seals off the outflowing energies of the body-mind, establishing an energy circuit between the man and the woman. Finally, it seals off the flow of the man's semen, which is arrested by the psychoenergetic continuum between the partners.

    To confuse matters further, the Sanskrit term *mudra* also denotes certain ritualistic hand gestures and bodily poses (such as the yogic headstand), which are all recognized means of manipulating the flux of the body's life-force (*prana*).

7. M. Anand, *The Art of Sexual Ecstasy: The Path of Sacred Sexuality for Western Lovers* (Los Angeles: Jeremy P. Tarcher, 1989), pp. 2–3.

8. Ibid., p. 386.

9. H. Bettenson, trans., *Augustine: Concerning the City of God Against the Pagans* (Harmondsworth, England: Penguin Books, 1972), p. 577.

10. G. Krishna, *The Biological Basis of Religion and Genius* (New Delhi: Kundalini Research and Publication Trust, 1971), p. 89.

11. See S. Freud, *Civilization and Its Discontents* (New York: W. W. Norton, 1961), p. 32.

12. B. Bhattacharya, *The World of Tantra* (New Delhi: Munshiram Manoharlal, 1988), p. 325.

13. S. Grof, *Beyond the Brain: Birth, Death and Transcendence in Psychotherapy* (New York: SUNY Press, 1985), pp. 228–29.

CHAPTER 11

1. This interpretation is found in Richard Wilhelm's rendering of the *Secret of the Golden Flower: A Chinese Book of Life* (London: Routledge & Kegan Paul, 1931), p. 11.

2. The rendering is by Ellen M. Chen, *The Tao Te Ching: A New Translation with Commentary* (New York: Paragon House, 1989), p. 51. Chen's translation is, in my view, the finest available to date, and her commentary affords the lay reader important insights into this often cryptic scripture.

3. E. M. Chen, *The Tao Te Ching*, p. 55. The verse quoted is II. 3.

4. The translation is by A. C. Graham, *Chuang-Tzu: The Inner Chapters* (London: Unwin Paperbacks, 1989), p. 265.
5. *See* H. S. Levy and Akira Ishihara, *The Tao of Sex: The Essence of Medical Prescriptions (Ishimpo)* (Lower Lake, CA: Integral Publishing, 1989).
6. Ibid., pp. 5–6.
7. For an interesting autobiographical rumination on this subject from the Christian point of view, *see* R. Gilman, *Faith, Sex, Mystery* (New York: Simon & Schuster, 1986). This is perhaps also the place for some cautionary remarks about excessive seminal retention. There are certain medical conditions, such as prostratitis, which make seminal retention undesirable. Moreover, the Taoist and Tantric techniques of stopping ejaculation by applying finger pressure on the perineum can be risky.
8. A. Carrel, *Man the Unknown* (London: Burns & Oates, 1961), p. 78.
9. Ibid., p. 118.
10. Cited in Ly K'uan Yu, *Taoist Yoga: Alchemy and Immortality* (London: Rider, 1970), p. 28.
11. Ibid., p. 19.
12. J. Durden-Smith and D. deSimone, *Sex and the Brain* (New York: Warner Books, 1983), p. 211.
13. D. P. Reid, *The Tao of Health, Sex and Longevity: A Modern Practical Guide to the Ancient Way* (New York: Fireside Books, 1989), pp. 261–62.
14. *See* S. T. Chang, *The Tao of Sexology: The Book of Infinite Wisdom* (San Francisco: Tao Publishing, 1986).
15. *See* M. Chia, with M. Winn, *Taoist Secrets of Love: Cultivating Male Sexual Energy* (New York: Aurora Press, 1984), and Mantak Chia and Maneewan Chia, *Healing Love Through the Tao: Cultivating Female Sexual Energy* (Huntington, NY: Healing Tao Books, 1986).
16. Ly K'uan Yu, *Taoist Yoga*, p. 115.
17. *See* R. Wilhelm, trans., *The Secret of the Golden Flower*, p. 9.
18. G. Heard, *Pain, Sex and Time: A New Hypothesis of Evolution* (London: Cassell, 1939), p. 199.
19. The translation is by E. M. Chen, *The Tao Te Ching*, p. 91.

CHAPTER 12

1. For some other contemporary sexual myths, *see* Eugene C. Kennedy, *The New Sexuality: Myths, Fables, and Hang-ups* (New York: Image Books, 1973).
2. Cited in I. P. Couliano, *Eros and Magic in the Renaissance* (Chicago, IL: University of Chicago Press, 1987), p. 87.
3. Ibid., p. xviii. *See also* W. Shumaker, *The Occult Sciences in the Renaissance: A Study in Intellectual Patterns* (Berkeley: University of California Press, 1979).
4. *See* E. Neumann, *The Great Mother: An Analysis of the Archetype* (Princeton, NJ: Princeton University Press, 1972), p. 114.
5. Ibid., p. 42.
6. Ibid., p. 172.

7. *De vinculis in genere,* p. 683. Cited in I. P. Couliano, *Eros and Magic in the Renaissance,* p. 98.
8. *See* L. T. Culling, *Sex Magick* (St. Paul, MN: Llewellyn Publications, 1988).
9. Ibid., p. 21.
10. *See* C. Wilson, *Aleister Crowley: The Nature of the Beast* (Wellingborough, England: Aquarian Press, 1987), p. 93. *See also* the fictionalized account by Colin Wilson entitled *Sex Diary of a Metaphysician,* in which the leading figure, "Cunningham," is none other than Crowley. This complements Somerset Maugham's novel *The Magician,* published in 1908, which is likewise based on Crowley's life.
11. C. Wilson, *Aleister Crowley,* p. 109.
12. *See* D. M. Kraig, *Modern Magick: Eleven Lessons in the High Magickal Arts* (St. Paul, MN: Llewellyn, 1988).
13. M. Adler, *Drawing Down the Moon: Witches, Druids, Goddess-Worshippers, and Other Pagans in America Today* (Boston, MA: Beacon Press, rev. ed. 1986), p. 4.
14. In an interview conducted by Margot Adler in 1979, the California witch Sharon Devlin remarked nostalgically that the movement was lacking in the ancient practice of "ritual drunkenness and sex." Adler felt that this indicated a certain sacramental inefficiency, a loss of skill in the use of music, dance, and drugs. The situation appears to be little different a decade later: the Neo-Pagan movement is still rather tame, which is perhaps understandable in light of today's conservative public attitudes. We need, of course, not condone the use of drugs to espouse the value of a more Dionysian outlook on life.
15. R. Lawlor, *Earth Honoring: The New Male Sexuality* (Rochester, VT: Park Street Press, 1989), p. 84.
16. Starhawk, *The Spiral Dance: A Rebirth of the Ancient Religion of the Great Goddess* (San Francisco: Harper & Row, 10th-anniversary edition, 1989), p. 97.
17. Ibid.

CHAPTER 13

1. *See* A. W. Watts, *Nature, Man and Woman* (New York: Pantheon Books, 1958), pp. 158ff.
2. A. Watts, *Behold the Spirit: A Study in the Necessity of Mystical Religion* (New York: Vintage Books, 1971), p. 99. First published in 1947.
3. Ibid., p. 210.
4. Ibid., p. 216.
5. A. M. Greeley, *Sexual Intimacy* (New York: Crossroad Books/Seabury Press, 1975), p. 64.
6. Ibid.
7. A. M. Greeley, *Love and Play* (New York: Seabury Press, 1977), p. 43.
8. Ibid., p. 45.
9. Ibid., p. 60.

10. J. Moore, *Sexuality and Spirituality: The Interplay of Masculine and Feminine in Human Development* (San Francisco: Harper & Row, 1981), p. 1.

11. D. H. Donnelly, *Radical Love: An Approach to Sexual Spirituality* (Minneapolis, MN: Winston Press, 1984).

12. Ibid., p. 34.

13. Ibid., p. 42.

14. P. A. Campbell and E. M. McMahon, *Bio-Spirituality: Focusing as a Way to Grow* (Chicago, IL: Loyola University Press, 1985).

15. Ibid., p. 8.

16. P. Tillich, "The Importance of New Being," *Man and Transformation: Papers from the Eranos Yearbooks,* ed. Joseph Campbell (Princeton, NJ: Princeton University Press, 1964), p. 174.

17. P. A. Campbell and E. M. McMahon, *Bio-Spirituality,* pp. 110–11.

18. Ibid., p. 66.

19. M. Fox, *The Coming of the Cosmic Christ* (San Francisco: Harper & Row, 1988), p. 218.

20. Ibid., pp. 163–64.

21. Ibid., p. 164.

22. Ibid.

23. Ibid., p. 172.

CHAPTER 14

1. See D. Loye, *The Sphinx and the Rainbow: Brain, Mind and Future Vision* (Boulder, CO: Shambhala, 1983).

2. Rolfing is a form of bodywork named after its inventor, Ida Rolf. A more technical designation for this approach is *structural integration.*

3. See D. Leder, *The Absent Body,* (Chicago, IL: University of Chicago Press, 1990).

4. M. Berman, *Coming to Our Senses: Body and Spirit in the Hidden History of the West* (New York: Simon & Schuster, 1989).

5. Ibid., p. 343.

6. S. Freud, *Drei Abhandlungen zur Sexualtheorie* (Frankfurt, Germany: Fischer Bücherei, 1961), p. 86. My translation.

7. See C. G. Jung, *On the Nature of the Psyche* (Princeton, NJ: Princeton University Press, 1969).

8. See W. E. Mann, *Orgone, Reich, and Eros: Wilhelm Reich's Theory of Life Energy* (New York: Simon & Schuster, 1973).

9. See, e.g., Barbara Ann Brennan, *Hands of Light: A Guide to Healing Through the Human Energy Field* (New York: Bantam Books, 1988); Shafica Karagulla and Dora van Gelder Kunz, *The Chakras and the Human Energy Fields* (Wheaton, IL: Quest Books, 1989), which is a fascinating account of Karagulla's studies with the clairvoyantly talented Gelder Kunz; and Hiroshi Motoyama, *Theories of the Chakras: Bridge to Higher Consciousness* (Wheaton, IL: Quest Books, 1981), which contains an attempt to integrate Hindu esoteric anatomy with the system of Far Eastern acupuncture. *See also* the photographic research invented by the Russian

electronics engineer Semyon Kirlian, which has given rise to experiments around the world, leading to the formulation of the concept of bio-plasma. Good overviews of these intriguing matters are provided in the two books by John Davidson, *Subtle Energy* (Saffron Walden, England: C. W. Daniel, 1987) and *The Web of Life* (same publisher, 1988).

10. G. Heard, *Pain, Sex and Time: A New Hypothesis of Evolution* (London: Cassell, 1939), p. 197.

11. Ibid., p. 66.

12. A similar argument from an evolutionary perspective has more recently been made by the Kashmiri pandit Gopi Krishna in his work *Kundalini: The Evolutionary Energy in Man* (London: Robinson & Watkins, 1971) and his numerous other publications.

13. *See* G. G. May, *Will and Spirit: A Contemplative Psychology* (San Francisco: Harper & Row, 1983), p. 188.

14. *See* J. Gebser, *The Ever-Present Origin* (Athens, OH: Ohio University Press, 1985), p. 55. *See also* G. Feuerstein, *Structures of Consciousness: The Genius of Jean Gebser—An Introduction and Critique* (Lower Lake, CA: Integral Publishing, 1987).

15. *See* the excellent survey of parapsychology by S. Holroyd, *PSI and the Consciousness Explosion* (New York: Taplinger Publishing, 1977). For a slightly more technical account, *see* R. A. McConnell, *An Introduction to Parapsychology in the Context of Science* (Pittsburgh, PA: University of Pittsburgh, 1983).

16. *See Brihad-Aranyaka-Upanishad* (IV.5.6).

17. Cited in M. Eliade, *The Two and the One* (London: Harvill Press, 1965), p. 106.

CHAPTER 15

1. M. Berman, *Coming to Our Senses: Body and Spirit in the Hidden History of the West* (New York: Simon & Schuster, 1989), p. 310.

2. *See* A. Maslow, *The Farther Reaches of Human Nature* (New York: Viking, 1971).

3. *See* J. Gebser, *The Ever-Present Origin* (Athens, OH: Ohio University Press, 1985). *See also* G. Feuerstein, *Structures of Consciousness: The Genius of Jean Gebser—An Introduction and Critique* (Lower Lake, CA: Integral Publishing, 1987).

4. B. Davis, *Monastery Without Walls* (Berkeley, CA: Celestial Arts, 1990), pp. 167–68.

5. F. A. Wolf, *Taking the Quantum Leap: The New Physics for Nonscientists* (San Francisco: Harper & Row, 1981), pp. 249–50. *See also* F. A. Wolf, *Star Wave: Mind, Consciousness, and Quantum Physics* (New York: Macmillan, 1984).

6. J. Singer, *Seeing Through the Visible World: Jung, Gnosis, and Chaos* (San Francisco: Harper & Row, 1990), p. 155.

7. Ibid., p. 165.

8. *See* J. Campbell, *Hero with a Thousand Faces* (Princeton, NJ: Princeton University Press, 1968).

9. *See,* e.g., J. S. Bolen, *Goddesses in Everywoman: A New Psychology of Women* (San Francisco: Harper & Row, 1984) and *Gods in Everyman: A New Psychology of Men's Lives and Loves* (San Francisco: Harper & Row, 1989).

10. *See* M. L'Engle, *A Wind in the Door* (New York: Dell, 1973).

11. L. M. Savary and P. H. Berne, *Kything: The Art of Spiritual Presence* (Mahwah, NJ: Paulist Press, 1988), p. 86.

12. R. N. Brock, *Journeys by Heart: A Christology of Erotic Power* (New York: Cross Road, 1988), p. 26.

13. M. Douglas, *Natural Symbols: Explorations in Cosmology* (Harmondsworth, England: Pelican Books, 1973), p. 19.

14. *See* L. Yablonsky, *Robopaths: People as Machines* (Baltimore, MD: Penguin Books, 1972).

Recommended Reading

Anand, Margo. *The Art of Sexual Ecstasy: The Path of Sacred Sexuality for Western Lovers.* Los Angeles: Jeremy P. Tarcher, 1989. A step-by-step practical introduction to sacred sex, containing a wide range of methods.

Berman, Morris. *Coming to Our Senses: Body and Spirit in the Hidden History of the West.* New York: Simon & Schuster, 1989. An important critique of the body-negative orientation of Western civilization.

Brown, Gabrielle. *The New Celibacy: A Journey to Love, Intimacy, and Good Health in a New Age.* New York: McGraw-Hill, 1989. A lively book on the advantages of a celibate life.

Bubba Free John [Da Love-Ananda]. *Love of the Two-Armed Form.* Middletown, CA: Dawn Horse Press, 1978. A bulky volume of informative essays on the theory and practice of sacred sexuality by a modern spiritual adept.

Douglas, Nik, and Penny Slinger. *Sexual Secrets: The Alchemy of Ecstasy.* Rochester, VT: Destiny Books, 1979. A profusely illustrated large-format book about the philosophy and practice of Tantrism.

Evola, Julius. *The Metaphysics of Sex.* New York: Inner Traditions International, 1983. A scholarly but significant study of eros and sex as positive forces in spiritual life.

Feuerstein, Georg, ed. *Enlightened Sexuality: Essays on Body-Positive Spirituality.* Freedom, CA: Crossing Press, 1989. An anthology comprising wide-ranging essays and several interviews with prominent representatives of a body- and sex-positive spirituality.

Goldberg, B. Z. *The Sacred Fire: The Story of Sex in Religion.* New York: Black Cat Books/Grove Press, 1958. A popularly written historical survey showing how various religions have approached sexuality.

Greeley, Andrew M. *Ecstasy: A Way of Knowing.* Englewood Cliffs, NJ: Prentice-Hall, 1974. A stylish introduction to mysticism and mystical experience, including a chapter on "Ecstasy through Sex."

_____. *Sexual Intimacy.* New York: Crossroad Books/Seabury Press, 1975. An original treatment of intimacy, affirming the importance of values over behavioristic techniques.

Henderson, Julie. *The Lover Within: Opening to Energy in Sexual Practice.* Barrytown, NY: Station Hill Press, 1987. A practical workbook for unblocking sexual-emotional obstructions.

Henriques, Fernando. *The Pretence of Love: Prostitution and Society.* Vol. 1: *Primitive, Classical & Oriental.* London: Panther Books, 1965. A popular survey of prostitution in the ancient world.

Keen, Sam. *The Passionate Life: Stages of Loving.* San Francisco: Harper & Row, 1983. A thoughtful and well-written book about the need for a more erotic, rather than sexual, orientation to life.

Kelsey, Morton, and Barbara Kelsey. *Sacrament of Sexuality: The Spirituality and Psychology of Sex.* Warwick, NY: Amity House, 1986. A discussion of sexuality and spirituality from a liberal Christian perspective.

Leonard, George. *Adventures in Monogamy: Exploring the Creative Possibilities of Love, Sexuality and Commitment.* Los Angeles: Jeremy P. Tarcher, 1988. Formerly published under the title of *The End of Sex,* a book written in Leonard's characteristically animated style.

Lewinsohn, Richard. *A History of Sexual Customs: From Earliest Times to the Present.* New York: Perennial Library/Harper & Row, 1971. A very readable comprehensive history of sexual mores and practices throughout the ages.

Lilar, Suzanne. *Aspects of Love in Western Society.* London: Panther Books, 1967. An exceptional historical study of erotic love, calling for a resacralization of sexuality.

Meldman, Louis William. *Mystical Sex: Love, Ecstasy, and the Mystical Experience.* Tucson, AZ: Harbinger House, 1990. A popular account of sacred sexuality, in some respects complementing the present work.

Monick, Eugene. *Phallos: Sacred Image of the Masculine.* Toronto: Inner City Books, 1987. An examination of the symbol of the phallus from the perspective of Jungian psychology.

Offir, Carole Wade. *Human Sexuality.* New York: Harcourt Brace Jovanovich, 1982. A comprehensive sexological college textbook.

Qualls-Corbett, Nancy. *The Sacred Prostitute: Eternal Aspect of the Feminine.* Toronto: Inner City Books, 1988. A thoughtful account of temple prostitution from the Jungian point of view.

Ramsdale, David Alan, and Ellen Jo Dorfman. *Sexual Energy Ecstasy: A Guide to the Ultimate, Intimate Sexual Experience.* Playa del Rey, CA: Peak Skill Publishing, 1985. A popular practical workbook on the theoretical basis of Tantrism and Taoism.

Singer, June. *Androgyny: The Opposites Within.* Boston, MA: Sigo Press, repr. 1989. An important Jungian discussion of androgyny.

Tannahill, Reay. *Sex in History.* New York: Stein and Day, 1980. An impressive history of sexual customs, focusing on secular aspects.

Taylor, Gordon Rattray. *Sex in History.* New York: Vanguard, 1954. A history of sexuality, focusing on the medieval era.

Welwood, John, ed. *Challenge of the Heart: Love, Sex, and Intimacy in Changing Times.* Boston, MA: Shambhala Publications, 1985. A well-selected collection of essays celebrating male/female love.

Wyly, James. *The Phallic Quest: Priapus and Masculine Inflation.* Toronto: Inner City Books, 1989. A Jungian account of the destructive aspects of the phallus as a symbol of masculinity.

PERIODICALS

Ecstasy: The Journal of Divine Eroticism. A quarterly magazine dedicated to promoting the awareness that sexuality is inherently sacred. P. O. Box 862, Ojai, CA 93024.

Tantra: The Magazine. A quarterly publication that seeks to make Tantric ideas and practices accessible to Western readers. P. O. Box 79, Torreon, NM 87061.

Index

Wasson, R. G., 81
Watts, A. W., 179–180
Weizsacker, C. F. von, 148
Wilber, K., 24
Wild Man, 9
Wilhelm, R., 166
Wilson, C., 174
Wilson-Schaef, A., 22
wine, 83, 88
witch hunts, 114, 176
Wolf, F. A., 206
women
  and agriculture, 53
  in ancient Greece, 65, 77, 80, 82
  in Christianity, 104, 110, 116
  in Islam, 124
  in Judaism, 96–97, 110
  secretions of, 149–150, 163
  and sexual frustration, 6

in Stone Age, 45–46
and troubadours, 116
as vessels, 172
work, inner, 207
Wu Tze-tien, 165
wu-wei, 156

Xochipilli-Cinteotl, 172

Yablonsky, L., 212
Yajnavalkya, 198
yang. *See* yin
Yellow Emperor, 158–159
yin, and yang, 157, 162, 164, 165
Yoga, 196. *See also* Kundalini-Yoga
Yudhishthira, 106

Zeus, 82
Zohar, 122